AF540697

ECONOMIC TRANSFORMATION OF INDIA

A Journey Inconclusive

ECONOMIC TRANSFORMATION OF INDIA

A Journey Inconclusive

MANDEEP SINGH
B.A. (Hons), M.Phil., Ph.D.
Lecturer in Economics, G.N. Khalsa College,
Yamuna Nagar, Haryana

and

HARVINDER KAUR
M.Phil., Ph.D. (Commerce)
Lecturer in Commerce, G.N.G. College,
Yamuna Nagar, Haryana

DEEP & DEEP PUBLICATIONS PVT. LTD.
F-159, Rajouri Garden, New Delhi-110027

ECONOMIC TRANSFORMATION OF INDIA

A Journey Inconclusive

ISBN 978-81-8450-043-1

Typeset by ASHISH TECHNOGRAPHICS,
3190, Mohindra Park, Shakur Basti, Delhi-110034.

Printed in India at MAYUR ENTERPRISES,
WZ Plot No. 3, Gujjar Market, Tihar Village, New Delhi-110018.

Published by DEEP & DEEP PUBLICATIONS PVT. LTD.
F-159, Rajouri Garden, New Delhi-110027.
Phones: 25435369, 25440916
E-mail: ddpbooks@yahoo.co.in • ddpubs@gmail.com
Showroom:
2/13, Ansari Road, Daryaganj, New Delhi-110002 • Telefax: 23245122

Contents

The present book is the result of the inspiration and encouragement we received from

S. Bhupinder Singh Jauhar

(Chairman, Khalsa Educational Institutions, Yamuna Nagar), a visionary, philanthropist and a true human being who is always a guiding spirit for endeavour like the present book.

Preface

In the end of June 1991, India landed in an unprecedented economic crisis. Balance of payment situation was leading towards a crisis. Faith of international community in Indian economy was shaken. The balance of payment position was on the brink of disaster as in mid-January 1991 and again in late June 1991 the level of foreign exchange reserves dropped to levels which were not sufficient to finance imports of even ten days. The BOP crisis that hit India in 1990-91, had been building for at least a half a decade preceding that year. The rising fiscal deficit and gradually increasing over-valuation contributed to the rising imbalance. Inadequate exchange rate adjustment in response to the external and domestic shocks during 1990-91 triggered the crisis. The period from mid-1989 to mid-1991 was packed with a series of political developments, one following on another without let-up. The break-up of Soviet empire, the unification of Germany followed the policy of Glasnost. Iraq invaded Kuwait and set-off another oil shock. Domestically there were three changes of government and unprecedented socio-political upheaval. Underlying macro-economic imbalances that had been building up over the eighties came to a head as a result of these shocks and, along with the inadequate policy response, resulted in a BOP crisis in 1990-91.

In order to pull the economy out of economic crisis and to put it on the path to rapid and steady economic growth, it was most essential to correct financial disequilibrium, curb rising prices, correct adverse balance of payment and replenish foreign exchange reserves. To achieve all these objectives, introduction of economic reforms or appropriate economic policy was considered inevitable. On June 21, 1991 the government adopted a number of stabilization measures that were designed to restore internal and external confidence. The government adopted, as the centerpiece of economic strategy, a programme to bring about reduction in fiscal imbalance to be supported by reforms in economic policy that were essential to impart a new element of dynamism to the growth process in the economy. In his memorandum on Economic Policies submitted to IMF, Dr. Manmohan Singh proposed, "The thrust will be to increase the efficiency and international competitiveness of industrial production, to utilize foreign investment and technology to a much greater degree than in the past, to improve the performance and rationalize the scope of the public sector, and to reform and modernize the financial sector so that it can more efficiently serve the needs of the economy."

Reforms became necessary because the earlier regulatory model of development, which was followed for several decades after independence, did not deliver results up to expectations. There were important achievements during the period, notably the increase in life expectancy and the creation of an impressive reservoir of scientific and technical personnel. However, the growth rate of the economy remained much below the targets and progress in poverty reduction was very limited. In terms of basic social amenities such as safe drinking water, sanitation facilities and primary education, our achievements were also far from satisfactory.

Economic policies began to change in the 1980s and a much bolder programme of economic reforms was introduced in 1991 which has been continued by successive governments since then. These reforms are aimed at closing the gap between India's potentials and its actual performance. Many developing countries in

East Asia, with very different social and economic systems, were able to achieve a rapid rate of economic growth over extended periods and to reduce poverty dramatically. India is capable of no less, and economic reforms can be seen as an effort to achieve this potential.

The era of sixteen years of economic reforms has given us some indication of what is possible. The growth rate of the economy in the post-reforms period is higher than in the previous decades putting India among top ten fastest growing developing economies. However, the task of reforms is far from over. Our growth remains below the levels achieved by East-Asian Countries. We need to grow at much faster rates if we have to raise standard of living of the mass of our people, create a sufficient growth of high quality jobs for increasing better educated new entrants to labour force and bring about reduction in poverty.

The scope of reforms that are needed is wide, and in some ways extend beyond economics. But there is an underlying common rationale or philosophical basis for all of the interconnected set of policies that constitute economic reforms. This rationale has been amply vindicated by actual experience, both within and outside India. It is based on philosophical and practical insight that equitable and sustainable growth flourishes best in an environment of opportunity, freedom and individual incentive and enterprise. A free and competitive set of markets with opportunity for access to them by all citizens, encourages efficiency and growth, and harmonises best their interests as producers, consumers, workers, savers and investors.

The liberalisation initiatives undertaken are important, but they are only a part of the agenda for increasing free and fair competition. They have to be a supplemented by positive efforts to create the institutions that make competitive markets function and to make sure that all sections of society have access to the market economy and opportunities it creates. They also have to be accompanied by targeted poverty alleviation schemes aimed at those whom the markets cannot help.

It may be noted further that the kind of relationships that have developed among the various interest groups, club arrangement among ,brokers, big investors and political execution are strong impediments against the reform process. The political establishment in a democratic polity cannot evade its democratic accountability to move away from the kind of solutions and preferences that are breeders of inefficiencies. However, they cannot also be expected to simply alter the rules and change the policy parameters all too suddenly or experiment with an essentially irreversible programme. The priority is to generate a kind of political climate that encourages the growth of countervailing interest groups that have a stake in the changes to promote the kind of efficiencies that the economy is looking for. What one has to continually aim at is that the state and market driven institutions adapt to each other; neither the state nor the market should become destructively dominant to cripple the other. This, together with what has been covered across these pages, will, it is hoped give an indication of what the future is likely to hold and it is essential that we plan for the future than let events overtake us.

It is in this backdrop that we prompted to undertake this book to make appraisal of various aspects of Economic Reforms in India in detail and in an analytical manner so that it can help in focusing the attention of policy-makers to ground realities of Economic Reforms in India and the problems that need to be urgently redressed.

Framework

The write up of this book has been divided into Seven chapters.

Chapter 1: The chapter analyses background which made it necessary to initiate various measures of economic reforms in India.

Chapter 2: Investigates the background, objectives, features and evaluation of industrial policy 1991. The impact of industrial policy on industrial production has also been analyzed in detail.

Chapter 3: This chapter investigates public sector reforms very extensively. New role of public enterprise has been analysed in the light of industrial policy 1991. The important issues related to public enterprises such as disinvestment and privatization, working autonomy for public enterprises; their efficiency, profitability and performance appraisal have also been dealt thoroughly with critical appraisal.

Chapter 4: Deals with impact of economic reforms on agriculture in light of trends in agriculture production and productivity.

Chapter 5: Investigates foreign investment policy specifically since 1991. The chapter critically analyses the trend of foreign investment after 1991 substantiated with all possible statistical data.

Chapter 6: Deals with Financial Sector Reforms. The chapter incorporates the analysis of reforms in banking sector, Monetary Policy and Capital market since 1991. The Balance of Payment problem in post-reform period has also been covered in this chapter.

Chapter 7: Deals with vision for the future and challenges ahead.

Objectives

Economic Reforms in India were introduced in 1991 by the Congress (I) Government led by Mr. P.V. Narsimha Rao. There has been near unanimity among almost all major political parties on the direction and implementation of economic reforms. The agenda of two major political parties viz. the Congress (I) and Bhartiya Janata Party and again the UPA Government has shown a very large consensus about economic reforms. This consensus has been achieved in the country to introduce and implement economic reforms so as to accelerate the process of the development. The objective of the book is to analyse in detail the various measures of Economic Reforms in India and their effects on Indian economy. In short, the main objectives of the book are to focus attention on:

(1) Background and rationale of the Economic Reforms.
(2) Analytical evaluation of the salient features of Economic Reforms.
(3) Critical review of the Impact of economic reforms particularly on Industrial output, productivity and industrial outlook for the future.
(4) Analysis of policies and trends related to foreign investment in India.
(5) Study of work-performance and reorientation of public sector enterprises in the environment of Economic Reforms.
(6) Analysis of problems and limitations related to measures of economic reforms.
(7) Suggest necessary policy framework for effective and purposeful implementation of various measures of Economic Reforms keeping in view the experiences of first generation economic reforms.

Scope and Time Period

In the present study comprehensive and analytical study of Economic Reforms has been made and the study try to analyse the impact of first 15 years of Economic Reforms. The time period of study is 1991-92 to 2004-05. It may be mentioned that Economic Reforms is a very wide concept and it is not possible to study all aspects of reforms. Hence, only those aspects have been covered in this study which are closely related with industrial sector and Business Management. In all following aspects have been covered in the study:

(i) Industrial Policy.

(ii) Foreign Investment: Trends and Impact.
(iii) Public Enterprises: New Role and Working Performance.
(v) Financial Sector: Reforms in Banking and Capital Market.
(vi) Agricultural Sector: Need of Reforms.

The present book is primarily an analytical and critical study of the facts and figures related to various aspects of New Economic Reforms. For this purpose secondary data were collected from different government publications. The main government publication used in the present study are:

(a) Economic Survey of India—An annual publication of Ministry of Finance and Company Affairs, Government of India.
(b) Public Enterprises Survey—An annual publication of Department of Public Enterprises, Ministry of Heavy Industries and Public Enterprises.
(c) Annual Report of Ministry of Industry—An annual publication of Ministry of Industry.
(d) World Development Report—An annual publication of World Bank and Oxford University Press.
(e) Statistical Abstract of India—An annual publication of Ministry of Statistics and Programmes Implementation, Government of India.
(f) SIA Newsletter—Monthly publication of Secretariat of Industrial Assistance, Ministry of Industry, Government of India.
(g) Report on Currency and Finance—An annual publication of Reserve Bank of India.
(h) Budget speeches of Union Finance Ministers since 1991.

Beside these publications, various research Journals and reference books were consulted for getting desired information about various aspects of Economic Reforms. The relevant information available on various Ministry's Websites was also unloaded and incorporated at proper places.

The book is the result of help and co-operation of many persons. We wish to acknowledge, with a deep sense of gratitude, the inspiration and encouragement we received from S. Bhupinder Singh Jauhar (Chairman, Khalsa Educational Institutions, Yamuna Nagar), a visionary, philanthropist and a true human being who is always a guiding spirit for endeavour like the present book. We are extremely thankful to Dr. K.L. Gupta, Reader, Department of Business Administration, S.V. College, Aligarh, Dr. Davinder Singh Dhaliwal, Principal, G.N. Khalsa College, Karnal, Dr. B.S. Dhillon, Principal, G.N. Khalsa College, Yamuna Nagar and Dr. Tripat Kapoor, Principal, G.N.G. College, Yamuna Nagar for their useful comments and suggestions.

For this book, we have heavily drawn upon the material of several publications, we whole heartedly acknowledge our debt to authors of these publications. Last, but not the least, we are also grateful to Sh. G.S. Bhatia of Deep & Deep Publications Pvt. Ltd., New Delhi for promptly and so neatly bringing out this publication.

Yamuna Nagar

MANDEEP SINGH
HARVINDER KAUR

Acronyms

ACU	Asian Clearing Union
ADR	American Depository Receipt
ADs	Authorised Dealers
AEZs	Agri Export Zones
AIMO	All India Manufacturers Organisation
AMU	Asian Monetary Units
APFDA	Agricultural Processed Food Products Development Authority
BFRS	Board for Financial Regulation and Supervision
BIFR	Board for Industrial and Financial Reconstruction
BOT	Build-Operator-Transfer
CAMELS	Capital Adequacy, Assets Equality, Management, Earnings, Liquidity and Systems
CCFI	Cabinet Committee on Foreign Investment
CCS	Cash Compensatory Scheme
CDS	Comprehensive Development Strategy
CENVAT	Central Value Added Tax
CEO	Chief Executive Officer
CGE	Computable General Equilibrium.
CIS	Collective Investment Schemes
CRR	Cash Reserve Ratio

DAPR	Draft Agricultural Policy Resolution
DEPB	Duty Entitlement Pass Book
DGFT	Directorate General of Foreign Trade
DTA	Domestic Tariff Area
DTL	Demand and Time Liabilities
ECB	External Commercial Borrowing
ECGC	Export Credit Guarantee Corporation
EEFC	Exchange Earners Foreign Currency
EHTP	Electronic Hardware Technology Park
EOU	Export Oriented Units
EPCG	Export Promotion Capital Goods
EPZ	Export Processing Zone
FCI	Food Corporation of India
FDI	Foreign Direct Investment
FEMA	Foreign Exchange Management Act
FERA	Foreign Exchange Regulation Act
FIIA	Foreign Investment Implementation Authority
FIIs	Foreign Institutional Investors
FIOB	Freight on Board
FIPB	Foreign Investment Promotion Board
FIPC	Foreign Investment Promotion Council
FTA	Foreign Technology Agreement
GATT	General Agreement of Trade and Tariff
GCF	Gross Capital Formation
GDP	Gross Domestic Product
GDR	Global Depository Receipts
GIR	General Index Register
HACCP	Hazard Analysis and Critical Control Points
HYV	High Yielding Varieties
ICAR	Indian Council of Agricultural Research

ICICI	Industrial Credit and Investment Corporation of India
ICRR	Incremental Cash Reserve Ratio
IDBI	Industrial Development Bank of India
IFCI	Industrial Finance Corporation of India
IMF	International Monetary Fund
IRCBI	Industrial Reconstruction Bank of India
KVIC	Khadi and Village Industries Commission
LAC	Latin American Countries
LERMS	Liberalized Exchange Rate Management System
LPG	Liberalization, Privatization and Globalization
MAI	Market Access Initiatives
MDES	Modified Duty Exemption Scheme
MNC	Multinational Corporation
MODVAT	Modified Value Added Tax
MOU	Memorandum of Understanding
MRP	Maximum Retail Price
MRTP	Monopolies and Restrictive Trade Practice
MSP	Minimum Support Price
MTEs	Medium Term Export Strategy
MTFRP	Medium Term Fiscal Reform Programme
NABARD	National Bank for Agriculture and Rural Development
NAIS	National Agricultural Insurance Scheme
NBFC	Non-Banking Financial Companies
NFE	Net Foreign Exchange Earning
NHAI	National Highway Authority of India
NRI	Non-Resident Indian
NRNR	Non-Residential Non-Repairable
NSA	Net Sown Area

NSB	National Seeds Board
NTP	New Telecom Policy
OCBs	Overseas Corporate Bodies
OECD	Organisation for Economic Co-operation and Development
OGL	Open General Licence
OPEC	Organisation of Petroleum Exporting Countries
OTCEI	Over the Counter Exchange of India
PAN	Permanent Account Number
PIOs	Person of Indian Origins
PML	Prevention of Money Laundering (Law)
PSE	Public Sector Enterprise
QRs	Quantitative Restrictions
RIB	Resurgent India Bond
RIDF	Rural Infrastructure Development Fund
SAIL	Steel Authority of India
SAP	Structural Adjustment Programme
SAU	State Agricultural Universities
SBI	State Bank of India
SCB	Scheduled Commercial Bank
SEBI	Security and Exchange Board of India
SFC	State Finance Corporation
SIA	Secretariat for Industrial Assistance
SICA	Sick Industries Companies Act
SIDBI	Small Industries Development Bank of India
SIDC	State Industrial Development Corporation
SIDO	Small Industries Development Organisation
SIL	Special Import Licence
SLR	Statutory Liquidity Ratio
STP	Software Technology Park

CHAPTER

1

Economic Reforms

An Introduction

1.1: INTRODUCTION

In the end of June 1991, India landed in an unprecedented economic crisis. Balance of payment situation was leading towards a crisis. Faith of international community in Indian economy was shaken. The balance of payment position was on the brink of disaster as in mid-January 1991 and again in late June 1991 the level of foreign exchange reserves dropped to levels which were not sufficient to finance imports of even ten days. The BOP crisis that hit India in 1990-91, had been building for at least a half a decade preceding that year. The rising fiscal deficit and gradually increasing over-valuation contributed to the rising imbalance. Inadequate exchange rate adjustment in response to the external and domestic shocks during 1990-91 triggered the crisis. The period from mid-1989 to mid-1991 was packed with a series of political developments, one following on another without let-up. The break-up of Soviet empire, the unification of

Germany followed the policy of Glasnost. Iraq invaded Kuwait and set-off another oil shock. Domestically there were three changes of government and unprecedented socio-political upheaval. Underlying macro-economic imbalances that had been building up over the eighties came to a head as a result of these shocks and, along with the inadequate policy response, resulted in a BOP crisis in 1990-91.

1.2: BUILDING OF CRISIS

As in the case of most developing countries that have liberalized the economy in the last three decades of the 20th century, India's reforms too were preceded by a serious financial crisis. In 1990-91, the gross fiscal deficit of the government (center and states) reached 10 percent of GDP, and the annual rate of inflation peaked at nearly 17 percent in August 1991. Fiscal imbalances in India, which assumed serious proportions since the mid-1980s, had two important facets. First, the outpacing of the rate of growth of revenues by the expenditure growth considerably reduced the resources available for public investment in the economy. The increasing use of borrowed funds to meet current expenditures rendered the latter self-propelling.[1]

Second, the increasing diversion of household savings to meet public consumption requirements not only resulted in the expansion of public debt to unsustainable levels, but also reduced the resources available for private investment. An unprecedented balance of payments crisis emerged in early 1991. The current account deficit doubled from an annual average of $2.3 billion or 1.3 percent of GDP during the first half of the 1980s, to an annual average of $5.5 billion or 2.2 percent of GDP during the second half of the 1980s. For the first time in modern history, India was faced with the prospect of defaulting on external commitments since the foreign currency reserves had fallen to a mere $1 billion by mid-1991. The balance of payments came under severe strain from one liquidity crisis experienced in mid-January 1991 and another in late June 1991. On both occasions, the foreign exchange reserves dropped significantly and the government had to resort to emergency measures, such as using its stocks of gold to obtain foreign exchange, utilization of special facilities of the IMF, and emergency bilateral assistance from Japan and Germany among others. Having resorted to these measures, the government was able to avoid default in terms of meeting its immediate debt service obligations and the financing of imports.[2] The main causes of crisis in 1991 and subsequent reforms were:

(A) International Factors

Following international factors emphasized the need for economic reforms in India:

(1) International Scenario

Over the last two or three decades, centrally planned economies like Russia, Eastern Europe, Eastern Germany, etc. failed on economic front. These economies were hesitant in adopting the process of economic reforms. On the contrary, those developing economies like Korea, Thailand, Taiwan, Hong Kong, Singapore, etc. which adopted the process of economic reforms achieved new heights of economic success. China also succeeded in achieving high rate of economic growth by resorting to the process of economic reforms. These success stories of economic reforms inspired India to globalize its economy and adopt series of new economic reforms.

(2) International Pressure and Condition

India faced unprecedented balance of payment and foreign exchange crisis in 1991. There was no alternative before the government but to take loan from international financial institutions like IMF and World

Bank. These institutions granted loan on the condition that economic reform in the form of liberalization, privatization and globalization are to be immediately implemented. This resulted in the emergence of new economic reforms.

(B) Domestic Circumstances

Besides international factors the economic conditions prevailing within the country around 1991 also underlined the need for new economic reforms. These conditions may be analysed as follows:

(1) Increase in Fiscal Deficit

Fiscal deficit of the government had been mounting year after year on account of continuous increase in its non-developmental expenditure. This has been made explicit by Table 1.1. It is clear from Table 1.1 that from 1980-81 to 1990-91, the two conventional indicators of fiscal imbalance rose substantially. The budgetary deficit was 2.4 percent of G.D.P. in 1990-91 as against 2.0 percent in 1980-81. The revenue deficit registered a similar trend as it rose from 1.5 percent of G.D.P. in 1980-81 to 3.5 percent in 1990-91. The gross fiscal deficit rose alarmingly from 5.7 percent of G.D.P. in 1980-81 to 7.0 percent in 1990-91.

Such a fiscal situation became unsustainable because it resulted in the absorption of an increasing proportion of Government resources in servicing of past debts and thus pushing the Government into debt-trap. The debt situation of Government at that time is shown in Table 1.2.

It is clear from Table 1.2 that internal debt registered a sharp increase in eighties, from 35.6 percent of G.D.P. in 1980-81 to 52.8 percent in 1990-91. An offshoot of the growth in internal debt was the mounting burden of interest payments. The gross interest payments as a ratio of total government expenditure more than doubled between 1980-81 and

TABLE 1.1

Central Government Deficit

(% of G.D.P. at current Market Prices)

Year	*Budgetary Deficit**	*Revenue Deficit***	*Gross Fiscal Deficit****
1980-81	2.0	1.5	5.7
1981-82	0.9	0.2	5.4
1982-83	0.9	0.7	6.0
1983-84	0.7	1.2	6.3
1984-85	1.6	1.8	7.5
1985-86	2.0	2.2	8.3
1986-87	2.8	2.7	9.0
1987-88	1.7	2.7	8.1
1988-89	1.4	2.7	7.8
1989-90	2.4	2.6	7.9
1990-91	2.4	3.5	7.0

* Budgetary Deficit = Total Expenditure (Revenue + Capital) - Total receipts (Revenue + Capital)

** Revenue Deficit = Current Revenue Expenditure (Non-plan + Plan Expenditure) - Current Revenue Receipts (Net Tax Revenue + Non-Tax Revenue).

*** Gross Fiscal Deficit = Revenue Receipts (Net Tax Revenue + Non-tax Revenue) + Capital Receipts (only recoveries of loan and other receipts) - Total Expenditure (Plan and non-plan expenditure).

Source: *Economic Survey*, 1992-93, p. 10.

1990-91, i.e. from 11.6 percent to 26.2 percent. Such a fiscal situation being unsustainable required immediate corrective measures in form of new economic reforms.

(2) Deficit of Current Account and Increase in Foreign Debt

The decade of eighties saw increase in defence imports, negligible increase in exports and very slow progress in import substitution of Petroleum product. All these factors resulted in increase in deficit of current account and increase in foreign debt. The situation is shown in Table 1.3, 1.7 percent in 1990-91.

TABLE 1.2

Trends of Internal and External Debt of Central Government

(% of G.D.P.)

Year	*Internal Debt*	*Gross interest payment as % of total expenditure*
1980-81	35.6	11.6
1983-84	38.6	13.3
1984-85	41.8	13.1
1985-86	45.5	14.1
1986-87	49.9	14.4
1987-88	51.7	16.0
1988-89	51.7	17.5
1989-90	53.2	18.7
1990-91	52.8	26.2

Source: Economic Survey, 1991-92, p. 13.

Thus India which was caught in cob web of foreign debt burden required immediate remedial measures in form of new economic reforms.

(3) Balance of Payment Crises

The balance of payment situation was highly precarious in 1990-91. The current account deficit which was $2.4 billion or 1.2 percent of G.D.P. in 1980-81 rose to $4.9 billion or 2.3 percent of G.D.P. in 1985-86 The perusal of data in Table 1.3 shows that from 1980-81 to 1984-85 deficit of current account remained almost stable but after 1984-85 it started increasing and stood at 2.3 percent of G.D.P. in 1990-91. The burden of foreign debt was to tune of 23.8 million dollars in 1980-81 which was 14.3 percent of G.D.P. The debt rose to 62.3 million dollars in 1990-91 which was 23.8 percent of G.D.P. The resultant increase in cost of

TABLE 1.3

Trends in Current Account Deficit, Foreign Debt and Servicing of Foreign Debt

Year	*Deficit current account (% of G.D.P.)*	*Foreign Debt (in million $)*	*Foreign debt (as % of G.D.P.)*	*Foreign debt (as % of export)*	*Foreign debt servicing (% of receipts)*
1980-81	1.2	23.8	14.3	14.9	7.9
1981-82	1.4	24.3	14.2	13.5	7.7
1982-83	1.3	27.9	15.6	14.6	8.7
1983-84	1.1	31.1	16.0	17.2	10.3
1984-85	1.2	31.9	17.1	19.8	11.7
1985-86	2.3	37.0	17.4	26.7	15.9
1986-87	2.0	43.8	19.4	39.4	31.0
1987-88	1.9	50.8	19.5	41.3	26.4
1988-89	2.6	53.5	21.1	38.9	25.4
1989-90	2.2	57.7	21.6	31.1	21.5
1990-91	2.3	62.3	23.8	29.8	21.7

Source: Deepak Nayyar, Economic Liberalization in India (1996), p. 6.

servicing of foreign debt was amazing. It was only 7.9 percent of receipts in 1980-81 but rose to and further to $9.7 billion or 2.3 percent of 1990-91. These continuously growing deficits had to be financed by borrowing from abroad and as a consequence India's external debt rose from 14.3 percent of GDP at the end of 1980-81 to 23.8 percent of GDP at the end of 1990-91. This steadily growing external debt led to an increase in debt service burden from 7.9 percent of current account receipts and 14.9 percent of export earnings in 1980-81 to 21.7 percent of current account receipts and 29.8 percent of export earnings in 1990-91. These mounting strains during the 1980s stretched to the breaking point in 1991 due to the Gulf crisis. The balance of payment position was on the brink of disaster as in mid-January 1991 and again in late June 1991 the level of foreign exchange reserves dropped to levels which were not sufficient to finance imports of even ten days.

No doubt this was a very difficult situation from India's point of view, as default in terms of financing imports and meeting debt service obligations looked imminent. The country's balance of payments position was extremely vulnerable on account of two factors which were greatly influenced by perceptions and expectations. First, it was exceedingly difficult to prevent flight of short-term debt on account of adverse international perception of the situation. Second, the net outflow of non-resident deposits which added up to $ 1.64 billion in the period October 1990-September 1991 could further increase if the perceptions had worsened. In this extremely precarious situation, default could be averted only by recourse to last-resort measures, such as using stocks of gold to obtain foreign exchange, seeking emergency bilateral assistance from donor countries and borrowing under special facilities from IMF. Thus soft options which the government adopted during the 1980s had such repercussions that in 1991-92, it was left with no options but to resort to measures which, although helping the country to avert default in meeting payments obligations, pushed it into recessionary situation.

(4) Mounting Inflationary Pressure

The price situation was apparently not alarming during the second half of 1980's as the average rate of inflation was 6.7 percent per annum in terms of the wholesale price index. However, the rate of inflation rose to 10.3 percent per annum in 1990-91. In terms of the consumer price index the rate of inflation climbed to 11.2 percent per annum which was certainly a cause for concern. However, the most disquieting feature of this inflationary situation was that the prices of food rose substantially in spite of three good monsoons in a row. According to Deepak Nayyar, "inflationary pressures in the economy did not surface out of the blue. The build-up was attributable to the large deficits, which were inevitably associated with a monetisation of budget deficits and an excessive growth of money supply. This liquidity overhang, in conjunction with real disproportional ties and underlying supply demand imbalances was bound to fuel inflation."[3]

(5) Unsatisfactory Performance of Public Sector

The expansion of the public sector was based on Industrial Policy Resolution of 1956, which assigned a strategic role to the public sector. Development of heavy and basic industries and the provision of infrastructure were the main tasks of the public sector. Massive investments were made over the past 45 years to build the public sector. Many of these enterprises successfully expanded production, opened up new areas of technology and build up a reserve of technical competence in a number of areas. There is no doubt that the public sector established an industrial base of the economy which enabled the private sector to undertake investments in other areas as infrastructural facilities were made available by the public sector. "However, after the initial concentration of public sector investment in key infrastructure areas, public enterprises began to spread into all areas of the economy including non-infrastructure and non-core areas. This had resulted in poor general overall performance of the public sector which had manifested itself in low or negative returns to public investment."[4]

The operation of the public sector resulted in a number of failures. These failures were highlighted by a number of Committees and economists. Principal failures were: Over manning and low work ethics leading to low capacity utilization, over capitalization due to substantial time and cost overruns, political and bureaucratic interference stifling the ability to innovate and to take quick and timely decisions, burden of taken-over private sector sick units, excessive social welfare expenditure, absence of rational pricing policy based on economic calculus. All these factors resulted in a low rate of return which tarnished the image of the public sector.

On account of above compelling factors, it became inevitable for the government to adopt new economic reforms

1.3: BASIS OF ECONOMIC REFORMS

Although economic reforms were introduced under Rajiv Gandhi regime, they did not yield the desired results. In the end of June 1991, country landed in an unprecedented economic crisis. Reserves of foreign exchange were just sufficient to pay for two weeks imports. New loans were not available. Balance of payment situation was leading towards a crisis. Faith of international community in Indian economy was shaken. In order to pull the economy out of economic crisis and to put it on the path to rapid and steady economic growth, it was most essential to correct financial disequilibrium, curb rising prices, correct adverse balance of payment and replenish foreign exchange reserves. To achieve all these objectives, introduction of economic reforms or an appropriate economic policy was considered inevitable.

P.V. Narsimha Rao led Congress (I) Government after resumption of office on June 21, 1991 adopted a number of stabilization measures that were designed to restore internal and external confidence. The government adopted, as the centerpiece of economic strategy, a programme to bring about reduction in fiscal imbalance to be supported by reforms in economic policy that were essential to impart a new element of dynamism to the growth process in the economy. In his memorandum on Economic Policies submitted to IMF, Dr. Manmohan Singh proposed, "The thrust will be to increase the efficiency and international competitiveness of industrial production, to utilize foreign investment and technology to a much greater degree than in the past, to improve the performance and rationalize the scope of the public sector, and to reform and modernize the financial sector so that it can more efficiently serve the needs of the economy."[5]

The reforms programme was undertaken in the face of a balance of payments crisis which forced the country to seek IMF financial assistance. Though India adopted a more cautious and step-by-step approach to reforms and liberalization than most other similarly placed emerging economies, the programme bore the unmistakable stamp of the Washington consensus. The then prevailing perception among international financial bodies and the most influential section of Indian economists was that the proximate cause of the payments crisis was the faulty macro-economic policies the country had been pursuing during the 80s. More fundamentally, the malady was traced to growing inefficiency and non-competitiveness of the country's products due to subversion of market forces through a plethora of controls and quantitative restrictions and to the position assumed by the public sector for controlling the "commanding heights" of the economy. The problems faced by the country were accordingly sought to be solved through two sets of policies, the first macro-economic, the second efficiency promoting, though in a number of instances the distinction was far from clear cut.

The thrust of the macro-stabilization programme consisted in the following measures:[6]

(a) reduction in fiscal deficit with curbs on government expenditure including subsidies; privatization along with priority accorded to profitability in running public enterprises; and tax reforms for imparting buoyancy to revenue receipts;
(b) sharp devaluation (in two quick, successive steps) at the initial stage followed by (i) a fairly rapid transition to a more or less market driven exchange rate system; and (ii) encouragement of the inflow of foreign

capital through opening up avenues for foreign institutional investment (FII) and considerable relaxation of controls on FDI; and

(c) significant scaling down of net central bank credit to the government to meet its financing requirement and the large measure of autonomy granted to the RBI for maintaining the country's internal and external balance.

Also important for promoting the medium- and long-term viability of the balance of payments were abandonment of the import substitution policy and phased liberalization of trade, though the major impact of these policies were mostly allocative, their effects being primarily on composition of domestic production and absorption. Similarly, practically all financial sector measures have both efficiency and macro-economic implications. The most important of these measures are:[7]

(a) a cutback in the Statutory Liquidity Ratio (SLR) from 38.5% to 25%, along with moves to make interest rates on government securities market determined (so that there could be a level playing field for private sector borrowers and the government);

(b) adoption of international best practice (Basle) norms relating to capital adequacy, income recognition, asset classification and provisioning and these were sought to enforced by strengthening of the RBI's regulatory-*cum*-supervisory role;

(c) gradual abolition of the system of fixing banks' lending and borrowing rates of interest, except for the rate on short-term (savings) deposit; and

(d) abolition of control of capital issues by the government and constitution of the Securities and Exchange Board of India (SEBI) for making the issues easier and rule-based, and functioning of stock exchanges transparent.

While adoption of the Basle norms and strengthening of the regulatory and supervisory role of the RBI (as also of the SEBI) were intended to impart stability to or strengthen the shock absorptive capacity of the financial and hence of the macro-economic system, steps like cutbacks in SLR, removal of controls on interest rates, entry of private firms in the financial market, etc. were designed to raise allocative efficiency through greater flows of funds to the relatively productive lines of activity in the economy. Such measures were complemented by policies relating to de-reservation so that private entrepreneurs were now permitted to set-up production units in any sector except for a few defence or strategic industries.

Macro-economic stabilization involves returning to low and stable inflation and sustainable fiscal and balance of payment position. Stabilization is necessary to overcome a crisis but it assumes a special importance if structural reforms are also introduced together with stabilization. This is because structural reforms often add to macro-economic pressures. For example, in the short-run, trade liberalization may increase deficit, in the balance of payments and financial sector reforms may worsen fiscal position by raising the cost of public borrowing. Therefore, stabilization must accompany structural reforms and stabilization policies have to be bold and effective, otherwise extra macro-economic strains generated in the reform process can disrupt the latter completely. Vijay Joshi and I.M.D. Little have argued that in the longer run, structural reform is as helpful for stabilization as stabilization is for structural reform. In the absence of reform, losses of public enterprises would continue to burden the budget, trade restriction would hamper the exports and compulsory government capture of private savings would erode fiscal discipline.[8]

The Congress Government which assumed office at the end of June 1991 responded quickly to growing economic crisis. Beside, committing itself to a comprehensive structural reform, it accorded an overriding priority to stabilization of the economy. The main elements of the strategy of new economic reforms adopted in 1991 are summarized below:

(1) Integration of National Economy with World Economy

This aspect may be referred as globalization of the economy. By the term globalization, we mean opening up of the economy for world market by attaining international competitiveness. Thus, the globalization of the economy simply indicates interaction of the country relating to production, trading and financial transactions with the developed industrialized countries of the world. According to eminent economist Deepak Nayyar,[9] "Globalization may be defined as a process associated with increasing openness, growing economic interdependence and deepening economic integration in the world economy." In the words of Rubens Ricuperio, "Globalization is the integration of the world economy as the result of following three main forces:

(i) increase in trade in goods and services;
(ii) the increase in the investment of transnational companies and the consequent, change in the nature of production. Production becoming no longer national but as a process that takes place in different countries; and
(iii) international financial and exchange rate transactions."[10]

Globalization of the economy offers both challenges and opportunities to the developing countries. While facing the trend of globalization, the developing countries can prepare themselves to face the challenge of international competitiveness.

With the introduction of new economic reforms, Indian economy has accepted the challenge of integrating national economy with world economy or globalisation of the economy.

(2) Control on the Role of Government in the Economy

Soon after independence, there was a widespread belief that without increasing the role of the State, it was not possible either to accelerate the process of growth or to create an industrial base for sustained economic development of the country. The Second Five Year Plan stated in unequivocal terms, "the adoption of the socialist pattern of society as the national objective, as well as the need for planned and rapid development, require that all industries of basic and strategic importance, or in the nature of public utility services, should be in the public sector. Other industries which are essential and require investment on a scale which only the State in the present circumstances, could provide, have also to be in the public sector. The state has therefore, to assume direct responsibility for the future development of industries over a wider area."[11]

Prior to 1991, government had imposed several types of controls on Indian economy e.g., industrial licensing system, price control or financial control on goods, import license, foreign exchange control, restrictions on investment by big business houses, etc. However, it was realized by the government that several shortcomings had crept into the economy on account of these controls. These had dampened the enthusiasm of the entrepreneurs to establish new industries and had given rise to corruption, red-tapism, undue delays and inefficiency. Rate of economic growth of the economy was not in accordance with targets and high-cost economic system came into being. Economic reforms, therefore, made a bid to reduce restrictions imposed on the economy. In fact, economic reforms are based on the assumption that market forces can guide the economy in a more effective manner than government control. New economic reforms took certain bold steps to reduce the role of government, by policy decisions under economic reforms. Some of these are as follows:

(a) Number of industries reserved for the public sector has been reduced from 17 to 3 only, and the remaining industries have been opened for private sector. This measure will increase the flow of investible resources to priority sectors. It is hoped that competition and efficiency will increase in these sectors.

(b) Public enterprises that were chronically sick and unlikely to be turned around would be referred to the Board for Industrial and Financial Reconstruction (BIFR) for rehabilitation or restructuring.

(c) Government equity in selected public enterprises is being disinvested through mutual funds, financial institutions, public and workers.

(d) The existing system of monitoring public enterprises through Memorandum of Understanding (MOU) has been strengthened with primary emphasis on profitability and rate of return.

(e) Consequent upon the policy of less government control, the office of Controller of Capital Issue was abolished in 1992 and the capital market was put under the control of Securities and Exchange Board of India (SEBI).

(3) Dominant Role of Market Forces in Economy

As mentioned earlier, economic reforms are based on the assumption that the market forces can guide the economy in more effective manner than government control. Examples of countries like Korea, Thailand, Singapore, etc. that had achieved rapid economic development as a result of free play of market forces, are worthy of emulation. Following measures taken under economic reforms in this regard are noteworthy:

(a) Under new economic reforms private sector has been freed, to a large extent, from the yoke of licenses and other restrictions. In July 1991, a new Industrial Policy was announced in this respect. According to it, with the exception of 6 industries, industrial licensing has been abolished for all other industries. Industries for which licenses are still necessary are Liquor; Cigarette; Defence Equipment; Industrial Explosives; Dangerous Chemicals and Drugs.

(b) The Government has accepted the policy of liberalization in all economic activities and accordingly it is relaxing controls on prices and distribution of goods. At the same time the government is aware that free competition and free prices are not fully applicable in India because:

   (i) There are still serious demand-supply gaps in some essential goods.

   (ii) Investment has to be guided into particular channels.

   (iii) Special consideration has to be shown to the needs of the vulnerable section of the community.

Necessarily, therefore prices will have to be regulated and administered to some extent, though price controls and regulation have to be kept to the minimum level. Infact, price control has been removed in respect of most commodities and now exist only for bulk drugs and certain varieties of paper.

(4) Relaxation to Large Indian and Foreign Business Houses

In new economic reforms the government is guided by policy of facilitating investment by big business houses rather than imposing a ceiling on their assets. Accordingly, the provision of Monopolies and Restrictive Trade Practices Act (MRTP Act) whereby, all those companies having assets more than 100 crore were declared MRTP firms and were subjected to several restrictions has been done away with. These firm are now no longer required to obtain prior approval of the Government, at the time of taking investment decisions. They are free to expand themselves. Large concession has been granted to companies falling under MRTP Act. Capital investment limit fixed earlier has been removed. As a result, there would be no restriction on dominant companies and industrial houses for setting up new industries or expansion of industries, taking over and amalgamation. However, under this policy more emphasis will be laid on checking unfair trade practices to safeguard the interests of the consumers. The newly empowered Monopoly Board is authorized to investigate any matter 'suo motu' or on complaints received from individual consumers.

The policy and procedures pertaining to direct foreign investment has been progressively liberalized over the years. At present all foreign direct investment are permitted under the automatic approval route, except for a small negative list. The existing upper limit of Rs.1500 crore for FDI in projects involving electricity generation, transmission and distribution (other than atomic reactor plants) has been dispensed with. In the oil refining sectors the ceiling for foreign direct investment under the automatic route has been increased to 100 percent from 49 percent. In special economic zones 100 percent foreign direct investment has been allowed in all manufacturing industries.

(5) Fiscal and Financial Reforms

Fiscal and Financial Reforms occupy prominent place in new economic reforms. For achieving fiscal and financial stability government intend to strictly control public expenditure and aim at higher tax and non-tax revenues. The government intends to impose fiscal discipline both on the central and state governments. Government has initiated steps to control subsidies and also intend to move towards more objective system of administered prices taking into account market development and domestic supply condition. The Government is making determined effort for developing a more efficient expenditure system.

The theme of new fiscal reforms summarized by Shankar Acharya is as follows:[12]

- A systematic effort to simplify both the tax structure and the tax laws.
- A deliberate shift to a regime of reasonable direct tax rates, combined with better administration and enforcement, to improve compliance and raise revenues.
- The fostering of a stable and predictable tax policy environment.
- Greater recognition and weight given to the resource allocation and equity consequences of taxation.
- More reliance on non-discretionary fiscal and financial instruments in managing the economy, as compared to *ad hoc*, discretionary fiscal controls.
- Concerted efforts to improve tax administration and reduce the scope for arbitrary harassment.
- Growing appreciation of the links between fiscal and monetary policy.
- Fresh initiative to strengthen methods of expenditure control.

Economic reforms introduced in India since 1991 has already created mixed reactions at different levels. Although it is too early to make a complete appraisal of these economic reforms in India but it is nothing wrong to consider both the positive and negative aspects of economic reforms in order to have a wise and successful implementation of these policy reforms. In ensuing chapters the implementation, effects and evaluation of new economic reform has been undertaken.

Notes and References

1 Bajpai, Nirupam, "A Decade of Economic Reforms in India: the Unfinished Agenda", Centre for International Development, Harved University, Working Paper No. 89, April 2002.

2. *Ibid.*

3. Nayyar, Deepak, "Indian Economy at Cross Roads—Illusions and Realities", *Economic and Political Weekly*, April 10, 1993, p. 639.

4. Ministrry of Finance, Public Enterprise Survey, 1992-93, Vol. I, p.1.

5. Memoradum of Economic Policies for 1991-92 to 1992-93, submitted by the finance minister to IMF dated August 27, 1991.

6. Rakshit Mihir, "Some Macro-economics of India's Reforms Experience—An Outline."

7. *Ibid.*

8. Joshi, Vijay and Little, I.M.D., "Economic Reforms, 1991-2000", Delhi, 1996, p. 32.

9. Nayyar, Deepak, "Economic Liberalization in India", 1996, p. 34.

10. Rubens Ricupero, Secretary-General of UNCTAD.

11. Government of India, Planning Commission, Second Five Year Plan, 1956, p. 29.

12. Acharya, Shankar, "India's Fiscal Policy," in Robert E.B. Lucas and Gustav, F. Papanek (eds.), "The Indian Economy—Recent Development and Future Prospects", p. 289.

CHAPTER

2

Industrial Sector Reforms

2.1: INTRODUCTION

The industrial sector in India has been undergoing significant changes in its both structure and pattern owing to the policy changes since the first industrial policy resolution of 1948 onwards. In pursuit of building an industrial base for the country, the policy-makers advocated a series of guidelines characterized by pervasive licensing, reservation of key areas for public sector, inward-oriented trade policy, control over large domestic firms, foreign direct investment, technology transfer and interventions in factor market. However, there emerged a view that the restrictive industrial policy regime, which roughly prevailed till 1985, created a high-cost industrial structure characterized by technological obsolescence, low rates of productivity, capacity utilization (CU) and growth. As the rough nature of this complex control system became more and more obvious, there emerged consensus over the need for a reorientation in planning. The increasing skepticism over the success of the import-substituting regime in the country resulted in a shift in the policy thinking towards a more liberal policy regime, based on the grounds of achieving efficiency and competitiveness. This resulted in a shift in the policy sphere since the late seventies,[1] nevertheless, it was in the second half of the 1970s that the government started relaxing the foreign trade regime and a number of imported items were placed on the open general license list. Significant changes were made in this direction during the 1980s. However, the key role played by the state in allocating resources remained decisive. The shift in the policy paradigm got further stimulus in 1991 with the introduction of new economic and industrial policies, where the market is allowed to play a decisive role. These major changes in the policy regimes created debates among economists regarding the impact of the liberal policy environment on industrial performance in India.[2] We, in this study examine the performance of Indian manufacturing sector in post-industrial policy 1991 phase.

The new Industrial Policy announced by the Government of India in July 1991 fulfilled a long felt demand of the corporate sector for declaring in very clear terms that licensing was abolished for all industries except 18 industries which included coal, petroleum, sugar, motor cars, cigarettes, hazardous chemical, pharmaceuticals and some luxury items.[3] Beside this, the Industrial Policy proposed to remove the limit of assets fixed for MRTP companies and dominant undertakings. Thus, business houses intending to float new companies or undertake substantial expansion were not required to seek clearance from MRTP Commission. Numerous cases of bottlenecks created by the bureaucracy were struck down by this singular decision of the Government. In this sense, the Industrial Policy was welcomed because it took bold decision to end the license-permit raj and save the entrepreneurs the harassment of seeking permission from the bureaucracy of the country to start an undertaking. This step enabled MRTP companies to establish new undertakings and effect plans of expansions, mergers, amalgamations and takeovers without prior government approval. In other words new Industrial Policy unshackled many of the provisions, which acted as brakes on the growth of the large private corporate sector. All these provisions were welcomed in business circles. There was thus an overall relief in the dismantling of industrial licensing and regime of controls.

Many economists hailed the new Industrial Policy as a cornerstone of industrial growth. According to J.C. Sandesra the new Industrial Policy seeks to raise efficiency and accelerate industrial production in five different ways[4]:

(1) A number of changes in industrial licensing policy, foreign investment, foreign technology agreements and MRTP Act are such as to do away with the prior clearance of the government. In such cases, project time and, therefore, project cost will be reduced. Material and human resources engaged in cultivating contacts and 'getting things done' will be released for more productive uses. Thus efficiency will improve.

(2) The changes in respect of foreign investment and foreign technology agreements are also designed to attract capital, technology and managerial expertise from abroad. This will raise the availability of such scarce resources in the country on the one hand, and will improve the level of efficiency of production on the other hand.

(3) Some changes as regards public sector may enhance the 'allocative efficiency'. Opening up of eleven areas (so far reserved for the public sector) to the private sector implies an opening for the sector which has, by and large, given a better account of itself. Closure, liquidation or rehabilitation, etc. of sick/weak public sector units will free resources for more productive use. Similarly, privatisation may make for improved efficiency of the public sector, through its being subjected to the stock market discipline.

(4) Other measures in this area such as purposeful formulation and implementation of Memorandum of Understanding and its monitoring, professionalisation and greater autonomy may be expected to improve the performance of the enterprises that will remain in the public sector.

(5) Greater emphasis in controlling and regulating monopolistic, restrictive and unfair trade practices and the strengthening of the powers of the MRTP Commission will curb anti-competitive behaviour of firms in the monopolistic, oligopolistic and ineffectively competitive markets and thus promote competition and efficiency.

Critics of the new Industrial Policy, however, point to the dangers of 'opening up' the economy to foreign influence. For instance, H.K. Paranjape argues that the list of high priority industries (in which direct foreign investment up to 51 percent will now be freely permitted) includes industries, which have been well established in the country for long and where technological development with indigenous Research and Development should not prove difficult. Invitation to foreign investors in these industries "would make it possible for large transnational to dominate certain growing areas of our economy and push to the wall any Indian concerns which attempts to stand out on their own. Indigenous Research and Development will be doomed.[5] Moreover, as correctly pointed out by Paranjape, "the past record of the multinationals operating in the country does not warrant much enthusiasm. None of the multinationals operating in this country has attempted to develop India as an important base for a significant part of its world-wide research and development work. Despite various tax concessions and incentives none of the multinationals tried to expand export markets. They undertook export activities only to the extent they were compelled to do so under export obligations, or when it was found necessary to do so in order to be able to earn foreign exchange for importing some of their essential requirements. In fact, instead of developing India as a major production and export base, many multinationals have only attempted to use their international trade capacities and contacts mainly for exporting goods manufactured by other—usually small scale units. Thus they have operated more as trading than as manufacturing and exporting concerns."[6] In light of two opposing views about the reforms in industrial sector it will be prudent to access the growth of industrial sector in post-reforms phase.

2.2: IMPACT OF INDUSTRIAL REFORMS ON INDUSTRIAL GROWTH RATE

The most important fundamental of evaluation of any Industrial Policy is the analysis of its impact on industrial growth rate. The impact of new Industrial Policy on industrial growth rate since 1991 is shown in Table 2.1.

Table 2.1 reveals that Industrial growth showed continuous improved and progressive trend up to 1995-96, when it reached to a record level of 13 percent. However, in the next year, i.e. in 1996-97, it fell down to only 6.1 percent. It slightly improved in 1997-98 but again declined to 4.1 percent in 1998-99. It recovered to 6.7 percent in 1999-2000 but was only at 5 percent in 2000-01 and fell further to 2.7 percent in 2001-02. Industrial recovery commenced from the second quarter of 2002-03 continued in the subsequent years. The rate of growth of industrial sector as measured in terms of Index of Industrial Production in 2005-06 was 7.8 per cent compared to a growth of 8.6 per cent in 2004-05. Impressive performance of the manufacturing sector, which grew at 8.9 per cent during this period, largely contributed to this performance. The yearly Growth of industrial production is also presented in the diagram.

In fact, the major contribution in this growth rate is that of manufacturing sector and the growth rate in

TABLE 2.1

Annual Growth Rate of Industrial Production in Major Sectors of the Industry

(per cent)

Period	*Mining*	*Manufacturing*	*Electricity*	*General*
1991-92	0.6	0.8	8.5	0.6
1992-93	0.5	2.2	5.0	2.3
1993-94	3.5	6.1	7.4	6.0
1994-95	9.8	9.1	8.5	9.1
1995-96	9.7	14.1	8.1	13.0
1996-97	-1.9	7.3	4.0	6.1
1997-98	6.9	6.7	6.6	6.7
1998-99	-0.8	4.4	6.5	4.1
1999-00	1.0	7.1	7.3	6.7
2000-01	2.8	5.3	4.0	5.0
2001-02	1.2	2.9	3.1	2.7
2002-03	5.8	6.0	3.2	5.7
2003-04	5.2	7.4	5.1	7.0
2004-05	4.4	9.2	6.4	8.6
2005-06	0.4	8.9	4.8	7.8

Source: *Economic Survey*, 2005-06, p. 132.

this sector has moved in the same trend. The conclusion is clear that economic reforms activated the industrial sector impressively but that activation has slowed down during the period of Ninth Plan. It is due to number of structural and cyclical as discussed below:

(A) Structural factors.
(B) Cyclical factors.

(A) Structural Factors[7]

The adjustment process of industry in response to increased competition in the form of Mergers and Acquisitions is taking longer time than expected.

- Infrastructural bottlenecks and high costs and inadequate and unreliable supply of services in transport, communications and the power sector.
- Low levels of productivity in the industry because of low volumes and inability to reap economies of scale, outdated technology and restricted labour laws.
- Lower speculative demand for sectors like automobiles and real estate due to expectation of lower prices and reduction of taxes and duties in the short and medium-term.
- High real interest rates.

(B) Cyclical Factors[8]

- Periodic investment cycles, reinforced by government's decision to reduce customs duties to levels in East Asian Countries by 2004, which might have deferred investment decisions.
- Business cycles affecting demand of some cyclical industries like cement, automobiles and steel.
- There is no pent up demand for consumer durables. The above cycles have been reinforced by reduction in inventory levels resulting from the introduction of e-business and e-commerce and better management of supply and demand by industry to cut costs.

Another way of judging industrial performance in post-reform period is to analyze the efficiency or productivity of resources in the process of growth. Number of studies have been conducted in India to judge factor productivity[9] in pre and post-reform period. The results of these studies have varied widely, but the overall conclusions appear to be: TFP is growing, but is growing at a slower rate than the pre-

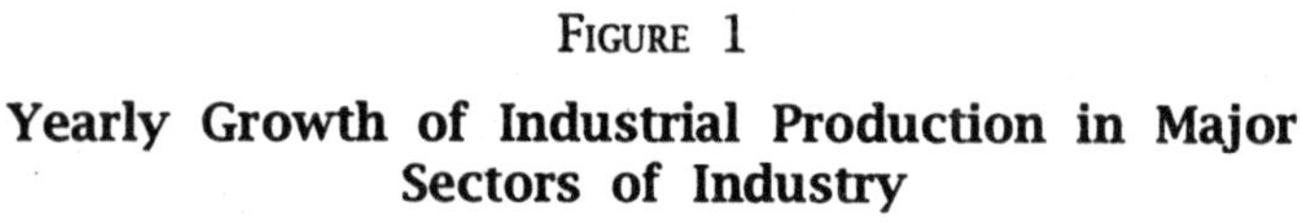

FIGURE 1

Yearly Growth of Industrial Production in Major Sectors of Industry

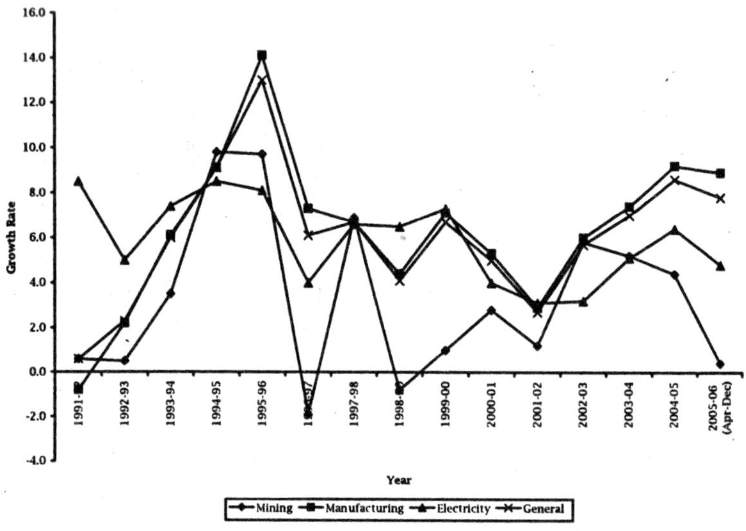

liberalisation period. However, most of these studies also conclude that there has been a decrease, not an increase, in the growth rate of TFP in Indian manufacturing in the post-reform period. This needs to be looked into and reversed. At the state level, various recent studies reveal that with respect to the overall manufacturing sector, the level of TFP was highest for Karnataka, Uttar Pradesh and Madhya Pradesh, whereas for Gujarat, Bihar and Rajasthan it was the lowest.

Trends in overall industrial growth, and by sectors and classes also suggest an all round slowdown in industrial activity after 1995-96 as shown in Table 2.3.

The Table 2.3 shows that industrial production, measured by the Index of Industrial Production, registered a significantly lower growth rate of 5.0 percent in 2000-01 compared to a growth rate of 13 percent in 1995-96. Growth rates also fell in both the basic goods and capital goods sector from 10.8 percent

TABLE 2.2

Total Factor Productivity Growth in Pre- and Post-Liberalization Period

Study	*Pre-liberalisation*	*Post-liberalisation*	*Methodology*
1	*2*	*3*	*4*
Unni *et al.* (2001)	1985-90 4.0 11.37	1990-95 -1.28 -3.13	Value Added Function Framework Organized Manufacturing, Unorganized Manufacturing
Srivastava (2001)	1980-81 to 1989-90 2.56 2.32	1990-91 to 1997-98 0.83 1.74	Estimates for aggregate economy With no corrections for capacity utilization made with adjustments made for capacity utilization (*Data Source*: CSO, NSSO; Methodology: GAA)
Goldar and Kumar (2003)	1981-82 to 1990-91 1.89 1.60	1990-91 to 1997-98 10.69 1.3	Gross Output Function Framework With no corrections for capacity utilization made with adjustments made for capacity utilization (*Data Source*: CSO, NSSO; Methodology: GAA)
Unel (2003)	1979-80 to 1990-91 1.8 3.2	1991-92 to 1997-98 2.5 4.7	Value Added Function Framework Based on actual income shares of labour as weights Based on constant labour elasticity of 0.6 (*Data Source*: ASI, Methodology: GGA)
Tata Services Ltd. TSL (2003)	1981-82 to 1992-93 0.68	1993-94 to 1999-2000 0.97	Gross Output Function Framework (*Data Source*: ASI)
Goldar (2004)	1979-80 to 1990-91	1991-92 to 1999-2000	Value Added Function

1	2	3	4
	2.14	1.57	
	1981-82 to 1990-91	1991-92 to 1999-2000	Gross Ouput Function
	0.92	0.65	
	1979-80 to 1990-91	1991-92 to 1999-2000	Using Translog Production Function
	2.23	1.65	(*Data Source*: ASI)
Banga and Goldar (2004)	1980-81 to 1989-90	1989-90 to 1999-2000	Based on random effects model inlcuding contribution of services as inputs to productivity (KLEMS model)
	1.3	0.5	
	1.5	1.1	Excluding services (KLEM model)
			(*Data Source*: ASI, Methodology, PFA)
Trivedi (2004)	1980-81 to 1991	1992-93 to 2000	Gross Output Function Framework
	-0.92	-0.1	(*Data Source*: ASI, Methodology: GAA)
	1.9	0.7	
Rodrik and Subramanian (2004)	1981-90	1991-2000	Econometric Approach (estimates for All India).
	2.5	1.6	

Source: *Economic Survey*, 2005-06, p. 137.

and 5.3 percent in 1995-96 to 3.7 percent and 1.8 percent respectively in 2001-02. The growth rate in the consumer good sector fell from 12.8 percent in 1995-96 to 8.0 percent in 2001-02. However industrial revival since 2002-03 is some consolation. In 2004-05 all the component activities of industrial sector witnessed a significant increase.

In the background of trends which suggest an industrial slowdown, the endeavor should be that the Indian industry must continue to strive to be an efficient and competitive one and able to stand on its own in the face of rising domestic and foreign competition. In order to ensure this, Government on its part must resist any attempts to delay the process of liberalization and deregulation and continue to deepen the reforms and remove all obstacles and bottlenecks

TABLE 2.3

Growth Rates of Industrial Production by Use-Based Classification

(per cent)

Sectors	*Weight*	*1995-96*	*1996-97*	*1997-98*	*1998-99*	*1999-00*	*2000-01*	*2004-05*
Basic Goods	35.5	10.8	3.0	6.9	1.6	5.5	3.7	5.5
Capital Goods	9.3	5.3	11.5	5.8	12.6	6.9	1.8	13.9
Intermediate Goods	26.5	19.4	8.1	8.0	6.1	8.8	4.7	6.1
Consumer Goods of which	28.7	12.8	6.2	5.5	2.2	5.7	8.0	11.7
(Consumer Durables)	(5.4)	(25.8)	(4.6)	(7.8)	(5.6)	(14.1)	(14.5)	14.3
(Consumer Non-Durables)	(23.3)	(9.8)	(6.6)	(4.8)	(1.2)	(3.2)	(5.8)	10.8
IIP (Index of Industrial Production)	100.00	13.0	6.1	6.7	4.1	6.7	5.0	8.4

Source: Economic Survey, 2005-06, p. 134.

for unleashing competitive forces in the industrial sector. This would entail removal of the remaining infrastructural constraints especially in power, transport and telecommunications; reducing bureaucratic controls in all spheres, liberalizing the labour and land market and removing other barriers to growth.

The industrial sector has gained in strength in many ways over the past fifteen years as a consequence of liberalising industrial controls and the gradual integration with the world economy. Automobile components, pharmaceuticals, special chemicals, textiles are recording unprecedented levels of global competitiveness and the recent surge in the Index of Industrial Production (IIP) also supports this assessment. However, there are numerous constraints that limit industrial performance and need to be addressed. Some of these constraints are as follows:

(a) Promoting Industrial Growth

The future Plan should aim at raising the rate of growth of the industrial sector to 10% and manufacturing growth to 12% per annum. The most critical short-term barriers to growth of the manufacturing sector are absence of world-class infrastructure and shortage of skilled manpower. The future plans should place special emphasis on infrastructure and skill formation. In addition, the Plan should give priority to take following initiatives to facilitate rapid industrial growth:

(i) Taxes and duties should be made non-distortionary and internationally competitive. Internally, the tax system must promote and be consistent with a unified national market, so that Indian industry can reap the benefit of economies of scale and scope. Externally, the gradual reduction of tariffs on non-agricultural products should continue. Negative protection which arises because of inverted duty structures must be minimised and, ideally, eliminated.

(ii) While initiatives to provide infrastructure in general are important, they should be supplemented by efforts to promote infrastructure development in local areas such as of Special Economic Zones and Special Economic Regions. The latter differ from SEZs in that they do not come with export tax benefits.

(iii) Technological modernisation is the key to high industrial growth. The growing interest of foreign direct investors in the economy provides a valuable method of injecting resources into the economy, upgrading our technological standards and building international partnerships, which can have many positive effects.

(iv) State governments should take steps to create an investor friendly climate. There is a need to ensure that delays in land registration, water and utility connections, environmental and other clearances are minimized through a single window clearance of applications for establishment of industrial units.

(v) Labour intensive mass manufacturing based on relatively lower skill levels provides an opportunity to expand employment in the industrial sector. China has done exceptionally well in this area and has opened up the world market in which we could compete effectively. A key issue in this context is the need for greater flexibility in some of the labour laws. In particular, there is the need to consider appropriate amendments in Section V-B of the Industrial Disputes Act, 1947 to facilitate exit and Contract Labour (Abolition and Regulation Act) to give to the industry the flexibility necessary to compete in international markets.

(vi) Another constraint affecting the growth of labour intensive manufacturing is the reservation of many of these industries for the small scale sector. With reduced barriers to trade, and the negotiation of free trade agreements with our neighbours and with ASEAN, our domestic producers have to compete with imports even if they don't aim for export markets. They cannot do so if reservation limits their ability to modernise. The policy of progressive de-reservation of industries for small scale production has reduced the list of reserved industries from about 800 to 326. This policy should continue in the 11th Plan at an accelerated pace.

(vii) Although industrial licensing has been virtually eliminated, residual entry barriers remain in sugar, petroleum refining, fertiliser and drug industry. These should be progressively eliminated. Equally important is the need to amend the Companies Act, 1956, in order to facilitate rehabilitation and liquidation procedures of industrial units, where necessary. While promoting industrial growth, protection of consumers, particularly illiterate and marginalised cross-sections of society in rural areas, should be accorded high priority in the future Plan. Competition is the best guarantee of consumer protection and should be strongly encouraged.

(b) Village and Small Enterprises

The dispersed and decentralised VSE Sector poses a special challenge and opportunity to our policy-makers. This sector has the second largest share of employment after agriculture and comprises a wide range including handlooms, handicrafts, sericulture, wool, powerlooms, khadi, village industries, coir and other agro and rural industry segments including food processing industries. It touches the lives of the weaker and unorganised sections of the society with more than half of those employed being women, minorities and the marginalised. Fifty-seven percent of the VSE units are owner run enterprises with one person. They account for 32% of the workforce and 29% of the value added in non-agricultural private incorporated enterprises. With the successful infusion of design skills, modern marketing and 24 appropriate technology, this segment can form the basis for a self-sustaining culture of creative and competitive industry. Several Ministries/ Departments/Institutions deal with activities falling within the domain of the VSE sector, and have a variety of schemes to support the VSEs. However, the benefits accrue to only a small fraction of VSEs as only 13% are registered. In the future we need to ensure that the unregistered small enterprises and units outside the cooperative fold are also able to benefit from government schemes. We need to change the approach from emphasis on subsidies to creating an enabling environment. A cluster approach can help increase viability by providing these units with infrastructure and support services of better quality at lower costs. The 11th Five Year Plan should restrict subsidies to those needed to create a level playing field and to reflect the costs or benefits that might be imposed on others in the society. It should incentivise innovation and creativity. It should mitigate business risk for start-ups, by removing all entry barriers. It should provide infrastructure and liberate VSEs from the inspector raj. Furthermore, in order to improve the competitiveness of small and medium enterprises, schemes for establishment of mini tool rooms, setting up of design clinics and providing marketing support should be evolved on a PPP basis.

(c) Mining

The mineral policy needs to be reviewed to bring it in line with contemporary realities. The Mines and

Minerals Act and the Mineral Concession Rules as wes the FDI policy have also been revised on several occasions with a view to attracting investment for exploration of mineral deposits and operation of mines but actual investment in this area has been very meager because of procedural hassles and numerous discretionary provisions in the laws, which discourage prospective investors. The provisions for rehabilitation are also unsatisfactory. A review of the policy and of the laws and procedures in this area is urgently needed to identify and eliminate the constraints in the way of investments in mining activities. The procedures should ensure that there is seamless transition from the stage of reconnaissance permit through prospective license to mining lease, and security of tenure is guaranteed to the maximum extent possible. The conditions for resettlement must also be made transparent and the rights of those whose lands are acquired must be suitably protected.

(d) Retailing Industry

Modern retailing can bring in new technology and reduce consumer prices, thus stimulating demand and thereby providing more employment in production. Foreign Direct Investment in retailing has been allowed to a limited extent and there is strong interest among foreign investors in being allowed to play a larger role, including in hyper markets and multi-brand retail stores. This is an area of policy where there are different views. We need to evolve a consensus keeping in mind the balance of advantages and disadvantages that exist with modern retailing with FDI in most other developing countries, including even China.

(e) Entertainment and Media Services

One of the sectors which has consistently outperformed the GDP growth year after year is the Entertainment and Media Services Sector which is expected to grow at a compound annual growth rate (CAGR) of 19% till 2010 and beyond during the 11th Plan period. This sector comprises Television CAGR (42%), Films (19%), Radio (1%), Music (2%), Print Media (31%), Live entertainment (2%) and Advertising (3%). It is a sector in which the demand grows faster than income. We can thus expect continued high growth. The 'convergence' of all forms of media to a common digital form, along with technological breakthroughs, provides scope for even higher growth. A facilitating policy environment needs to be created as the sector offers large scope for employment.

2.3: QUALITY CONSCIOUSNESS: R&D EFFORTS IN INDIAN MANUFACTURING SECTOR

In the increasingly knowledge-driven economy, quality consciousness is an integral part of international competition, representing a new strategic philosophy of enterprise towards the improvement of business performance and competitiveness. New products, technologies and creative designs appear regularly in the market as a result of continuous innovation and creativity, which needs to be enhanced by increasing research and development (R&D). A few common measures to enhance quality are Total Quality Management (TQM), Statistical Process Control (SPC), Six Sigma or quality function deployment. There are three main drivers that improve the quality of an organisation—quality planning (business excellence), quality improvement (Six Sigma) and quality control (ISO Standards). ISO standards assure a minimum standard of quality and do not provide competitive advantage or assure the long-term strength of a business. Six Sigma is a highly prescriptive approach for delivering quality in both the design of products and services and the work processes. TQM means consistently and predictably producing what the customer wants—a never ending process of improving the quality and not just an outcome. Six Sigma and SPC are part of TQM that focuses on creating a process that delivers quality products. In India, about 50 large companies have so far obtained ISO-9000 certification. The Quality Council of India (QCI) was set-up in 1997 as a joint initiative of the Government of India and the Indian industry to promote, coordinate, building confidence in Indian products and services and for improving the competitiveness of Indian industry. During 1996-2002, India's expenditure on R&D as a percentage of GDP was 0.85 per cent as compared with 1.11 per cent for East Asia and Pacific, and 2.36 per cent for the world. India's R&D expenditure as a percentage of GDP was, however, higher than other EMEs such as Malaysia, Mexico, Argentina and Thailand. India is identified as an emerging hub for outsourcing collaborative R&D in drugs, biotechnology and chemicals. Investment in pharmaceutical R&D has risen steadily from 2.0 per cent of the sector's turnover in 1999-2000 to around 5.0 per cent in 2004-05. In anticipation of the new challenges, Indian drugs and pharmaceutical companies have increased their R&D spending by around 400 per cent during the last four years, shifting towards more in-house innovative research rather than just copying drug molecules made by others. India is trying to build a golden triangle between traditional medicine, modern medicine and modern science, which holds great promise.[10]

2.4: COMPETITIVENESS OF THE INDIAN INDUSTRY

Competitiveness is the degree to which a nation can, under free trade and fair market conditions, produce goods and services, which meet the test of international markets while simultaneously maintaining and expanding the real income of its people over the long-term. At the global level, there are two leading surveys which compare the competitiveness of various countries on a regular basis, viz., Global Competitiveness Report (World Economic Forum,

Switzerland) and World Competitiveness Yearbook (International Institute for Management Development, Lausanne, Switzerland). In addition, the United Nations Industrial Development Organisation (UNIDO) also ranks the competitiveness of the industrial sector of various economies. The Global Competitiveness Report 2004 has ranked India 55th among 104 economies in terms of the Growth Competitiveness Index and 30th in terms of Business Competitiveness Index. According to recent international reports on competitiveness, labour productivity growth in India has been better than Australia, Germany, United Kingdom and United States. Wage rates in India are much lower than Thailand, Singapore, the Philippines, Malaysia and Korea. In terms of unit labour cost, India has a competitive edge over Singapore, Korea and Malaysia. The unit labour cost in India is higher in food products, electrical machinery and transport equipments as compared with some other emerging market economies. India fares better than Hong Kong, Indonesia, and Malaysia, both in terms of lower input costs and higher operating surplus, in the case of the iron and steel industry. India leads in skill-based manufacturing activity such as ability to reengineer equipment at lower capital costs, innovative process reengineering, availability of skilled technicians and quality mindset.[11]

2.5: INDIA'S INVESTMENT CLIMATE FROM INTERNATIONAL PERSPECTIVE[12]

A new report from the World Bank "Doing Business in 2005; Removing Obstacles to Growth", indicates that India has made the highest progress among the South Asian Nations in improving its investment climate last year and was rated among the top ten reformers in the world. India established a private credit registry and made improvements in enforcing debt contracts and bankruptcy laws. But India still has a heavy regulatory burden on business and, India still ranks in the bottom quartile on the ease of

TABLE 2.4

Doing Business Indicator

Procedure	*Brazil*	*China*	*India*	*Sweden*
Time required for starting a Business (Days)	152	41	89	16
Time required for registering a property (Days)	42	32	67	2
Time required for enforcing contracts (Days)	566	241	425	208
Time required to complete insolvency proceedings (Year)	10	2.4	10	2

doing business. The World Bank's "Doing Business" database shows that in China the average time taken to secure the necessary clearances for a start up, or to complete a bankruptcy procedure, is much shorter than in India. Also, Indian labour laws allow firms less latitude with their employees than the labour court does in China, Brazil or Mexico.

2.6: GROWTH CYCLES IN INDUSTRIAL PRODUCTION[13]

Macro-economic variables tend to exhibit cyclical behaviour, displaying phases of expansion and contraction. An analysis of the cyclical fluctuations provides useful information in predicting the sustenance/subsidence of expansion or contraction. For India, several studies have established synchronous movements in respect of a large number of key economic processes. Mohanty *et al.* (2000) using the composite leading indicator approach found that there have been 13 growth cycles in the Indian economy with varying durations between 1970-71 and 2001-02. According to Nilsson and Brunet (2006), industrial production in India registered seven growth cycles measured from trough to trough over the period 1978-

2004 and the average duration of the cycle was 38 months—with the expansion and contraction phases lasting for 20 months and 18 months, respectively.

Empirical analysis based on the cyclicity of the IIP growth behaviour since 1994 reveals that the industrial sector in India has seen several upswings and downswings. These can broadly be divided into four phases (Chart). Phase I marked eight quarters of expansion (1994Q2 to 1996Q1) which was supported by all round growth of the industrial sector. The cyclical downturn of the industrial sector in 1996Q2 was led by the slowdown in mining and electricity sectors on account of poor performance of crude oil and negative growth in hydro-electricity generation. Recovery in industrial growth in the second phase was supported by improved performance of all the three sub-groups, viz., manufacturing, mining and electricity sectors. However, this recovery phase lasted only for a short while. The industrial sector once again entered recession in 1998 which can be attributed to poor performances by mining and manufacturing sectors in an environment of slowdown in global demand following the Asian crisis.

In the third phase starting from the first quarter of 1999, the industrial sector witnessed some turnaround. Various supportive policies of the Government such as rationalisation of excise duties on intermediate goods and customs duty on imported raw materials, reduction in interest rates and extension of infrastructure status to telecommunications, oil exploration and industrial parks, fiscal incentives, such as tax holidays and concessional duties as well as cut in corporate tax rates across the board helped in rejuvenating industrial growth. Subsequently, marked slowdown in manufacturing sector as well as electricity and mining sectors led to the downswing of the industrial sector during 2001-02. The current phase of industrial resurgence, which started in 2002Q2, was buoyed by sharp rise in the production of capital goods, non-oil imports, higher level of manufacturing exports enabled by global recovery, and higher domestic demand for consumer durables in an environment of softer interest rate regime. Industrial recovery also benefited from growing efficiency and competitiveness of domestic production, emanating from various policy reforms and restructuring of the country's industrial sector since the early 1990s. The current cyclical upturn remains one of the longest in the last decade as it has continued for four years. The IIP growth reached a peak in 2005Q2. Although some signs of slowdown were visible in the third and fourth quarters of 2005, industrial activity recovered in 2006Q1. While contraction in industrial activity during 2005Q3 and 2005Q4 seemed to suggest that industrial growth might lose some of its momentum in the ensuing quarters, the phenomenal growth of capital goods sectors coupled with its imports and increased capacity additions across the industry suggest a buoyant investment climate

2.7: CONCLUSION

In retrospect, Indian industry upgraded technology and product quality to a significant degree and met the challenge of openness after being protected for decades. This was reflected in high growth of the industrial sector in the initial phase of reform. This exuberance reflected in high growth in investment and production in industry during 1993-94 to 1996-97, particularly in manufacturing, however, could not be sustained. Although the growth process has been to some extent influenced by global business cycles, the persisting deceleration in Indian industrial growth is, in part, attributed to the slowdown in reform momentum and inadequacy of certain major structural reforms. Today, the industrial sector confronts challenges of a continued slowdown. In the background of trends which suggest an all round industrial slowdown, the endeavour should be that the Indian industry must continue to strive to be an efficient and competitive one and able to stand on its own in the face of rising domestic and foreign competition. In order to ensure this, Government on its

CHART

Growth Cycles in Industrial Production in India

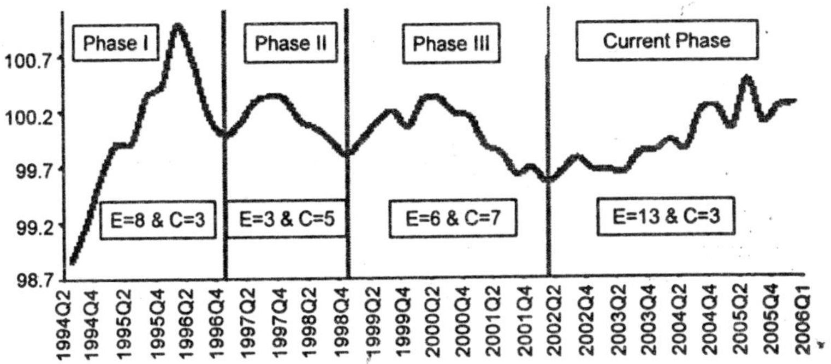

Note: E: Expansion and C: Contraction (in Quarters).
Source: Reserve Bank of india, Annual Report, 2005-06, p. 21.

part must resist any attempts to delay the process of liberalization and deregulation and continue to deepen the reforms and remove all obstacles and bottlenecks for unleashing competitive forces in the industrial sector. This would entail removal of the remaining infrastructural constraints especially in power, transport and telecommunications; reducing bureaucratic controls in all spheres, liberalizing the labour and land market and removing other barriers to growth.

NOTES AND REFERENCES

1. In the second half of 1970s the Government started relaxing the foreign trade regime and a number of imported items were placed on the open general license list.
2. Azeez, E.A., "Economic Reforms and Industrial Performance—An Analysis of Capacity Utilisation in Indian Manufacturing", Working Paper No. 339, Centre for Development Studies, Thiruvanthapuram.
3. At present only six industries are under compulsory licensing mainly on account of environment, safety and strategic considerations. These industries are: (i) Distillation and brewing of alcoholic drinks, (ii) Cigar and Cigarettes of

tobacco and manufactured tobacco substitutes, (iii) Electronic Aerospace and defence equipments, (iv) Industrial explosives, (v) Hazardous chemicals, and (vi) Drugs and Pharmaceuticals (according to modified Drug Policy, 1994 as amended in 1999), Annual Report of Department of Industrial Policy and Promotion, Govt. of India, 2001, p. 134.

4. Sandesara, J.C., "Industrial Policy: Questions of Efficient Growth and Social Objectives", *Economic and Political Weekly*, August 3-10, 1991, p. 1870.
5. H.K. Paranjape, "New Industrial Policy: A Capitalist Manifesto", *Economic and Political Weekly*, October 26, 1991, p. 2475.
6. *Ibid.*, p. 2476.
7. *Economic Survey*, 2001-02, p. 163.
8. *Ibid.*
9. There are many different productivity measures. The choice between them depends on the purpose of productivity measurement and, in many instances, on the availability of data. Broadly, productivity measures may be classified as single factor and multifactor productivity. Multifactor productivity can, further, be computed on the basis of:—
   - Gross output and value added productivity measures,
   - Single deflation and double deflation productivity measures, and
   - Growth accounting *versus* production function productivity approaches.

   While each of the method mentioned above has its own advantages and disadvantages, most of the studies in the Indian context has computed Total Factor Productivity (TFP), which is defined as the ratio of real output (or real value added) to a weighted sum of the inputs used in the production a useful process, is measure for this purpose
10. Annual Report, Reserve Bank of India, 2004-05, p. 18.
11. Annual Report, Reserve Bank of India, 2004-05, p. 19.
12. Doing business in 2005; World Bank, IFC and Oxford University Press.
13. 1. Nilsson, Ronny and Olivier Brunet, 2006, "Composite Leading Indicators for Major OECD Non-Member Economies: Brazil, China, India, Indonesia, Russian Federation, South Africa", OECD Statistics Working Paper, STD/DOC(2006)1, January 25.
    2. Mohanty, J., Bhupal Singh, and Rajeev Jain (2000), "Business Cycles and Leading Indicators of Industrial Activity in India", Reserve Bank of India Occasional Papers, Monsoon and Winter.
    3. Reserve Bank of India Annual Report, 2005-06, p. 21.

CHAPTER

3

Public Sector Reforms

3.1: BACKGROUND OF PUBLIC ENTERPRISE IN INDIA

The growth of public sector in India has been guided by Industrial Policy Resolution, 1956 which gave the public sector a strategic role in the economy. At the time of India's Independence in 1947, there were various problems confronting the country which needed to be tackled in a planned and systematic manner. India was basically an agrarian economy with a weak industrial base, low level of savings and inadequate investment and near absence of infra-structural facilities. A vast percentage of population was extremely poor. There existed considerable inequalities in income, level of employment as well as glaring regional imbalances in economic attainments and trained man-power in various fields of management. It was, thus, obvious that if the country was to speed up its economic growth and maintain it in the long-run at a steady level, a big push was required from the government. As such, State's intervention in all sectors of the economy was inevitable because private sector had neither the necessary resources in terms of funds, managerial and scientific skills nor the will to undertake risks involved in large long-gestation investments. Among the imperatives were removal of poverty, better distribution of income, expansion of employment opportunities, removal of regional imbalances, accelerated growth of agricultural and industrial production, better utilisation of natural resources and a wider ownership of economic power to prevent its concentration in a few hands. Given the type and range of problems faced by the country on its economic, social and strategic fronts and the various imperatives, it became a pragmatic compulsion to deploy the public sector as an instrument for self-reliant economic growth so as to develop a sound agricultural and industrial base, diversify the economy and overcome the economic backwardness."[1]

The predominant considerations for continued investments in public sector enterprises were to accelerate the growth of core sectors of economy; to serve the equipment needs of strategically important sectors like Railways, Telecommunications, Nuclear Power, Defence, etc., to enable the Government to exert a countervailing power on the operation of private monopolies and multinationals in selected areas; and to provide a springboard for the economy to achieve a significant degree of self-sufficiency in the critical sectors. Another category of a large number of public enterprises concerns essentially the consumer-oriented industries such as drugs, hotels, food industries, etc. The rationale for setting up such enterprises was to ensure easier availability of vital articles of mass consumption, to introduce check on prices of important products and services or help promote emerging areas like tourism, etc. Further, a large number of enterprises which were 'sick units', were taken over from the private sector in order to sustain production and protect employment. A number of public enterprises are also operating in national and international trade, consultancy, contract and construction services, inland and overseas communications, etc. The overall profile of public sector enterprises in India is, thus, a heterogeneous conglomerate of basic and infrastructural industries, industries producing consumer goods and engaged in trade and services, etc.

3.2: OBJECTIVES OF PUBLIC SECTOR

Some of the major objectives of setting up of public enterprises as envisaged originally could broadly be summarised to include the following:

- To ensure rapid economic growth and industrialization of the country and create necessary infrastructure for economic development;
- To earn return on investment and thus generate resources for development;
- To promote redistribution of income and wealth;
- To create employment opportunities;
- To promote balanced regional development;
- To assist the development of small-scale and ancillary industries; and
- To promote import substitutions, save and earn foreign exchange for the economy.

3.3: ECONOMIC REFORMS AND NEW ROLE OF PUBLIC ENTERPRISE

During the eighties, the disillusionment witnessed in the socialist economies accelerated the process of disenchantment with the public sector in the mixed capitalist enterprise systems in the world. The wave of economic reform under perestroika started in the USSR swept the economies of Eastern Europe. Although Communist China suppressed the opposition move to introduce democracy in its polity, but it has itself introduced economic reforms since it was felt that the public sector did not optimize efficiency and productivity of capital. The social economies were operating in a system of monopolistic control and acted on cost plus pricing policies suggested by the plant managers. The virtual absence of market did not provide a competitive environment to develop a system of efficiency pricing. Quite a large number of enterprises in mixed capitalist economies worked under conditions of monopoly and thus were the victims of excessive bureaucratisation and centralization in decision-making, resulting in inordinate delays which also led to escalation of costs.

In India, it was in middle of seventies, disenchantment with the public sector had started, but the voices of protest were feeble and were sporadic and unarticulated. The failure of the public sector to fulfil the role assigned to it resulted in the protest becoming louder and more articulate. Although even in the beginning of eighties, the opening of certain areas hitherto reserved for public sector was undertaken, but the government was still hesitant to make a clear statement. The first clear pronouncement on the public sector which outlined the change in policy was made by Prime Minister Rajiv Gandhi in his first broadcast to the Nation in 1984 when he said, "The public sector has spread into too many areas where it should not be. We will be developing our public sector to undertake jobs that the private sector cannot do. But we will be opening up more to private sector so that it can expand and the economy can grow more freely."[2] It is in this backdrop of liberalization throughout the world the new economic reforms were initiated in India. The policy of state control over production gave way to efficient utilisation of resources through privatisation.

3.4 DEVELOPMENT OF PUBLIC ENTERPRISES IN INDIA

On April 1, 1951 at the time of initiation of First Five Year Plan, the total number of public sector enterprises in India was just 5, which has increased to 237 in 2005. The growth of public sector and investment therein is shown in Table 3.1

About 55 percent of total investment in central public enterprises is in steel, coal, minerals and metals, power and petroleum groups of enterprises. These basic industries provide linkages to a host of other industries. The wide range of products and activities of central public enterprises include making of steel, mining of coal and minerals, extraction and refining of crude oil, manufacture of heavy machinery, machine tools, instruments, heavy machine-building equipment, heavy electrical equipment for thermal and hydel stations, transportation equipment, telecommunication equipment, ships, submarines, fertilizers, drugs and pharmaceuticals, petro-chemicals, cement, textiles and a few consumer items such as bread, newsprint, paper, footwear and contraceptives, operation of air, sea, river and road transport, operation in national and international trade, consultancy, contract and construction services, inland and overseas telecommunication services, hotel and tourist services, etc.

A long and arduous journey has been undertaken by the central public sector enterprises during its life span of about four decades. It has weathered many storm and successfully withstood much attacks on it. It has come to stay and will play an important role in future also. "The Public Sector", says the Seventh Plan document, "has initiated and sustained the industrial transformation of India and it shall continue to play this pivotal role in modernizing Indian industry and in reducing the concentration of economic power."[3]

3.5: PATTERN OF INVESTMENT

The statement showing the total investment for the last two years in various cognate groups, changes in investment during the year and percentange share of investment in each cognate group to the total investment is given in Table 3.2.

TABLE 3.1

Growth of Public Enterprises and Investment therein

Particulars	*Total Investment (Rs. in crores)*	*Enterprises (Numbers)*
At the commencement of the 1st Five Year Plan	29	5
At the commencement of the 2nd Five Year Plan (1.4.1956)	81	21
At the commencement of the 3rd Five Year Plan (1.4.1961)	948	47
At the end of 3rd Five Year Plan (31.3.1966)	2,410	73
At the commencement of the 4th Five Year Plan	3,897	84
At the commencement of the 5th Five Year Plan (1.4.1974)	6,237	122
At the end of 5th Five Year Plan (31.3.1979)	15,534	169
At the commencement of the 6th Five Year Plan (1.4.1980)	18,150	179
At the commencement of the 7th Five Year Plan (1.4.1985)	42,673	215
At the end of 7th Five Year Plan (31.3.1990)	99,329	244
At the commencement of the 8th Five Year Plan (1.4.1992)	1,35,445	246
At the end of 8th Five Year Plan (31.3.1997)	2,13,610	242
As on 31.3.1998	2,31,024	240
As on 31.3.2000	2,52,745	240
As on 31.3.2001	2,74,114	242
As on 31.3.2005	3,57,849	237

Source: *Public Enterprise Survey*, 2005-06, p. 11.

Fig. 3.1

Growth of Investment in Public Sector

(Rs. in crores)

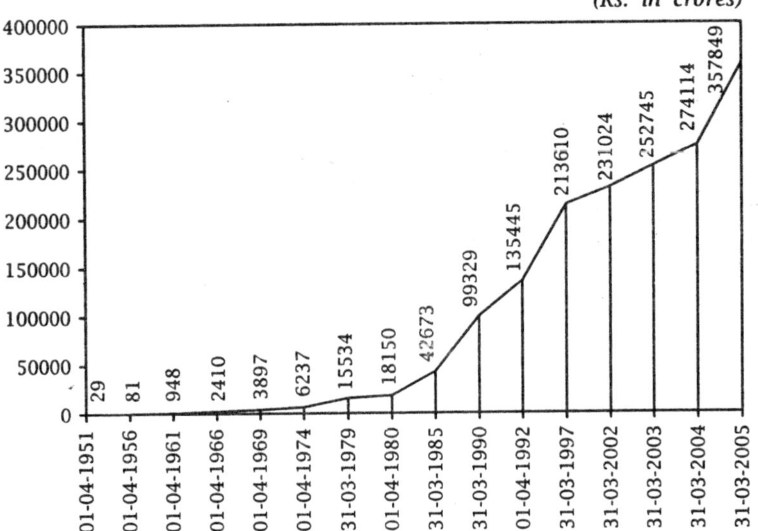

Source: *Public Enterprise Survey*, 2004-05.

The table shows that investment in some cognate groups have increased while in other cognate groups, it has come down. It is generally due to increase in share capital, increase/decrease in long-term loans, or capital restructuring by way of capitalization of reserves, waiver/write-off of equity or loan, or period of loan coming down less than one year. Generally, investment in steel cognate group has come down as the CPSEs under this group have repaid their loans from their internal resources, while power cognate group have shown increase in investment as equity (NTPC, NHPC, NEEPC) as well as long-term loans (NHEDC, NTPC, NPCIL, SJVNL) have increased. Decrease in investment in Fertilizer cognate group is due to restructuring of loan (FCI) and repayment of loan from internal resources by NFL. Decrease in Investment in Consumer Goods cognate group is due to change of nature of loan from

TABLE 3.2

Cognate Group-wise Pattern of Investment

(Rs. in crores)

Sl. No.	*Cognate Group*	*Investment as on*		*Investment during 2004-05*	*% Share as on 31.03.2005*
		31.03.2005	*31.03.2005*		
I.	**Enterprises under Construction**	**6618,19**	**6156.11**	**463.08**	**1.85**
II.	**Enterprises producing/Selling goods:**				
1.	Steel	18061.71	19939.96	-1878.25	5.05
2.	Minerals and Metals	3800.66	4361.56	-560.90	1.06
3.	Coal and Lignite	22931.73	23559.12	-627.39	6.41
4.	Power	75300.45	68012.10	7288.35	21.04
5.	Petroleum	34859.77	35259.77	-400.00	9.74
6.	Fertilisers	13710.13	22309.62	-8599.49	3.83
7.	Chemicals and Petrochemicals	2597.90	3439.03	-841.13	0.73
8.	Heavy Engineering	5783.73	5107.88	675.85	1.62
9.	Medium and Light Engineering	6928.45	6096.42	832.03	1.94
10.	Transportation Equipment	3221.27	3161.42	59.85	0.90
11.	Consumer Goods	4128.90	5542.53	-1413.63	1.15
12.	Agro-based Industries	70.66	63.59	7.07	0.02
13.	Textiles	19663.08	17456.42	2206.66	5.49

III. Enterprises Rendering Services:				
1. Trading and Marketing	6833.37	2763.55	4069.82	1.91
2. Transportation Services	4677.77	4659.76	18.01	1.31
3. Contract and Construction Services	8452.92	8554.90	-101.48	2.36
4. Ind. Dev. and Tech. Consul. Services	16719.91	16047.79	672.12	4.67
5. Tourist Services	187.65	187.58	0.07	0.05
6. Financial Services	80099.83	74165.43	5934.40	22.38
7. Telecommunications and Information Technology	21608.20	21624.43	-16.77	6.04
8. Section 25 Companies	1593.00	1526.22	66.78	0.45
Total (1 to 8)	140172.65	129529.70	10642.95	39.17
Grand Total (I + II + III)	357849.28	349994.23	7855.05	100.00

Source: Public Enterprises Survey, 2004-05, Vol. 1.

long-term to short term. Increase in investment in Trading and Marketing Group and Financial Group is due to increase in loans (Food Corpn. of India, REC, PFC) and increase in equity (HUDCO).

3.6: INDUSTRIAL POLICY, 1991: POLICY OF REFORMS IN PUBLIC ENTERPRISES

The new Industrial Policy was announced in July, 1991. The main aim of new Industrial Policy was to unshackle the Indian industrial economy from the cobwebs of unnecessary bureaucratic control, to introduce liberalisation with a view to integrate the Indian economy with the world economy. The public sector was assigned new role. The policy document underlined, "the Government will ensure that the public sector plays its rightful role in the evolving socio-economic scenario of the country. Government will ensure that the public sector is run on business lines and would continue to innovate and lead in strategic areas of national importance."[4]

Industrial Policy, 1991, outlines a new approach towards public sector. The resolution states, "There must be greater commitment to the support of public enterprises which are essential for the operation of the industrial economy. Measures must be taken to make these enterprises more growth-oriented and technically dynamic. Units which may be faltering at present but are potentially viable must be restructured and given a new lease of life."[5]

The Industrial Policy resolution identified priority areas for growth of public enterprises in future. These are:

1. Essential infrastructure goods and services.
2. Exploration and exploitation of oil and mineral resources.
3. Technology development and building of manufacturing capabilities in areas which are crucial in the long-term development of the

economy and where private sector investment is inadequate.
4. Manufacture of products where strategic considerations predominate such as defence equipment.

It is worth mentioning that new Industrial Policy Resolution attempts to give 'desirable role' to public enterprises in place of 'dominant role'. Consequently the list of industries reserved for public sector was revised and brought down to only 8 industries[6] in Industrial Policy, 1991. However, at present only following three industries are reserved for the public sector.[7]

1. Atomic Energy.
2. Substances of Atomic Energy.
3. Railway Transport.

In the later amendments private sector has been invited in the field of oil exploration and research.

In order to improve the portfolio and performance of public enterprises in a liberalized economy, the Government of India announced on 24th July, 1991 as a part of the 'Statement on Industrial Policy' a Statement on Public Sector Policy also. The statement contains the following decisions:[8]

(i) Portfolio of public sector investments will be reviewed with a view to focus the public sector on strategic, high-tech and essential infrastructure. Whereas some reservation for the public sector is being retained, there would be no bar for area of exclusivity to be opened upto the private sector selectively. Similarly, the public sector will also be allowed entry in areas not reserved for it.

(ii) Public enterprises which are chronically sick and which are unlikely to be turned around will, for the formulation of revival/ rehabilitation schemes, be referred to the

Board for Industrial and Financial Reconstruction (BIFR) or other similar high level institutions created for the purpose. A social security mechanism will be created to protect the interests of workers likely to be affected by such rehabilitation packages.

(iii) In order to raise resources and encourage wider public participation, a part of the government's share-holding in the public sector would be offered to mutual funds, financial institutions, general public and workers.

(iv) Boards of public sector companies would be made more professional and given greater powers.

(v) There will be a greater thrust on performance improvement through the Memoranda of Understanding (MOU) system by which managements would be granted greater autonomy and will be held accountable. Technical expertise on the part of the Government would be upgraded to make the MOU negotiations and implementation more effective.

(vi) To facilitate discussion on performance, the MOU signed between Government and the public enterprises would be placed in Parliament. While focusing on major management issues, this would also help place matters on day-to-day operations of public enterprises in their correct perspective.

As per the announcement in the Industrial Policy Statement and also in the Budget speech of July, 1991, in order to raise resources, encourage wider public participation and promote greater accountability, the Government equity in selected public enterprises was to be offered to mutual funds, financial institutions, workers and general public.

It is clear that Industrial Policy, 1991 was a corner

stone regarding scope, organisation, working and reforms of public sector. The policy documents enumerated the following policy initiatives with regard to public sector:

(i) Restructuring involving modernization, rationalisation of capacity, product-mix changes and selective exit and privatisation.

(ii) Increase in autonomy and performance accountability through an effective system of MOUs between administrative ministries and public enterprises.

(iii) Changes in management in specific enterprises to promote leadership, resourcefulness and innovation.

(iv) To streamline the working of public sector enterprises which are beset with interference and *ad hoc* investment and employment decisions.

(v) Technological upgradation through an integrated R&D effort and import of technology.

(vi) Re-orientation of approach in Ministries and other Government agencies corresponding to liberalisation and dismantling of regulation (price, distribution, investment and import controls) to develop a new institutional capability to facilitate operation of market forces, orchestrisation of integrated R&D effort and evolution of consensus and partnership among various stake-holders.

After 1991 there were major political changes but the new governments continued to pursue the policy of more reforms in public sector. The National Front government stated in its manifesto in 1996, "In respect of infrastructure and capital goods industries we shall modify the conditions and parameters to ensure efficiency in investment planning and relevance to national priorities. The commanding position will remain with the public sector but every effort will be made to make the public sector industries more efficient, providing them with professional management.[9]

Bhartiya Janata Party which came into power in 1998, stated the following in respect of public sector and deregulation in its election manifesto.

1. Debureaucratise the industry, cut down the plethora of controls which have mushroomed over the years, and which breed corruption and dampen enterprise. We will clear projects promptly and quickly. Industrial Development and Regulation Act will be replaced by Industrial Development Act.
2. Reconsider the role of the public sector in the light of its contribution to development and society and draw up firm guidelines for its re-organisation into a more efficient, productive, profitable and people-oriented sector.
3. Improve the efficiency and profitability of crucial public sector units like railways, oil and gas production, ports, nuclear energy, defence, etc. through better management.
4. Encourage people's initiative in public sector units involving trading, hotels, tourism, consumer goods, etc. by offering them to the public in capital market with appropriate safeguards.
5. Foreign capital will be encouraged in high-tech, import substitution and strictly export-oriented areas.[10]

3.7: DISINVESTMENT AND PRIVATISATION IN PUBLIC ENTERPRISES

In the recent past, privatisation has emerged as one of the most revolutionary innovations in economic policy of almost all countries of the world. As a reaction to the inefficient working of the state-owned enterprises, the wave of privatisation spread all over the world. The disequilibrium in the macro-economic balance of the socialist economies as well as the developing countries led to disequilibrium in their balance of payments. The dependence of these economies on the advanced capitalist economies of the west, especially USA, hastened the process of economic reform. The unrelenting pressure from the USA and other capitalist economies on the World Bank, IMF and other international financial institutions to bail them out of economic crises also forced them to accept privatisation as the new philosophy of regeneration.

The most important form in the process of privatisation of public sector enterprises in India is disinvestment of capital in public sector enterprises. The policy of the government on disinvestment has evolved over a period is briefly stated in the form of following policy statements made in the chronological order in Table 3.3.

TABLE 3.3

Chronology of the Evolution of the Policy on Disinvestment since 1991-92

Date	*Event*
1991-92 Interim Budget	Government announced its intention to divest up to 20% of government equity in selected PSEs in favour of public sector institutional investors.
Industrial Policy statement dated 24.7.1991	In the case of selected enterprises, part of government holdings in the equity share capital of the enterprises will be disinvested in order to provide further market discipline to the performance of public enterprises.
Rangarajan Committee, April, 1993	It emphasized the need for substantial disinvestment and stated that while the percentage of equity to be divested should be not more than 49% for industries explicitly reserved for the public sector, it should be either 74% or 100% for others.

Budget speech, 1998-99	"Government have also decided that in the generality of cases, the Government shareholding in public sector enterprises will be brought down to 26%. In cases of public sector enterprises involving strategic considerations, Government will continue to retain majority holding. The interest of workers shall be protected in all cases."
Budget speech, 1999-00	"Government strategy towards public sector enterprises will continue to encompass a judicious mix of strengthening strategic units, privatizing non-strategic ones through gradual disinvestment of strategic sale and devising viable rehabilitation strategies for weak units."
Cabinet decision dated 16.3.1999	Public sector enterprises have been classified into strategic and non-strategic areas for the purpose of disinvestment. Strategic PSEs would be those in the areas of: (a) Arms and ammunitions and the allied items of defence equipment, defence aircrafts and warships; (b) Atomic energy (expect in the areas related to the operation of nuclear power and applications of radiation and radio-isotopes to agriculture medicine and non-strategic industries). (c) Railway Transport. All other PSEs were to be considered as non-strategic. For the non-strategic PSEs, it was decided that the reduction of government stake to 26% would not be automatic. Decision in regard to the percentage of disinvestment i.e., Government's stake going down to less then 51% or 26% would be taken on the following considerations: (a) Whether the industrial sector requires the presence of the public sector as a countervailing force to

	prevent concentration of power in private hands; and (b) Whether the industrial sector requires a proper regulatory mechanism to protect the consumer interests before Public Sector Enterprises are privatized.
Budget Speech, 2000-01	Government announced its decision to reduce its stake in the non-strategic PSEs even below 265, if necessary. There would be increasing emphasis on strategic sale and the entire proceeds from disinvestment/privitisation would be deployed in social sector, restructuring of PSEs and retirement of public debts.
Decision dated 23.6.2000	In order to secure the presence of the public sector as a countervailing force, the government took the decision of not going for disinvestment of GAIL, IOC and ONGC, and retaining them as flagship companies.
Decision dated 7.9.2002	Central public enterprises, central government owned Cooperative Societies (where Government Ownership is 51% or more) should not be permitted to participate in the disinvestment of other PSEs as bidder. If in some specific cases any deviation from these restrictions is considered desirable in public interest. The ministry may bring an appropriate proposal for consideration of the Core Group of Secretaries on Disinvestment.
Budget Speech, 2003-04	Details about the already announced Disinvestment Fund and Asset Management company, to hold residual shares post-disinvestment, shall be finalized early in 2003-04.
Budget Speech, 2004-05 (July)	The disinvestment and privitisation are useful economic tools. Government will selectively employ these tools, consistent with the declared policy. Government will establish a Board for Reconstruction of public Sector Enter-

	prises. The board will advise the Govt. on the Measures to be taken to restructure PSEs, including cases where disinvestment or closure or sale is justified. The disinvestment revenues will be a part of the Consolidated Fund of India. While presenting the budget for 2005-06, the manner in which the said revenues have been or will be applied for specified social sector schemes will be reported to the House.
Decision dated 27.01.2005	(i) Government decided, in principle, to list large, profitable Public Sector Enterprises on domestic stock exchanges and to selectively sell a minority stake in listed, profitable PSEs while retaining at least 51% of the shares along with full management control so as not to disturb the Public Sector character of the companies. (ii) Government has also decided to constitute a "National Investment Fund" into which the realization from sale of minority shareholding of the government in Profitable PSEs would be channelised. The Fund would be maintained outside the Consolidated Fund of India. The income from the fund would be used for the following broad investment objectives: (a) investment in the social sector projects which promote education, health care and employment; (b) Capital investment in selected profitable and revivable PSEs that yield adequate returns in order to enlarge their capital base to finance expansion/diversification.

Source: *Public Enterprise Survey*, 2004-05, pp. 63-65.

TABLE 3.4

Actual Disinvestment from April 1991 onwards and Methodologies Adopted

Year	*No. of companies in which equity sold*	*Target receipt for the year (Rs. in Crore)*	*Actual receipts (Rs. in crore)*	*Methodology*
1	*2*	*3*	*4*	*5*
1991-92	47 (31 in one tranche and 16 in other)	2,500	3,038	Minority shares sold by auction method in bundles of "very good", "good", and "average" companies.
1992-93	35 (in 3 tranches)	2,500	1,913	Bundling of shares abandoned. Shares sold separately for each company by auction method.
1993-94	—	3,500	Nil	Equity of 7 companies sold by open auction but proceeds received in 1994-95.
1994-95	13	4,000	4,843	Sale through auction method, in which NRIs and other persons legally permitted to buy, hold or sell equity, allowed to participate.
1995-96	5	7,000	168	Equities of 4 companies auctioned and Government piggy backed in the IDBI fixed price offering for the fifty companies.

(Contd.)

TABLE 3.4 *(Contd.)*

1	*2*	*3*	*4*	*5*
1996-97	1	5,000	380	GDR (VSNL) in international market.
1997-98	1	4,800	902	GDR (MTNL) in international market.
1998-99	5	5,000	5,371	GDR (VSNL)/Domestic offerings with the participation of FIIs (CONCOR, GAIL). Cross purchase by 3 Oil sector companies i.e. GAIL, ONGC and Indian Oil Corporation
1999-00	2	10,000	1,829	GDR-GAIL, VSNL-domestic issue, BALCO restructuring, MFIL's strategic sale and others
2000-01	4	10,000	1,870	Strategic sale of BALCO, LMC; Takeover—KRL (CRL), CPCL (MRL), BRPL
2001-02	10	12,000	5,632	Strategic sale of CMC—51%, HTL—74%, VSNL—25%, IBP—33.58%, PPL—74%, and sale by other modes; ITDC and HCI ; surplus reserves: STC and MMTC
2002-03	8	12,000	3,347.98	Strategic sale of HZL, IPCL and sale of hotel properties of HCI and ITDC; Control premium from renunciation of rights issue from MUL; Put option of MFIL; sale of shares to employees of HZLl and CMC
2003-04	2	14500	15547.41	Strategic sale of JCL; call option of HZL; IPO/offer for sale of MUL, IBP, IPCL, CMC, DCI, GAIL and ONGC; Sale of shares of ICI Ltd.
2004-05	3	4000	2664.87	Offer for sale of NTPC; sale of shares to IPCL employees, etc.
Total		96800	47671.62	

Source: Disinvestment Ministry website: www.disinvest.nic.in

The total disinvestments in public sector enterprises since 1991 is shown in Table 3.4.

The table shows that in total the disinvestments till now has yielded Rs. 47671.62 crores to the Government against targeted Rs. 96800 crores.

3.8: REDUCTION IN INDUSTRIES RESERVED FOR PUBLIC SECTOR

Initially in the economic development of India, public sector was accorded prime importance. Priority was given to the public sector in the hope that it would help capital accumulation, industrialisation, development and removal of poverty. But none of these objectives could be realised. Policy of contraction of public sector was adopted under the scheme of privatisation number of industries exclusively reserved for public sector is reduced from 17 in 1956 to 8 in 1991. The number was reduced to 6 in 1993 and now only three industries are exclusively reserved for public sector namely:

(a) Atomic energy,
(b) Mining of atomic minerals, and
(c) Railways.

3.9: EFFICIENCY, PROFITABILITY AND PERFORMANCE APPRAISAL OF PUBLIC ENTERPRISES AFTER ECONOMIC REFORMS

The study of efficiency, profitability and performance appraisal of public enterprises can be undertaken under following heads:

(1) Profitability in Public Enterprises

Initially little attention was paid to profitability aspect of public sector enterprises, as these were considered as engine of social welfare and objective was to promote welfare instead of profitability. But since

1990's the profitability aspect has gained prominence and the efficiency of enterprise is judged by its profitability. The profitability of the public sector enterprises is shown in Table 3.5.

TABLE 3.5

Profitability of Public Sector Enterprises

(Rs. in crores)

Year	*Gross Margin**	*Gross Profit***	*Net Profit****
1981-82	4,012	2,654	446
1991-92	22,223	13,675	2,355
1995-96	40,526	27,989	9,878
2000-01	69,288	48,768	15,652
2004-05	1,08,491	86,063	65,429

* Gross Margin—Profit before depreciation, interest and tax.
** Gross Profit—Profit before interest and tax.
*** Net Profit—Profit after interest and tax.
Source: *Public Enterprise Survey,* 1991-2005.

The table shows that there is remarkable improvement in the profitability of public sector enterprises. The gross margin was Rs. 4,012 crores in 1981-82 which increased to Rs. 22,223 crores in 1991-92 and jumped to Rs. 1,08,491 crores in 2004-05. Similarly, the gross profit rose from Rs. 2,654 crore in 1981-82 to 13,675 crores in 1991-92 and to Rs. 86,063 crores in 2004-05, Net profit stood at Rs. 65,429 crores in 2004-05.

The number of profit-making and loss-making enterprises are shown in Table 3.6.

Table 3.6 shows that in 1991-92 and 1995-96 the number of profit-making and loss-making enterprises is almost same and the same picture holds good in 2004-05 where profit-making enterprises are 143 while loss-making enterprises are 73.[11]

TABLE 3.6

Profit-making and Loss-making Public Sector Enterprises

Year	*Profit-making enterprises*	*Loss-making enterprises*	*No profit/ No loss enterprises*	*Total*
1981-82	104	83	1	188
1991-92	133	102	2	237
1995-96	134	101	4	239
2000-01	122	111	1	234
2004-05	143	73	1	224

Source: Public Enterprise Survey, 1981-82 to 2004-05.

(2) Dividend

An important measure of performance appraisal of public enterprises is the declaration of dividend by these enterprises. It is worth mentioning that in 1971-72, the total amount of dividend declared by these enterprises was just Rs. 15 crores. While in 1981-82 it was 109 crores. It rose to Rs. 687 crores in 1991-92 while in 2004-05 the dividend declared stood at Rs. 20713 crores. The total number of enterprises declaring dividend was 79 in 1995-96 while in 2004-05, 122 public sector enterprises declared dividend.[12]

(3) Growth of Turnover/Operating Income

The turnover/operating income of public enterprises has grown significantly over the period as may be seen from Table 3.7.

It may be seen from the Table 3.7 that the public sector enterprises have shown consistent growth in the turnover/operating income. It has increased from Rs. 1,33,906 crores in 1991-92 to Rs. 4,58,227 crores during 2000-01 showing an increase of 242.2 percent during post-reform period. Turnover has improved every

FIG. 3.2

Dividend of Public Sector Enterprise

(Rs. in crores)

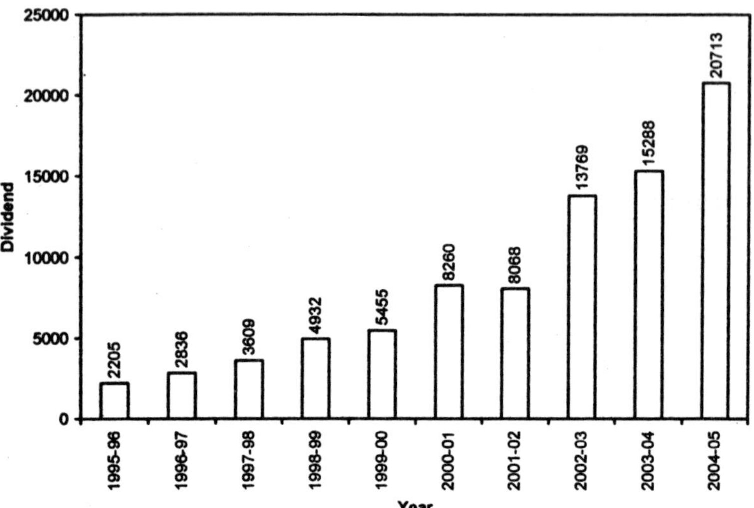

TABLE 3.7

Growth of Turnover

Year	*Rupees in crores*		*Turnover to Capital Employed*	*Growth of Turnover (%)*
	Turnover/ Operating Income	*Capital Employed*		
1991-92	1,33,906	1,17,991	113.49	12.83
1992-93	1,47,266	1,40,110	105.11	9.98
1993-94	1,58,049	1,59,836	98.88	7.32
1994-95	1,87,355	1,62,450	115.33	18.54
1995-96	2,26,919	1,73,948	130.45	21.12
1996-97	2,60,735	2,31,178	112.79	14.90
1997-98	2,76,002	2,49,855	110.46	5.86
1998-99	3,10,179	2,65,093	117.01	12.38
1999-00	3,89,199	3,02,867	128.50	25.48
2004-05	7,00,862	5,04826	138.83	19.39

***Source*: *Public Enterprise Survey*, 2004-05. Vol. I, p. 24.**

year. However, rate of growth has varied from 5.86 percent in 1997-98 to 25.48 percent in 1999-2000. The trend of increase has been quite impressive in 1994-95, 1995-96, 1999-2000 and 2004-05. On the whole performance on the basis of turnover can be assessed as satisfactory during post-reform period.

FIG. 3.3

Turnover/Operating Income of Public Sector Enterprise

(Rs. in crores)

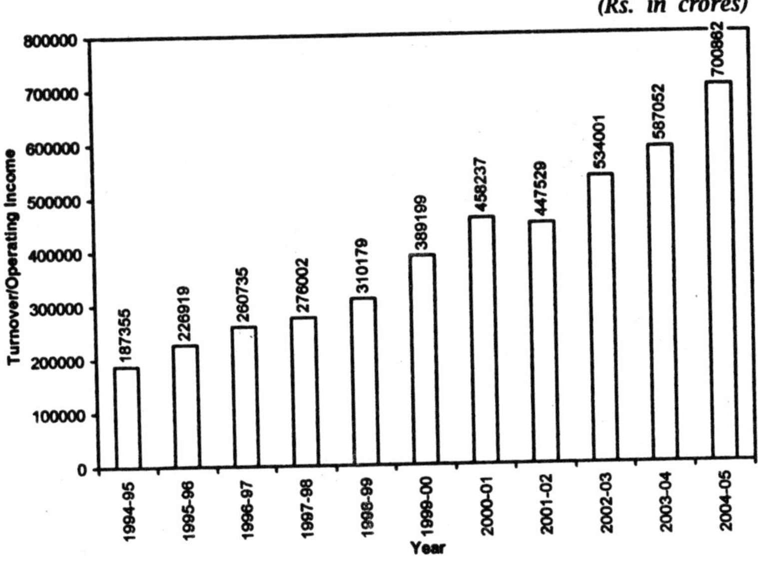

(4) Internal Resources

The internal resources generated by central public sector enterprises since 1992-93 is shown in Table 3.8.

Table 3.8 reveals that there has been no encouragement from the point of view of number of enterprises generating internal resources but the amount generated has improved significantly from Rs. 14,792 crores in 1992-93 to Rs. 37,802 crores in 2000-01. The matter of satisfaction is that the share of retained profit in total resources generated has also improved from 43.12 percent in 1992-93 to 47.86 percent in

2000-01. It is definitely a sign of improvement in efficiency.

TABLE 3.8

Internal Resources Generation

(Rs. in crores)

Year	*No. of Enterprises Generating Internal Resources*	*Details of Internal Resources*			*Total*
		Deprecia-tion	*DRE Written Off*	*Retained Profits*	
1992-93	146	7,184	1,199	6,409	14,792
1993-94	135	8,113	287	8,376	16,676
1994-95	140	9,718	449	9,825	19,992
1995-96	143	11,777	462	11,959	24,198
1996-97	144	12,827	299	12,428	25,554
1997-98	144	15,280	289	15,623	31,192
1998-99	136	14,411	285	16,606	31,302
1999-00	135	17,521	247	18,165	35,933
2000-01	134	19,364	344	18,094	37,802

Source: Public Enterprise Survey, 2000-01, Vol. I, p. 27.

(5) Capacity Utilisation

The capacity utilisation of manufacturing/ production enterprises indicating the number of enterprises which achieved more than 75 percent, between 50 percent and 75 percent and below 50 percent capacity utilisation for 2000-01 and previous two years is given in Table 3.9.

The table shows that number of enterprises using more than 75 percent capacity utilisation is showing steady increase, i.e. from 69 in 1980-81 to 121 in 1994-95 and 98 in2004-05. The number of enterprises using capacity between 50 percent and 75 percent has decreased continuously. However, the number of enterprises using capacity less than 50 percent increased to 69 in 1998-99 from 52 in 1994-95. Though the position has improved in this strata, about 25 percent of total enterprises were not in a position to utilize even 50 percent of their capacity in 2004-05.

TABLE 3.9

Capacity Utilisation in Public Enterprises

Capacity Utilisation	*Number of Enterprises*				
	1980-81	*1994-95*	*1998-99*	*1999-00*	*2004-05*
A. More than 75%	69	121	119	133	98
B.B etween 50% and 75%	39	47	46	30	28
C. Less than 50%	42	52	69	65	59
Total	150	220	234	228	236

Source: *Public Enterprise Survey*, 2004-05, Vol. I, p. 31.

(6) Contribution to the Country's Economy

Public sector occupy a key position in the nation's economy in several sectors, specially in the production of fuel, basic metal, non-ferrous metal and fertilizers as can be seen from Table 3.10.

(7) Balanced Regional Development

Industrialisation plays an important role in correcting regional imbalances and accelerating industrial growth. The pace of economic development of different States and Regions in the country has not been uniform over the years owing to historical reasons and a number of other factors. Even the states which are fairly well developed, have pockets and areas which have not been able to keep pace the progress achieved elsewhere. The lack of industries in different parts of the country is often due to factors such as non-availability of raw-materials or other resources. In this

TABLE 3.10

Public Sector's Contribution in Total Industrial Production

Item	*National Production (NP)*		*Public Sector's Production (PSP)*		*PSP to NP (%)*	
	1968-69	*2004-05*	*1968-69*	*2004-05*	*1968-69*	*2004-05*
Fuel (Million Tonnes)						
Coal	71.4	382.62	12.61	358.88	17.66	93.8
Lignite	3.98	30.34	3.98	21.57	100	71.09
Petroleum (Million Tonnes)						
Crude Oil	6.06	33.98	3.08	29.68	50.83	87.34
Natural Gas	NA	31.76	NA	24.98	NA	78.65
Refined Crude	16.55	127.12	8.09	92.81	48.88	73.01
Basic Metals (Million Tonnes)						
Finished Steel	4.58	40.64	2.55	12.32	55.68	30.31
Non-Ferrous Metals (000 Tonnes)						
Aluminium	125.3	886.26	NIL	338.48	Nil	39.19
Primary Lead	1.9	15.89	1.9	Nil	100	Nil
Zinc	17	212.28	13.7	Nil	80.6	Nil
Fertilizers (000 Tonnes)						
Nitrogenous	563	11339	401	3054	71.23	26.93
Phosphatic	213	4067	53	266	24.86	6.54

Source: *Public Enterprise Survey*,2004-05, Vol. I, p. 26.

context, public sector enterprises have a vital role to play since the setting up of large industries in public sector help in improving employment opportunities, growth of small scale and ancillary industries, development of infra-structural facilities, etc. While deciding the location of central public sector enterprises, due consideration is given to the requirements of various regions subject to the over-riding consideration of techno-economic feasibility. The quantum of investment in terms of gross block in different States/Union Territories, percentage share of different states to the total and the ranking of each state.

(8) Contribution to Central Exchequer

Apart from generation of internal resources, public enterprises have been making substantial contribution

TABLE 3.11

Contribution to Central Exchequer on Actual Basis

(Rs. in crores)

Sr. No.	*Particulars*	*2004-05*	*1999-01*	*1998-99*
1.	**On investment by Central Govt. in PSEs**			
	A. Dividend	9496.12	3765.75	2486.67
	B. Interest	1367.12	2252.81	2563.75
2.	**Taxes and Duties**			
	A. Excise Duty	40000.3	26509.7	18765.5
	B. Custom Duty	7344.81	10676.1	9350.04
	C. Corporate Tax	17976.6	7974.52	8479.41
	D. Dividend Tax	320.13	708.38	449.59
	E. Sales Tax	4164.07	1606.07	2351.99
	F. Other Duties and Taxes	1197.02	2663.24	2487.35
	Total (2)	71003	50138	4188391
3.	**Total contribution (1+2)**	**60978**	**56156.6**	**46934.3**

Source: Public Enterprise Survey, 2004-05, Vol. I, p. 28.

to augment the resources of the Central Government through payment of dividends, interest, corporate taxes, excise duty, customs duty and other duties, thereby helping in mobilization of funds for financing the needs for planned development of the country. Contribution of public sector enterprises to central exchequer on actual basis for the last three years is given in following table.

3.10: CONCLUSION

In the liberalisation era and the post-1991 Industrial Policy Resolution period, competitiveness of industry, be it public or private, assumes great importance for their very survival. The PSEs no longer enjoy any special privileges or facilities. In fact they have to bear the burden of past legacies and social considerations and at the same time, they have to compete with the private enterprises. Today, private initiative is being encouraged even in the development of infrastructure like power, roadways, telecommunications, etc. It may be worthwhile to determine whether public sector presence is required in markets, which are fully matured. There is, perhaps, good justification in withdrawal of government presence in such areas, and public sector should remain confined to a few restricted areas.

Those PSEs which have comparative advantages *vis-a-vis* global markets should be identified and supported. Other profit-making enterprises should be further strengthened. The management of these public sector enterprises should be professionalised and encouragement be given to workers' participation in management. As the lack of autonomy has historically created a somewhat unequal playing field for the public sector, in an increasingly competitive environment, they should be given full autonomy and encouraged to conduct their business on commercial lines only. Relationship between public enterprises and government should be very clearly defined in terms of MOUs, if necessary, and there should be no political interference in the decision-making processes. It would be unfair not to acknowledge the great contributions made by a large number of public sector undertakings to the nation-building process. There are today a number of examples of successful enterprises and their case studies would be an eye-opener, to be emulated by others.

Today there is a lot of debate on the merits of disinvestment of public sector enterprises. There is a case for Government's withdrawal from non-core sectors on considerations of long-term efficient use of capital, growing financial non-viability and the compulsions of these enterprises to operate in an increasingly competitive and market-oriented environment. In certain other key and core sectors of the economy, the public sector should be called upon to continue to play an important role. However, they should be managed on sound commercial lines and must generate adequate surpluses and make contribution commensurate with the quantum of public resources invested in them.

Unlike the experience in many other countries, like Great Britain, which went in for wholesale privatisation, public sector in India continues to be an important component of the Indian industry, even after liberalisation. Viewed in this scenario, disinvestment has larger implications than just selling government equity at the best price.

Therefore, a long-term disinvestments strategy should include strengthening of certain public sector enterprises as well as selective disinvestments in certain others. In such a strategy, protection of employees interests should be of paramount importance. While the surplus workforce should be provided adequate and fair compensation through Voluntary Retirement Schemes, the sustaining of long-term employment can only be ensured by financial turnaround of loss-making enterprises.

There is an increasing consensus today that the government has no business to engage itself in business and industry and should instead concentrate on social sectors like health, education and social security. With a view to ensure higher return on public investments which are locked up in industries, there is a need to adopt a strategy for restructuring of these enterprises encompassing a wide range of components namely, restructuring of ownership, organisational, financial and personnel restructuring, restructuring of the board of directors and the relationship between the Government and the public enterprises. These should include the closure and winding up of terminally sick PSEs and selling of their assets. Such terminally sick PSEs are mostly restricted to those which were earlier taken over from the private sector as sick units, and which are a major contributory factor for the overall unsatisfactory performance of the public enterprises.

Unless the public sector enterprises respond quickly to the dynamic changes which are taking place globally, following liberalisation and opening up of our economy under WTO dispensations, they will be left behind and become irrelevant.

Notes and References

1. Public Enterprises Survey, 2000-01, Vol. I, pp. 1-2.
2. Rajiv Gandhi address to the Nation, quoted by Dutt and Sundharam (1988), Indian Economy, 25th edition, p. 233.
3. Draft Seventh Five Year Plan, p. 6.
4. Industrial Policy Resolution, 1991, para. 15.
5. Industrial Policy Resolution, 1991, para. 32.
6. Annex. I—Arms and ammunition and allied items of defence equipment, defence aircraft and warships; Atomic Energy; Coal and lignite; Mineral oils; Mining of iron ore, manganese ore, gypsum, sulphur, gold and diamond; Mining of copper, lead, zinc, tin, molybdenum and wolfram; Minerals specified in the Schedule to the Atomic Energy (Control of Production and Use) Order, 1953; Railway Transport.
7. Annual Report of Deptt. of Industrial Policy and Promotion, Govt. of India, 2001-02, p. 20.
8. Public Enterprise Survey 2000-01, Vol. I, pp. 3-4.
9. The National Front Manifesto, 1996, p. 25.
10. BJP Election Manifesto "Towards Ram Rajya", 1998.
11. Public Enterprise Survey, 2004-05, Vol. I, p. 22.
12. Compiled from Public Enterprise Survey, 1990-91 to 2000-01.

CHAPTER

4

Agriculture Sector Reforms

4.1: STATUS OF AGRICULTURE

Agriculture continues to be an important sector of the economy with a 24.8% share in the Gross Domestic Product (GDP). Its contribution in terms of providing employment to nearly two-third of the work force has been critical in maintaining livelihoods especially in the rural areas. The planned approach to development has helped the country to reach a stage where the country is self-sufficient in food grains and has a comfortable buffer stock. These achievements have been possible mainly through the favourable policy framework. The policy of Indian Agriculture was to achieve food security by providing incentive for growth along with equitable access to food. As a result, terrible famines have become events of the past and the agricultural production does not show large variation even in the event of adverse climatic condition. It is, however, revealed that the growth rate of agricultural production declined from 3.72% in eighties to 2.35% in the nineties indicating towards the need of sustainability in agriculture. Indian agriculture is still beset with problems like inadequate capital formation, low productivity, high cost of production, uneven growth, etc.[1]

4.2: ECONOMIC REFORMS AND AGRICULTURE

India initiated the process of economic reforms in 1991 in response to the changes in the external and internal economic environment. The major objectives of economic reforms were market orientation of the economy, increasing private sector initiative, improving efficiency in Government spending, enhancing export competitiveness, foreign capital inflow, stabilizing balance of payment and revamping many sectors of the economy such as Industry, Trade, Finance, Infrastructure, etc. The response of the economy to the reform efforts has been both positive and not so positive in different sectors. Not many reforms were initiated in the agriculture sector on account of the perception that in the early phase of reforms, food security and agricultural growth should be maintained.

Reforms, on account of unexpected consequences that they might produce should not be allowed to threaten food security. The agriculture sector has seen very little direct reform efforts though the rest of the economy has been undergoing reforms and restructuring. But the reforms in the other sector have had an impact on the agriculture sector. The changes brought about in the monetary policy, banking policy, credit policy, trade policy, exchange rate policy and the like have had different effects on agriculture sector.

A major criticism of the process of economic reforms is the neglect of agriculture. The economic reforms initiated in 1991 largely focused on fiscal adjustment, foreign trade and investment, industry and financial sector. Some of the measures—notably reduction of subsidies, tariff reduction and trade liberalisation have impact on Agriculture for e.g. the reduction in fertilizer subsidies has raised the input costs for agriculture giving rise to apprehensions that fertilizer use and therefore agricultural product will be adversely affected. Tariff reduction and import liberalisation is expected to have reduced the cost and improved the availability of imported materials and product, entering agricultural production. The relaxation in restrictions on import and export of farm products surely must also have benefited agriculture. The magnitude of the impact of these measures however remains to be established. It may however, be held that no attempt at a comprehensive revamp in agricultural strategy is made in first generation economic reforms. A major cause of concern in recent years has been deceleration in agriculture in the post-reform period. To highlight this fact the agriculture growth is analyzed in terms of following indicators:[2]

(A) GDP and Agriculture Growth Rates.
(B) Annual Growth Rates in Area, Production and Productivity in 1980s and 1990s.
(C) Gross capital formation in Agriculture.
(D) Annual growth rates of various Development Programmes.

(A) GDP and Agriculture Growth Rates

The deceleration in agriculture is best reflected in fluctuating growth rates of Agriculture Sector in post-reform period. It is shown in Table 4.1.

Table 4.1 shows that growth rate of agriculture and allied sector has shown wide fluctuations in post-reform period. The growth rate of Agriculture and Allied sector was 5.8 percent in 1992-93. It turned into negative growth of 0.9 percent in 1995-96. It jumped to 9.6 percent in 1996-97 on account of good monsoon, but it again registered negative movement of 2.4 percent in 1997-98. This rate again rose to 6.2 percent in 1998-99 but was only 0.3 percent in 1999-2000 and -0.4 percent in 2000-01. It recovered in the form of 5.7 percent in 2001-02 but again slipped to -3.1 percent in the year 2002-03 and subsequently to 1.1 percent in 2004-05.

TABLE 4.1

G.D.P. and Agriculture Growth Rates (at 1993-94 Prices)

(Percent)

Year	*G.D.P.*	*Agriculture and Allied Sector*
1992-93	5.1	5.8
1993-94	5.9	4.1
1994-95	7.3	5.0
1995-96	7.8	-0.9
1996-97	7.8	9.6
1997-98	4.8	-2.4
1998-99	6.5	6.2
1999-00	6.1	0.3
2000-01	4.4	-0.4
2001-02	5.6	5.7
2002-03	4.4	-3.1
2003-04	8.5	9.6
2004-05	6.9	1.1

Source: Economic Survey, 2004-05, p. 171.

From the above analysis it can be fairly concluded that in 15 years of post-reform period the growth of agriculture and allied sector has not been stable. It is still more or less dependent on monsoon which shows the backwardness of the agriculture sector and failure of new reforms to develop the strongness of agricultural sector.

(B) Annual Growth Rates in Area, Production and Productivity in 1980s and 1990s

The deceleration of agricultural growth can be better analyzed by analyzing the annual growth rates of production of food grains in Pre and Post-reform period. It is clear from the table that the rates of growth of production of rice, wheat, coarse cereals, and pulses have all declined in the nineties *vis-a-vis* the eighties. The overall growth rate of production of rice and wheat which was 3.59 percent per annum during the eighties fell to only 2.27 percent per annum during nineties which is just marginally above the rate of growth of population. Pulses and cereals have recorded little or no growth in the 1980s and 1990s. Some area expansion under non-food crops in the 1990's is attributable mainly to the growth in area under cotton and sugarcane, perhaps at the cost of shrinkage in area under coarse cereals. However, the growth in yield of non-food crops in the 1990's has been lower than that in 1980s.

It will be worthwhile if we compare the productivity of crops in India with some other countries of the world. The comparison is presented in Table 4.2.

TABLE 4.2

Annual Compound Growth Rate of Crop Area, Production and Productivity

(Percent)

Crop	*1980-81 to 1989-90*			*1990-91 to 2002-03*		
	Area	*Production*	*Yield*	*Area*	*Production*	*Yield*
Rice and Wheat	**0.43**	**3.59**	**3.15**	**0.84**	2.27	**1.42**
• Rice	0.41	3.62	3.19	0.63	1.79	1.16
• Wheat	0.47	3.57	3.10	1.21	3.04	1.81
Coarse Cereals	-1.34	0.40	1.62	-1.84	0.06	1.62
Pulses	-0.09	1.52	1.61	-1.02	-0.58	0.27
Total Foodgrains	-0.23	2.85	2.74	-0.20	1.66	1.34
Non-Food Crops	**1.12**	**3.77**	**2.31**	**0.84**	**1.86**	**0.59**
• Oilseeds	-1.51	5.20	2.43	0.44	0.66	0.61
• Sugarcane	1.44	2.70	1.24	1.72	2.62	0.89
• Cotton	-1.25	2.80	4.10	2.21	0.92	-1.26
All Crops	0.10	3.19	2.56	0.08	1.73	1.02

Source: *Economic Survey*, 2002-03, p. 189.

The data Indicates that India's Share to World Area And Production is significant in case of paddy and groundnut, however the share in production for all the selected crops is more or less stable over the period of 2001-03.

(C) Gross Capital Formation in Agriculture

The pace and pattern of agricultural development are largely conditioned by growth of infrastructural facilities of irrigation, road, market, power, cold storage, etc. Infrastructure plays a critical role on both input and output sides, while on the input front, it helps to integrate local markets with national and international markets whereas on the output front it is the base for increasing productivity. Therefore, an adequate and efficient infrastructure system is essential for realizing the potential of the sector. However, one of the most disquieting developments in agricultural sector during post-reform period has been the neglect of capital formation, particularly in public sector. It is indicated by Table 4.3.

Table 4.4 reveals that investment in agriculture declined from 1.6 percent of G.D.P. in 1993-94 to 1.3 percent in 2000-01. The decline was due to fall in public investment from Rs. 4,457 crore in 1993-94 to Rs. 3,869 crore in 1998-99. There has infact, been a continuous decline in public investment in agriculture from 1995-96 till 1998-99. Although the declining trend in public investment was halted in 1999-2000 with the public sector capital formation rising to Rs. 4,222 crore from Rs. 3,869 crore in the preceding year, there has not been any improvement in the share of investment in agriculture as percentage of GDP from the preceding year's level of 1.7 percent. The estimates for year 2004-05 also present a dismal picture with the share of investment in agriculture to GDP remaining at 1.3 percent. This calls for review of policies which led to diversion of scarce resource away from the creation of productive assets to subsidies for fertilizers, small

TABLE 4.3

Area and Production of Principal Crops in the World and India's Share

(Area: in '000 ha. Production in '000)

Crops	*Area*			*Production*		
	2001	*2002*	*2003*	*2001*	*2002*	*2003*
Rice (paddy)	151679 (29.4)	147552 (27.2)	153522 (28.7)	598174 (23.4)	569527 (18.9)	589126 (22.4)
Wheat	214690 (12.0)	213716 (12.3)	208765 (11.9)	590520 (11.8)	573513 (12.7)	556349 (11.7)
Coarse grains	309925 (9.6)	300899 (8.8)	312051 (9.5)	919832 (3.6)	886015 (2.9)	929835 (3.8)
Total cereals	676293 (32.3)	662127 (30.9)	674338 (31.6)	2108526 (26.4)	2029055 (23.3)	2075309 (25.0)
Groundnut in shell	24041 (25.9)	24105 (24.7)	26463 (30.2)	36083 (19.5)	33303 (13.1)	35658 (21.0)
Cotton seed	34587 (26.3)	30725 (24.3)	32168 (26.1)	60674 (9.8)	52875 (9.0)	56097 (11.2)
Tea	2359 (18.7)	2406 (17.9)	2410 (18.4)	3068 (27.6)	3125 (27.1)	3207 (27.6)
Tobacco	3767 (7.7)	3790 (8.6)	3938 (11.0)	6192 (7.9)	6229 (6.2)	6195 (9.6)

Note: Figures in Parenthesis denote India's share to World Area and Production.
Source: FAO Production Yearbook, Vol. 57, 2003.

TABLE 4.4

Gross Capital Formation in Agriculture (At 1993-94 Prices)

(Percent)

Year	*Gross Capital Formation*				*Percentage Share of*			*Investment in Agriculture as Percentage of GDP*
	Agriculture	*Total economy*	*Public sector in agriculture*	*Private sector in agriculture*	*Public sector in agriculture*	*Private sector in agriculture*	*Agriculture to total*	
1993-94	13,523	181.133	4,457	9,056	33.0	67.0	7.47	1.6
1994-95	14,969	229,879	4,947	10,022	33.0	67.0	6.51	1.6
1995-96	15,690	2,74,557	4,849	10,841	30.9	69.1	5.51	1.6
1996-97	16,176	2,48,631	4,668	11,508	28.9	71.1	6.51	1.5
1997-98	15,942	2,56,551	3,979	11,963	25.0	75.0	4.77	1.4
1998-99	14,895	2,43,697	3,869	11,026	26.0	74.0	6.11	1.3
1999-00	17,304	2,68,374	4,222	13,082	24.4	75.6	6.18	1.3
2000-01	38176	—	7018	31158	18.4	81.6	—	1.9
2001-02	46744	—	8529	38215	18.2	81.8	—	2.2
2002-03	45867	—	7849	38018	17.1	82.9	—	2.1
2003-04	47883	—	12809	35024	26.8	73.2	—	2.0
2004-05	43123	—	12591	30532	29.2	70.8	—	1.7

* The estimates from 2001 onwards at 1999-00 prices.

Source: *Economic Survey*, 2005-06, p. 170.

TABLE 4.5

Share of Agriculture and Allied Sector in Total Gross Capital Formation

(Percent)

Year	*Pre-Reform Period*			*Year*	*Post-Reform Period*		
	Public Sector	*Private Sector*	*Total*		*Public Sector*	*Private Sector*	*Total*
1980-81	17.7	13.6	15.4	1990-91	7.1	11.9	9.9
1981-82	14.1	9.2	11.2	1991-92	6.6	9.9	8.7
1982-83	13.1	12.3	12.7	1992-93	6.7	10.5	9.1
1983-84	13.5	14.4	13.9	1994-95	6.7	9.4	8.4
1984-85	11.8	11.5	11.7	1995-96	6.7	7.7	7.3
1985-86	10.2	9.5	9.8	1996-97	7.0	7.5	7.4
1986-87	8.9	10.1	9.6	1997-98	6.2	7.5	7.1
1987-88	10.1	13.2	11.7	1998-99	5.7	7.8	7.2
1988-89	8.8	9.7	9.3	1999-00	5.1	8.2	7.2
1989-90	7.5	9.1	8.4	2000-01	4.9	8.2	7.1

Source: Government of India, Planning Commission, 10th Plan, p. 519.

electricity, irrigation, credit and other agricultural inputs.

Another disturbing fact is that not only the public and private investment in agriculture is declining but the share of agriculture and allied sector in total gross capital formation of the economy has also shown declining trend in post-reform period as indicated by Table 4.5.

The table shows that share of Agriculture and allied sector in total G.C.F. was 9.9 percent in 1990-91 which declined to 8.4 percent in 1994-95 and ultimately to 7.1 percent in 2000-01. Over the same period the public sector contribution declined from 7.1 percent in 1990-91 to 4.9 percent in 2000-01, while the share of private sector declined from 11.9 percent in 1990-91 to 8.2 percent in 2000-01.

The declining trend in capital formation will need to be reversed by better targeting of subsidies, increasing investment in productive assets such as irrigation, power, credit and developing rural infrastructure. According to Economic Survey, 1999-2000[3] "the decline in public investment in agriculture is mainly due to the diversion of resources to current expenditure in the form of subsidies for food, fertilizers, electricity, irrigation, credit and other agriculture inputs rather than as creation of assets."

(D) Annual Growth Rates of Various Development Programmes

One of the important method of assessing development of agriculture in post-reform period is to assess the growth of various development programmes inagriculture *vis-à-vis* in pre-reform period. In the present analysis the assessment is made with respect of three important variables, namely:

(a) High Yield Varieties.
(b) Irrigated Area.
(c) Fertilizer Consumption.

The annual growth rates of these three programmes is shown in Table 4.5. The table reveals that during the decade 1970-71 to 1980-81, irrigated area indicated an annual average growth rate of 3.6 percent which declined to 2.7 percent during the decade 1980-81 to 1990-91 and further to merely 2.1 percent during 1990-91 to 2002-03. Since irrigation is the basic input which helps the fuller utilization of other inputs —seeds and fertilizers, we also observe declining growth rates in irrigated area under rice and wheat from seventies to eighties and nineties. In case of pulses also, irrigated area growth experienced a declining trend (From 2.7 percent in the decade of eighties to 1.8 percent in the decade of nineties). A similar trend was observed in case of extension of area under HYV in case of paddy and rice. The growth rate of fertilizer consumption indicated a sharp decline from 8.5 percent annual average growth rate during the eighties to just 3.7 percent during the nineties.

In this connection, it is relevant to consider the trend in major and minor irrigation. Major irrigation acts as a supplement to minor irrigation in keeping the water level high, while minor irrigation provides water security to the peasant in case of failure of rains. The slowing down of the growth rate of irrigated area under minor irrigation from 3.5 percent during eighties to 2.3 percent during nineties is another contributing factor to slow down of over-all agricultural growth. Economic reforms did not pay adequate attention to expansion of irrigation and this is a major sin responsible for low growth of agricultural production and productivity during nineties.

An analysis of India's agriculture position in the world is Table 4.7 depicts that India lag behind the world in all the major indicators of agricultural growth.

TABLE 4.6

Annual Growth Rate of Various Development Programmes

	1970-71 to 1980-81	*1980-81 to 1990-91*	*1990-91 to 2002-03*
High Yield Varieties			
Total HYV	10.5	4.2	4.4
Paddy	12.5	4.1	2.3
Wheat	9.5	2.7	1.1
Irrigated Area	3.6	2.7	2.1
Rice	1.4	1.7	1.6
Wheat	4.6	2.3	1.1
Total Cereals	2.4	1.7	2.0
Pulses	0.0	2.7	1.8
Major Irrigation	2.7	1.3	1.2
Minor Irrigation	4.2	3.5	2.3
Fertilizer Consumption	9.6	8.5	3.7

Source: Compiled from the data given in *Economic Survey* (2002-03).

4.3: INTERNATIONAL COMPARISONS OF YIELD OF SELECTED COMMODITIES, 2003[4]

Low productivity has afflicted growth of Indian agriculture (Table 4.8). For example, though India accounted for 21.8 per cent of global paddy production, the yield per hectare in 2002 was less than that in neighbouring Bangladesh and Myanmar, and only about a third of that in Egypt, which had the highest yield level in the reference year. India, while accounting for 12 per cent of global production in wheat, had average yield levels higher than the global average, but only a third of the highest level achieved in the UK in 2002. However, in maize and groundnut, while accounting for 2 per cent and 18 per cent of global output, yield levels were only 39 per cent and 57 per cent of the global

TABLE 4.7

India's Position in World Agriculture

Item	*India*	*World*	*India's*		*Next to*
			Share %	*Rank*	
1	*2*	*3*	*4*	*5*	*6*
1. Area** (million ha)					
Total area	329	13431	2.4	Seventh	Russian Federation, Canada, U.S.A., China, Brazil, Australia
Land area	297	13068	2.3	Seventh	Russian Federation, China, Canada, U.S.A., Brazil, Australia
Arable land	162 F	1402	11.6	Second	U.S.A.
Irrigated area	55 F	272	20.2	Second	China
2. Population (million)					
Total	1025	6134	16.7	Second	China
Agriculture	739	3211	23.0	Second	China
3. Economically active population (million)					
Total	451	2993	15.1	Second	China
Agriculture	267	1327	20.1	Second	China
4. Crop production (million t)					
Total Cereals	214	2029	10.5	Third	China, USA

(Contd.)

TABLE 4.7 *(Contd.)*

1	*2*	*3*	*4*	*5*	*6*
Wheat	72	573	12.6	Second	China
Rice (Paddy)	117	576	20.3	Second	China
Coarse grains	25	8880	2.8	Sixth	U.S.A., China, Brazil, Russian Federation, France
Total pulses	14	55	25.5	First	
Groundnut	5*	34	14.7	Second	China
Rapeseed and Mustard	5	33	15.2	Second	China
5. Fruits and Vegetables (million t)					
Vegetables and Melons	78	787	9.9	Second	China
Fruits excluding Melons	47	476	9.9	Second	China
Potatoes	24	307	7.8	Third	China, Russian Federation
Onion (Dry)	6F	52	11.5	Second	China
6. Commercial crops (million t)					
Sugarcane	279	1288	21.7	Second	Brazil
Tea	0.83*	3.10	26.8	First	
Coffee (green)	0.32*	7.37	4.3	Sixth	Brazil, Vietnam, Colombia, Indonesia, Mexico
Jute and allied fibres	1.99	3.22	61.8	First	
Cotton (lint)	1.86*	18.59	10.0	Third	China, USA
Tobacco leaves	0.58	6.35	9.1	Third	China, Brazil
7. Livestock (million head)					
Cattle	222*	1367	16.2	First	
Buffaloes	95*	167	56.9	First	

Camels	0.90F	18.48	4.9	Fourth	Somalia, Sudan, Mauritania
Sheep	59F	1034	5.7	Third	China, Australia
Goats	124F	743	16.7	Second	China
Chicken	824F	115854	5.2	Fifth	China, USA, Brazil, Indonesia
8. Implements (000' numbers)**					
Tractors-in-use	1525F	26854	5.7	Fourth	USA, Japan, Italy
9. Animal Products					
Milk ('000 Mt)	85000*	597403	14.2	First	
Eggs ('000 Mt)	2000*	58102	3.4	Fifth	China, U.S.A., Japan, Russian Federation
Total meat ('000 Mt)	5743F	245047	2.3	Sixth	China, U.S.A., Brazil, France, Germany

Source: *Agricultural Statistics at a Glance, 2005,* Directorate of Economics and Ministry of Agriculture, Govt. of India.

levels. In sugarcane, yield was in excess of average global levels critical for achieving accelerated agricultural growth.

4.4: AGRICULTURAL TRADE BEFORE AND AFTER REFORMS[5]

India initiated liberalisation of its economy and trade with economic reforms in June 1991. As a part of these reforms India adjusted its exchange rate to market rate and relaxed restrictions on agricultural exports. This created a favourable environment for agricultural exports. From 1993-94, agricultural exports started increasing in leaps and bounds. Export earning doubled in three years between 1992-93 and 1995-96. Imports also increased at almost the same pace and net surplus generated by agriculture trade increased from $ 2 billion during 1992-93 to 4.33 billion during 1995-96.

High growth in agricultural exports that resulted from domestic liberalization during 1992-93 to 1994-95, witnessed further increase in the initial years of WTO and reached historical peak of $ 6.8 billion in 1996-97. However, after 1996-97 earnings from agricultural exports started moving downward (Table 4.7 and Fig 1) and dropped to $ 5.8 billion by the year 1999-2000. This happened despite further liberalisation in agricultural exports announced in the Export-Import policy, 1997-2002. Once again agricultural exports started growing from year 2000-01. Provisional figure for the year 2003-04 shows that agricultural export reached $ 8 billion which is about 30 percent higher than exports during 2000-01. The decline in exports during late 1990s was caused due to sharp fall in global prices and is in keeping with the global trend. However, this dip in prices did not cause decline in value of India's imports during late 1990s.

The growth in imports and exports after 1990-91 was much higher than the growth in GDP. As a result, share of import and export in GDP followed increase.

TABLE 4.8

International Comparisons of Yield of Selected Commodities, 2003

(Kg/Hectare)

Rice/Paddy	
Bangladesh	3448
Egypt	9135
India	2915
Japan	6582
Myanmar	3582
Pakistan	2882
Thailand	2597
USA	7372
World	3916
Wheat	
Bangladesh	2164
China	3885
France	7449
India	2770
Iran	1905
Pakistan	2262
USA	8043
World	2720
Maize	
China	5022
Egypt	7789
France	8813
India	1705
Italy	9560
Pakistan	1769
Philippines	1803
World	4343

Sugarcane	
Bangladesh	39890
China	66353
Colombia	94789
Egypt	119893
Guatemal	94032
India	68049
Pakistan	48042
World	65802
Tobacco Leaves	
Bangladesh	1233
Canada	2600
France	2778
India	1353
Indonesia	829
Italy	3333
Pakistan	1848
World	1589
Groundnut (in shell)	
Argentina	2329
Brazil	2043
China	2986
India	794
Sudan	630
USA	2869
Uganda	701
World	1381

Imports accounted for less than 1 percent of India's agricultural GDP during early 1990s and now they are close to 4 percent. Similarly, share of exports in GDP agriculture increased from less than 4.5 percent in early 1990s to more than 6.5 percent in the recent years. These changes indicate that there has been significant increase in trade orientation of Indian agriculture after 1990-91 as trade to GDP ratio has increased from around 5 percent in early 1990s to more than 10 percent in the recent years. Despite this increase in agriculture trade import of agriculture is relatively small compared to the total import of the country. In most of the recent years agricultural imports comprised around 6 percent of India's total imports. Share of agricultural exports in total exports is about double the share of agricultural imports. After 1990-91 there is decline in the share of agricultural export but increase in share of agriculture imports.

Trend in import and export shows that integration of Indian agriculture with global economy has improved considerably during last 13 years after 1990-91 but still ratio of trade to GDP is very low compared to most of the developing south-east Asian countries. Initial years of liberalization were arable for growth of export and import but post-WTO years turned out to be highly adverse for India's agriculture exports. Exports have seen some recovery again in the recent years.

There were considerable variations in export performance of various commodities (Table 4.10 and Fig. 2). Export of non-basmati rice picked up during 1995-96 when lot of stock was released for export. However, non-basmati rice and wheat could not face global competition and their export was promoted by providing some subsidies like transport and marketing. Export of oil meal, which was the second biggest item of export after marine products, increased from $ 377 million in early 1990s to close to $ 1 billion by 1996-97, but suffered serious setback due to decline in international prices and East Asia financial crisis during late 1990s. Likewise, export of most of the commodities first followed increase with liberalization and then followed decline during late 1990s. Export earnings from traditional group consisting of tea, coffee, spices, tobacco suffered mainly due to sharp fall in international prices as quantity of export in most cases did not decline. Export (value in $) of marine products, and groups of livestock and horticultural products maintained the tempo of growth, continuing from pre-WTO period. This shows that post-WTO situation was

TABLE 4.9

Agriculture Trade and its Share in GDP Agriculture and Total Trade

Year	*Agricultural trade $ Million*		*Share in GDP agriculture %*		*Share in total trade %*	
	Import	*Export*	*Import*	*Export*	*Import*	*Export*
1990-91	672	3352	0.75	3.76	2.79	18.49
1991-92	604	3203	0.80	4.24	3.09	17.8
1992-93	938	2950	1.38	4.34	4.54	16.84
1993-94	742	4013	0.96	5.2	3.18	18.05
1994-95	189142	11	2.13	4.74	6.6	15.99
1995-96	176160	98	1.94	6.73	4.8	19.18
1996-97	186368	06	1.82	6.66	4.76	20.33
1997-98	236466	85	2.27	6.42	5.7	19.09
1998-99	346260	64	3.29	5.77	8.17	18.25
1999-00	370858	42	3.48	5.48	7.45	15.91
2000-01	264662	73	2.58	6.12	5.29	14.23
2001-02	340862	34	3.11	5.70	6.63	14.22
2002-03	3 542	7161	3.45	6.80	5.92	13.58
2003-04	476580	29	3.91	6.58	6.19	12.62

Source: Ramesh Chand, "India's Agro Food Trade Policies and W.T.O. Negotiations," National Centre for Agriculture Economies and Policy Research, New Delhi.

favourable to export of high value food products. Moreover, this growth was mainly market-driven as there is little direct government intervention in these products. Export of cotton almost dried up in the post-WTO period due to increased demand from domestic textile industry and decline in domestic production. Sugar exports remained occasional as the surplus arose temporarily. Except some commodities there is sharp year to year fluctuation in export. In the case of imports, liberalisation of trade in the initial years of implementation of WTO agreement did not cause much difficulty because international prices of bulk products were quite high in the first three post-WTO years. Imports hovered around $1.8 billion during 1994-95 to 1996-97. Subsequently, as international prices started

FIG. 1

India's agriculture Trade before and after WTO

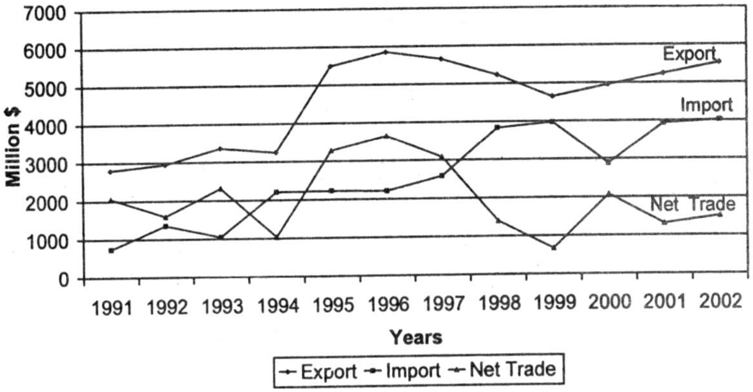

falling, India's imports started rising. Level of imports doubled in three years between 1996-97 and 1999-00 and reached peak of $ 3.7 billion. This caused lot of disappointment to the country which expected big gain in export earning in the post-WTO period through increased market access into developed countries' market. Domestic production of staples came under threat of disruption. International prices of cereals towards the year 2000 and 2001 turned out to be almost half of what they were in the beginning of WTO. This happened when India was having very large stock of rice and wheat. Tariffs were not found adequate to keep a check on import of cereals and India had to resort to desperate measures like reimposing QRs on imports of foodgrains to keep a check on cheap imports. Important lessons from this experience is that India was not able to safeguard domestic production against imports with usual tariff when international prices went very low. In order to deal with this kind of situations, India seeks either high bound tariff so that applied tariffs can be raised appropriately, or, special safeguards to regulate imports of sensitive products.

Composition of imports show that most of the

TABLE 4.10

Export of Major Agricultural Products During Reforms and Post-WTO Period

($ million)

Commodity	*1991-92*	*1992-93*	*1993-94*	*1994-95*	*1995-96*	*1996-97*	*1997-98*	*1998-99*	*1999-00*	*2000-01*	*2001-02*	*2002-03*	*2003-04*
Basmati rice	204	276	338	276	255	352	454	446	411	472	387	426	434
Non-basmati rice	105	60	72	108	1113	543	454	1046	311	170	279	782	467
Wheat	52	3.5	0.07	13.5	110	197	0.11	*	*	91	280	365	513
Cotton raw inc. waste	125	63	208	45	61	444	221	49	18	48	9	10	177
Pulses	**	18	23	29	39	37	97	53	97	118	77	71	70
Oil meal	377	534	740	573	703	985	925	461	378	448	474	308	714
Sugar and mollases	64	122	57	20	152	304	69	6	9	111	375	376	266
Marine products	590	602	813	1127	1012	1129	1207	1038	1184	1396	1218	1435	1324
Groundnut	3	3	54	32	69	92	153	33	86	69	53	37	119
Spices	152	136	182	195	238	339	380	388	408	355	312	343	333
Tea	495	337	337	311	351	292	505	538	412	392	360	342	348
Coffee	136	130	174	335	450	402	457	411	332	260	229	206	236
Tobacco Mfd.	154	164	147	81	134	213	288	181	233	190	170	211	238
Cashew	274	257	333	369	370	362	377	387	568	449	374	425	370
Castor oil	57	40	92	141	222	177	155	160	247	209	131	126	139
Guargum meal	38	36	45	45	68	100	147	173	188	130	84	101	110
Poultry and dairy prod.	**	**	**	**	18	35	32	23	28	47	73	74	89

Meat and prep.	94	89	110	128	188	200	218	187	189	322	251	285	350
Floriculture product	6	5	6	10	18	18	23	25	27	26	27	37	48
Fresh fruits	**	**	**	60	69	69	75	63	71	85	85	93	166
Fresh vegetables	143	108	132	79	89	94	84	65	77	100	121	133	205
Processed fruit/veg.	36	41	49	79	104	92	105	109	129	172	152	172	154

* Less than 0.5 million $.

** Data not available.

Source: Agricultural Statistics at a Glance, Ministry of Agriculture, GOI, various issues.

increase in agriculture imports took place due to increase in import of edible oil. Vegetable oils accounted for more than three-fourth of total increment in agriculture imports in the post-WTO period. The other items whose imports increased significantly are pulses, spices and cotton. There is also noticeable increase in imports of fruits and nuts. In this group increase in cashew nut import is mainly for re-export of processed cashew nuts.

Experience with agricultural imports indicates that because of high volatility in international prices in some years even high bound tariff is not adequate to regulate imports. Because of such situation India seeks special safeguard or protection. Similarly, due to volatility in international prices, domestic prices of exportables also got depressed. Price volatility is the most important factor in affecting India's export and import and in turn domestic prices and production, the country should suggest in AOA negotiations measures to reduce volatility and to guard against it.

Imports of items like vegetable oils have depressed domestic prices and caused adverse impact on domestic production. In the case of pulses imports did not help in lowering domestic prices. Imports of edible oil was much more than the reduction in production of edible oil. This is evident from the per capita availability of edible oil in the country which remained between 5 to 5.8 kg for a decade till 1992-93 and then steadily increased to more than 9 kg by 2002-03. Thus, edible oil import have been quite favourable for consumers as they could increase consumption due to low prices.

4.5: TRADE FLOWS IN TERMS OF QUANTITY FOR SELECTED COMMODITIES[6]

Year-wise data on export and import of selected products shows that except basmati rice, tea, and coffee there was very large fluctuations in quantity sent for exports. In the case of bulk products like wheat, non-

TABLE 4.11

Import of Major Agricultural Products During Reforms and Post-WTO Period

($ million)

Commodity	*1991-92*	*1992-93*	*1993-94*	*1994-95*	*1995-96*	*1996-97*	*1997-98*	*1998-99*	*1999-00*	*2000-01*	*2001-02*	*2002-03*	*2003-04*
Spices	0	0	24	18	22	27	36	71	68	56	106	121	127
Cotton Raw	84	6	162	166	9	9	22	91	290	260	432	256	343
Pulses	99	109	181	189	205	251	322	168	82	109	665	567	491
Vegetable oil	96	54	53	199	676	826	745	1803	1859	1310	1360	1819	2547

Source: Agricultural Statistics at a Glance, Ministry of Agriculture, GOI, various issues.

basmati or common rice, groundnut, sugar and cotton in some years India used to export very large quantity and in some years exports reduced to almost nil. Despite being exporter in most of the years India frequently used to import large volume of products like wheat, sugar and cotton mainly because of fluctuations in production and poor management of demand and supply. Because of the fluctuations in volume of trade India is not a consistent and permanent player in export market of these products. (Table 4.12). The Table shows that India's wheat exports increased from 252.6 thousand tonnes during early 1990s to 593.3 thousand tonne in next 5 years. During the first three years of 21st Century average wheat exports have crossed 2.378 million tonne. Wheat imports, which exceeded exports till mid-1990s have almost banished in the recent years. There has been a very consistent increase in export of basmati rice which have doubled in last 12 years. India created a surprise by capturing almost one-fourth of global rice export market after rice exports were freed. The country exported more than 4 million tonne of common rice during 1995-96, 1998-99 and 2002-03. Triennium averages show that India exported less than 340 thousand tonne rice in early 1990s. Since mid-1990s average annual export of non-basmati rice have remained more than 2 million tonne while total rice exports remained close to 3 million tonne.

Like wheat, exports of sugar also increased sharply after 1990-91. Annual exports in the beginning of 1990s were at 377 thousand tonne which have increased to 1.15 million tonne in the recent years.

From few hundred tonne export of maize increased to 25 thousand tonne during triennium 1995/96 to 1997/98. Maize export further trebled in next five years. Exports of tea followed moderate decline and then small increase. Present level of tea export is placed at 183 thousand tonne. India's coffee exports doubled between early 1990s and the early years of 2000. In the same period coffee import increased from 14 hundred tonne to 38 hundred tonne but imports are mere 2

FIG. 2

Export of Agricultural Products: 1991-92 to 2003-04

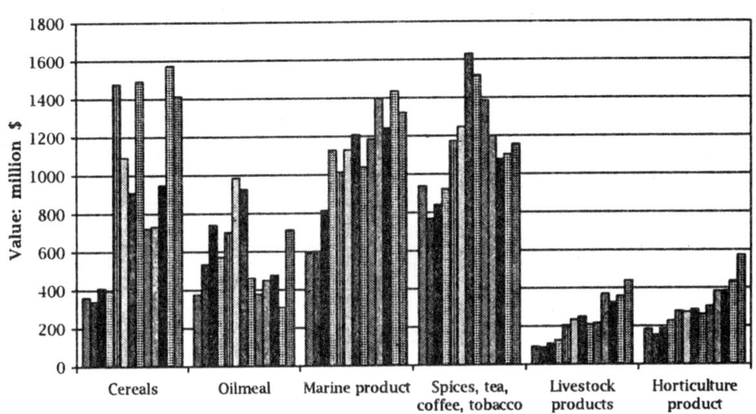

FIG. 3

Import of Selected Agricultural Products: 1991-92 to 2003-04

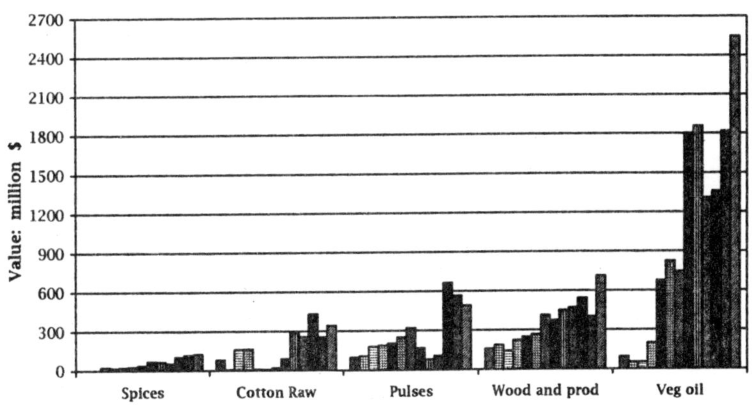

percent of export. Recent triennium has seen emergence of tea imports to the tune of 15 thousand tonne. Export of rapeseed/mustard and soyabean have emerged from nowhere to sizable amount. Groundnut exports first increased but then declined.

FIG. 4

Real Prices of Selected Agricultural Products Adversely Affected by WTO

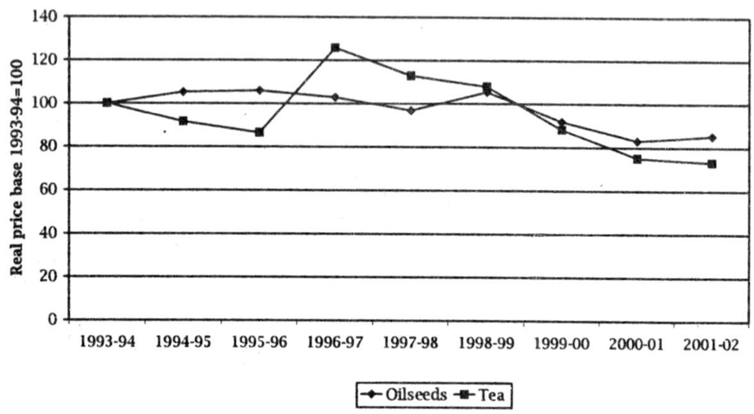

In early 1990s India was net importer of milk. The situation reversed in next five years with exports turned out to be more than double the import. In the recent years imports have plummeted to below 200 tonne and

FIG. 5

Production of Oilseeds and Raw Cotton in India, before and after WTO

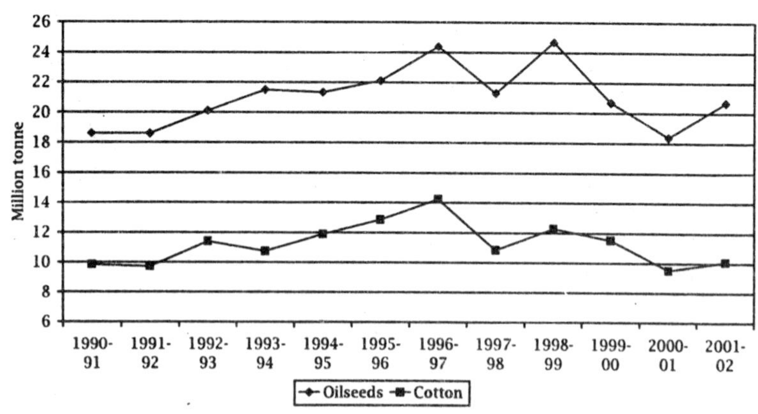

TABLE 4.12

Changes in Export and Import of Selected Commodities, 1990-91 to 2002-03

(00 tonne)

Commodity	*Export*			*Import*		
	TE 1992-93	*TE 1997-98*	*TE 2002-03*	*TE 1992-93*	*TE 1997-98*	*TE 2002-03*
Wheat	2526	5933	23780	7148	7022	28
Maize	4	252	747	—	—	111
Rice: Basmati	3729	4967	7416			
Rice: Non-basmati	3338	27751	21609	602	1	161
Soyabean	1	43	259	—	1	1
Rapeseed/ Mustard	—	9	102	—	4	18
Groundnut	651	1710	1273	—	—	—
Sugar	3772	5681	11525	53	1666	325
Cotton	2404	1535	165	1381	275	2777
Tea	1955	1773	1833	—	—	149
Coffee	995	1598	1820	14	19	38
Milk	2	19	109	26	7	2
Sheep meat	16	22	12	—	—	—
Eggs			114	—	—	—
Poultry meat	—	—	1	—	—	—

— Very small, less than 51 tonne.
Source: Agricultural Statistics at a Glance, Ministry of Agriculture, GOI, various issues.

exports have risen to about 11 thousand tonne. Export of sheep meat witnessed setback in the recent years and has declined to 1200 tonne. India exports about 11.4 thousand tonne of eggs. Cotton is the only commodity whose exports have hit very badly after 1990-91 and imports have risen to high level. Import of groundnut and poultry meat remained negligible. Trade flows in selected products show a very favourable growth of export volume except cotton and sheep meat. Imports of cereals, sugar, rapeseed/mustard, soyabean and milk show sharp decline whereas tea, coffee and cotton imports showed increase.

4.6: TRADE DESTINATIONS AND ORIGIN

India export most of its agricultural products to diverse destinations but export of some products is concentrated in 2-3 countries. All countries which accounted for more than 2 percent share in India's total agricultural exports are shown in Table 4.13. USA has remained the biggest and very stable trade partner for India's agricultural exports. Its share in the recent years varied between 12.66 to 14.18 percent. Bangladesh has emerged as the second biggest export destination and its share has increased from below 4 percent during 2000-01 to more than 9 percent during 2003-04. UAE is the third most important destination for India's agricultural exports with around 5.5 percent share. Till three years ago Japan used to be the second biggest destination for India's agricultural products but its share dropped sharply in the last three years which has relegated its rank to fourth place. Saudi Arab competes closely with Japan with its share remaining at little more than 5 percent. Indonesia and Malaysia each account for more than 4 percent of India's agro-export while share of UK has come down to 3.83 percent during 2003-04. Other important destinations are Sri Lanka, China, Germany, Russia and Netherlands. These 13 countries account for more than 60 percent of India's agricultural exports.

TABLE 4.13

Destination of Indian Exports: Total Agriculture and Allied Products

Destination	*(% Share of the country)*			
	2000-01	*2001-02*	*2002-03*	*2003-04*
USA	13.22	12.66	14.18	12.87
Bangladesh	3.85	5.04	6.06	9.26
UAE	6.36	5.55	5.20	5.99
Japan	10.89	7.56	6.54	5.23
Saudi Arabia	6.23	5.51	4.65	5.05
Indonesia	2.3	4.25	3.67	4.24
Malaysia	2.82	3.72	4.75	4.15
UK	5.23	4.12	4.06	3.83
Sri Lanka	1.6	2.52	2.54	2.73
China	2.69	2.13	2.25	2.64
Germany	2.62	2.18	2.29	2.52
Russia	3.82	3.48	2.34	2.27
Netherlands	3.7	3.11	2.43	2.19
Total of above	65.33	61.83	60.96	62.97

Source: Agricultural Statistics at a Glance, Ministry of Agriculture, GOI, various issues.

In short, it can be said that after reforms trade growth in agriculture sector has remained lackluster and there was not much change in traditional trade partners of India.

4.7: CAUSES FOR DECELERATING GROWTH IN AGRICULTURE SECTOR DURING 1990'S

The Tenth Plan document has stated that there are region-specific causes for the decelerating growth in agriculture sector during the 1990's. Some of these are:[7]

- Low public investment in irrigation and poor maintenance.

- Poor maintenance of rural infrastructure, specially canals and roads.
- Decline in investments in rural electrification and in its availability. This has greatly affected production in eastern India, where huge groundwater potential remains untapped.
- Rising level of subsidies for power, water, fertilizers and food are eating into public sector investments in agriculture, besides encouraging inefficient use of scarce resources such as water. This further aggravates environmental problems leading to loss of soil fertility and decline in groundwater, which reduces return on capital. Farmers then demand further subsidies to maintain the same level of production.
- Inadequate credit support.
- Continuing imbalanced use of NPK fertilizers, (6.69:2.59:1.0) in 2001-02 as against the desirable norm of 4:2:1) and increasing deficiency of micro-nutrients in the soil.
- Stringent controls on movement, marketing, credit, stock and export of agri-products that affect their profitability. In the face of pressure from the WTO, there is apprehension that without speedy domestic market reforms, an opportunity to capture world markets would be converted into a threat to the future growth of Indian agriculture. The classic case is that of sugar where imports were opened at zero duty when controls on domestic markets remained widespread.
- Demand constraints (slow growth of the urban economy, restriction on exports, lack of land reforms, failure of poverty alleviation schemes, slow growth in rural wages).
- Controls on the agro-processing industry.
- Poor extension service.

4.8: NEGLECT OF AGRICULTURE: THE MAJOR SIN OF ECONOMIC REFORMS

Mahesh V. Joshi stated that in Economic Reforms[8] "Agriculture is being neglected although it is the decisive field in the economy of our country. The Government approved the policy of urban development at the cost of rural and industrial expansion and at the cost of agriculture. This is suicidal policy and yet no concrete or effective steps have been taken to boost agriculture which is facing a great crisis. The India economy is burdened with foreign domination, industrial expansion and the Indian farming and farmers are decapitating the villages dedication and the country is in the grip of economic, social and political whirlpool. The time is ripe for us to ask what will happen to the rural economy and the Indian farmer on whose shoulder rests the future of the country."

The upshot of the entire analysis is that the major sin of economic reforms is gross neglect of agriculture—the mainstay of livelihood of over two-third of the population. Although the Tenth Plan has fixed a target of over 4 percent for annual growth in agriculture, this target appears to be somewhat difficult to achieve. This is more so in view of the fact that though India had seven good monsoon years in succession, agricultural production indicated year-to-year fluctuations. This casts a shadow on sustainability of agricultural growth, unless there is a re-orientation of priorities with much greater

4.9: ACCELERATING AGRICULTURAL GROWTH[9]

Accelerating GDP growth in agriculture to around 4% as envisaged in this study, is not an easy task. Actual growth of agricultural GDP, including forestry and fishing, was only 1% per annum in the first three years of 10th Plan and even the most rosy projections for 2005-06 and 2006-07 would limit this below 2% for the full five year period. The challenge posed is to more than double the growth rate achieved in the 10th Plan. This will require action on both the demand side and the supply side.

(a) Demand Side Intervention

On the demand side there is evidence that farmers face adverse demand conditions. Not only has agricultural growth been low in the last decade, the prices received for agricultural products have also failed to keep pace with the costs or the general price level and, as a consequence, profitability has declined. Several modeling exercises suggest that a 4% growth of agriculture will not be sustainable from the demand side unless aggregate GDP growth is much higher than 8%. Some of the steps already taken, such as the recently introduced National Rural Employment Guarantee Programme, will help the demand side in the 11th Plan. The emphasis on expanding access and improving quality of public sector schools and health facilities may also help by reducing the need for private expenditure on these items by lower income groups and some of this expenditure will be redirected to generate demand for agriculture. Improved rural connectivity envisaged through Bharat Nirman can also trigger growth of an integrated national market where rural people are more able to meet each other's demand. In its sheer size and scope, such expanded rural-rural trade is likely to be as important in the initial years as other efforts of demand support such as promoting agricultural exports, or strengthening support to agricultural diversification for domestic processing. The latter of course have the advantage of being able to attract private corporate investment into rural areas once essential infrastructure is in place and their importance is likely to grow over time. A very large private expenditure shift has occurred over the last decade from food to health, education and conveyance, some of which should be reversible.

(b) Supply Side Strategy

The supply side challenge of doubling agricultural growth is also formidable.

This is especially so because no dramatic technological breakthrough comparable to the "green revolution" is presently in sight. We are also not exploiting the potential of existing technology. In fact, most of the growth required in cereals, pulses and oilseeds is possible merely through plausible yield increase in currently low yield regions. It is however necessary to identify the specific constraints and policy distortions that have produced these yield gaps. The National Commission on Farmers has drawn attention to the knowledge deficit which constrains agricultural productivity. To overcome this, farmers will need effective links to universities and best practices. A good extension system is the means for achieving this linkage but unfortunately the extension system has virtually collapsed in most states, partly as a result of constraints on non-plan expenditure. Krishi Vigyan Kendras set-up by ICAR have very little interaction with the ATMA model of extension being promoted by DAC. The result is that farming practices in large parts of the country are sub-optimal. Soil testing to determine optimal nutrient requirements is hardly practiced and fertilizer application is often highly unbalanced with excessive use of nitrogenous fertilisers, often leading to a negative effect on productivity of the soil over time, a consequence that farmers are not fully aware of these imbalances are themselves to some extent the result of a system of fertilizer subsidy which is irrational and focuses excessively on nitrogenous fertilizers. Lack of credit at reasonable rates is a persistent problem, in large part, reflecting the collapse of the cooperative credit system. The failure of the organized credit system in extending credit has led to excessive dependence on informal sources usually at exorbitant interest rates. This is at the root of farmer distress reflected in excessive indebtedness. Accelerated agricultural growth will require diversification into horticulture and floriculture which in turn imply structural changes in the relation between agriculture and non-agriculture. Diversification requires effective marketing linkages, supported by modern marketing practices including introduction of grading, post-harvest management, cold chains, etc. There is a need to encourage the development of modern agricultural markets and for this purpose it is necessary to amend the APMC Acts. Although this has begun, the process needs to be accelerated. Diversification also means the product must meet the specific requirements of the different markets being serviced, and these requirements vary depending on whether the market is domestic consumption, agro-processing or exports. Contract farming is a potentially effective way of attracting corporate investors to help establish these linkages with markets and also provide farmers with necessary inputs, extension and other advice. Although very limited at present, many states have already taken steps to facilitate this potential to assist the process of diversification. A greater focus is, however, necessary on enabling small farmer participation by encouraging group formation and providing suitable and effective regulatory frameworks. Existing vested interests in traditional trade channels often oppose these changes but they must be overcome. As farmers adopt new and untried technology, and increase input intensities, they also face larger risks. These risks are often not well understood owing to lack of knowledge of the requirements of new seeds and new technology. All farmers do not have the ability to bear downside risks. Thus, we have seen farmer suicides when new seeds fail to deliver expected output, or when expenditure on bore wells proves in fructuous, or when market prices collapse. Farmers should be protected against such risks by appropriate measures. Insurance is one way of doing this, but the financial cost of existing and proposed crop insurance schemes is very considerable, and recurring, so that these are not appropriate as plan schemes. These and related issues of risk management need to be addressed in the 11th Plan.

The agricultural strategy for the 11th Plan must be based on recognition of the need for strategies specific to different agro-climatic zones. The nature of the technical constraints and crop development possibilities vary considerably across zones. Viable policy packages must be devised for each zone keeping these variations in mind. This will need to be incorporated in the design of future plan schemes with corresponding improvements in plan implementation and in administrative structures to optimize region-specific benefits. While the strategies can emerge through consultation between the Centre and the States, the task of implementing these strategies on the ground falls almost wholly on the state governments.

(c) Agricultural Research

In the longer run, growth in agricultural productivity can be sustained only through continuous technological progress. This calls for a well considered strategy for prioritized basic research, which is now all the more urgent in view of mounting pressure on scarce natural resources, climate change and also the shrinking availability of spill-over from international public research. The 11th Plan will have to focus the National Agricultural Research System (NARS) to strengthen its basic research component through properly anticipated identification of strategic research pathways. This must go hand in hand with clearer demarcation of responsibilities within NARS between such basic research, which may not contribute immediately to growth, and the more immediate requirement to adapt and disseminate existing technology and provide region-specific problem-solving capacity. The recently established National Strategic Agricultural Research Fund must be expanded in the 11th Plan and oriented to stimulate research responding to a well defined strategy of prioritization. New generation technologies based on rapidly evolving scientific developments will play a pivotal role in achieving new levels of productivity in agriculture. The country's large agricultural research system which successfully launched the green revolution in the past will now be called upon to address newer and more formidable challenges. In this endeavor, business as usual has no place whatsoever. The system needs to be thoroughly revamped and restructured in the light of the advice rendered by the high powered committees chaired respectively by Dr. Swaminathan and Dr. R.A. Mashelkar.

(d) Water Management and Irrigation

Water is a critical input for agriculture and this calls for expansion of irrigation, where it is possible and better water management in rain fed areas where assured irrigation is not possible. This is clearly an area where past policies have been inadequate. Performance in expanding irrigation has been disappointing with resources being spread thinly over many projects and a large number of irrigation projects remaining under construction for many years. The Bharat Nirman programme *inter-alia* envisages creation of 10 m. ha. additional assured irrigation during the 4 years period (2005-09). To achieve this, the pace of potential creation will have to be scaled up from 1.42 m. ha. per year in recent years to 2.5 m. ha./year. Of the new potential envisaged under Bharat Nirman, about half is planned for 2007-08 and 2008-09 i.e., first 2 years of the 11th Plan. Assuming the same rate of creation of continues thereafter, a total of about 11 m. ha. of new potential can be expected in the 11th Plan consisting of 5.5 m. ha. in major and medium irrigation, 3.5 m.ha. through minor irrigation and about 2.0 m. ha. through ground water development. In addition, another 3-4 m. ha. of land is to be restored through modernisation of major, medium and minor projects and restoration of tanks. Investments in the major and medium irrigation sector will require large resources from the state governments supported by Central Assistance under AIBP. However, implementation of these projects by state governments is also important. Monitoring the pace of creation of potential assumes special importance. Besides regular monitoring by Central Water Commission, it is proposed to expand usage of remote sensing techniques for this purpose which has been initiated on a pilot basis in the 10th Plan.

Along with expansion of irrigation facilities, steps need to be taken to ensure that water is distributed equitably and that it is used efficiently. The past pattern where tailenders are denied water because upper end users appropriate it for highly water intensive crops must be avoided. Participatory Irrigation Management (PIM) by democratically organised water user associations empowered to set water charges, collect and retain substantial part of it, would help to maintain field channels, expand irrigated area, distribute water equitably and provide the tailenders their just share of water. Experience in Gujarat has shown the effectiveness of such PIM. The 11th Plan must expand reliance on PIM on a large scale. Water is also critical for the more than 60% of cultivable land that is unirrigated and rainfed. Ground water management is critical for these areas and will therefore need much more focused attention in the 11th Plan. Unless this is done we run the risk of a deepening agricultural crisis in dryland areas. Water must be recognised as a scarce resource and every drop needs to be used efficiently. In this context, it must be recognised that some existing policies followed by state governments contribute to the problem. Continued provision of free power by some states and highly subsidised power by all states is leading to an increase in semi-critical, critical and over-exploited areas of groundwater use, which already cover 29% of the blocks in the country.

Watershed management, rainwater harvesting and ground water recharge can help augment water availability in rainfed areas. Building structures for water management and managing them also provides opportunities for employment generation in rural areas. In addition, the enhanced productivity of land will generate its own employment. The National Rainfed Areas Authority to be set-up in the current year provides a vehicle for developing concerted action plans for rainfed areas in close consultation with state governments. With an estimated 80 million hectares needing treatment, and average expenditure of Rs. 10,000 per hectare, the total requirement of funds is about Rs. 80,000 crore. For this magnitude of funding to be feasible during the 11th Plan, it is absolutely essential that these programmes be converged with or at least supplemented by the Employment Guarantee programme funding local level schemes which conserve moisture and recharge ground water.

(e) Animal Husbandry and Fishery

The livestock and fisheries sectors together account for about 30% of the value of the output of Agriculture and Allied Sector and provide full time and part time employment to 5.5% of the total working population. Their contribution to total GDP in 2003-04 was 6.3%. The 11th Plan must evolve viable strategies for these sectors to expand rapidly. The effort to revive agricultural dynamism must therefore pay sufficient attention to this sector. India continues to be the largest producer of milk in the World with a total production of 91 million tonnes in 2005-06 and the contribution of milk alone was higher than paddy, wheat and sugarcane in the year 2003-04. Yet the per capita availability of milk at 231 gm. per day during 2003-04 is still very low. Matters are even worse regarding meat, with abattoir conditions pathetic and utilization of by-products inefficient. Poultry development in the country has shown better progress over the years, primarily because research and development schemes of the government have been complemented with effective management and marketing by an organized private sector. Some of the important initiatives that are needed are:

Promotion of appropriate crossbreeds while conserving indigenous breeds of livestock. Establishment of livestock marketing system. Promotion of rural backyard poultry in a cooperative marketing set-up. Development of cooperative dairy firms enhancing livestock extension services. Encouraging private veterinary clinic. Institutionalising a framework for utilizing synergy between restoration and creation of water bodies for water harvesting and fishery.

(f) Provision of an Insurance Package to Avoid Distress

The survival of pastoralism is crucial for sustainable land use. Besides conserving domestic biodiversity, it is a means of producing food in dry lands without depleting groundwater resources. However, there are many constraints on expansion in this area. Grazing permits are denied in traditional grazing sites that have been converted into protected areas/wildlife sanctuaries, national parks/Joint Forest Management (JFM) programme. Original pasture lands or stipulated animal drinking water ponds are encroached upon, or used for other purposes. Bio-diesel (Jatropha) planting is being promoted through state agencies without seeing all the consequences such as blocking the migration routes of animals and encroaching upon herd-passing pathways.

4.10: VISION 2020[10]

The future of agriculture Growth in India will rest only on embarking on path where some radical changes are made not only in prevailing system but also on bringing some dynamic changes in our thinking. The future plan must consider following changes:

(a) Enhancing Yield of Major Commodities

Yield of major crops and livestock in the region is much lower than that in the rest of the world.

Considering that the frontiers of expansion of cultivated area are almost closed in the region, the future increase in food production to meet the continuing high demand must come from increase in yield. There is a need to strengthen adaptive research and technology assessment, refinement and transfer capabilities of the country so that the existing wide technology transfer gaps are bridged. For this, an appropriate network of extension service needs to be created to stimulate and encourage both top-down and bottom-up flows of information between farmers, extension workers, and research scientists to promote the generation, adoption, and evaluation of location specific farm technologies. Ample scope exists for increasing genetic yield potential of a large number of vegetables, fruits as well as other food crops and livestock and fisheries products. Besides maintenance breeding, greater effort should be made towards developing hybrid varieties as well as varieties suitable for export purposes. Agronomic and soil researches in the region need to be intensified to address location specific problems as factor productivity growth is decelerating in major production regimes. Research on coarse grains, pulses and oilseeds must achieve a production breakthrough. Hybrid rice, single cross hybrids of maize and pigeonpea hybrids offer new opportunities. Soybean, sunflower and oil palm will help in meeting future oil demands successfully. Forest cover must be preserved to keep off climatic disturbances and to provide enough of fuel and fodder. Milk, meat and draught capacity of our animals needs to be improved quickly through better management practices.

(b) Integrated Nutrient Management

Attention should be given to balanced use of nutrients. Phosphorus deficiency is now the most widespread soil fertility problem in both irrigated and unirrigated areas. Correcting the distortion in relative prices of primary fertilizers could help correct the imbalances in the use of primary plant nutrients—

nitrogen, phosphorus, and potash and use of bio-fertilizers. To improve efficiency of fertilizer use, what is really needed is enhanced location-specific research on efficient fertilizer practices (such as balanced use of nutrients, correct timing and placement of fertilizers, and, wherever necessary, use of micronutrient and soil amendments), improvement in soil testing services, development of improved fertilizer supply and distribution systems, and development of physical and institutional infrastructure.

(c) Arresting deceleration in Total Factor Productivity

Public investment in irrigation, infrastructure development (road, electricity), research and extension and efficient use of water and plant nutrients are the dominant sources of TFP growth. The sharp deceleration in total investment and more so in public sector investment in agriculture is the main cause for the deceleration. This has resulted in the slow-down in the growth of irrigated area and a sharp deceleration in the rate of growth of fertiliser consumption. The most serious effect of deceleration in total investment has been on agricultural research and extension. This trend must be reversed as the projected increase in food and non-food production must accrue essentially through increasing yield per hectare. Recognising that there are serious yield gaps and there are already proven paths for increasing productivity, it is very important for India to maintain a steady growth rate in total factor productivity. As the TFP increases, the cost of production decreases and the prices also decrease and stabilise. Both producer and consumer share the benefits. The fall in food prices will benefit the urban and rural poor more than the upper income groups, because the former spend a much larger proportion of their income on cereals than the latter. All the efforts need to be concentrated on accelerating growth in TFP, whilst conserving natural resources and promoting ecological integrity of agricultural system. More than half of the required growth in yield to meet the target of demand must be met from research efforts by developing location specific and low input use technologies with the emphasis on the regions where the current yields are below the required national average yield. Literacy had a positive and significant relation with crop productivity and a strong link exists between literacy and farm modernisation. A recent study (Kumar and Mittal, 2000), has shown that literacy emerged as an important source of growth in adoption of technology, use of modern inputs like machines, fertilisers, and yield. Recognising that in the liberalised economic environment, efficiency and growth orientation will attract maximum attention. Literacy will play a far more important role in the globalised world than it did in the past. Contribution of literacy, through TFP, will be substantial on yield growth and domestic supply. As future agriculture will increasingly be science-led and will require modern economic management, high return to investment on education is expected. The investments that are good for agricultural growth-technology and its dissemination, rural infrastructure (roads), education and irrigation amount to a 'winwin' strategy for reducing rural poverty by also increasing the non-farm economy and raising rural wages. Creating infrastructure in less developed areas, better management of infrastructure and introduction of new technologies can further enhance resource productivity and TFP. Generation and effective assessment and diffusion of packages of appropriate technologies involving system and programme based approach, participatory mechanisms, greater congruency between productivity and sustainability through integrated pest management and integrated soil-water-irrigation nutrient management, should be aggressively promoted to bridge the yield gaps in most field crops. Besides this, efforts must be in place to defend the gains and to make new gains particularly through the congruence of gene revolution, informatics revolution, management revolution and eco-technology. Many observers have expressed concern that technological gains have not occurred in a number of crops, notably coarse cereals, pulses and in rainfed areas.

Recent analysis on TFP growth based on cost of cultivation data does not prove this perception (Table 4.14). In all the 18 major crops considered in the analysis, several states have recorded positive TFP growth. This is spread over major cereals, coarse grains, pulses, oilseeds, fibers, vegetables, etc. In most cases, in the major producing states, rainfed crops also, showed productivity gains. There is thus strong evidence that technological change has generally pervaded the entire crop sector. There are, of course, crops and states where technological stagnation or decline is apparent and these are the priorities for present and future agricultural research. Farming system research to develop location specific technologies and strategy to make grey areas green by adopting three-pronged approach—watershed management, hybrid technology and small farm mechanisation will accelerate growth in TFP. It is necessary to enlarge the efforts for promoting available dry land technologies. Promoting efficient fertiliser practices, improving soil-testing services, strengthening distribution channel of critical inputs specially quality seed and development of physical and institutional infrastructure will help resource-poor farmers.

(d) Bridging Yield Gaps

Vast untapped potential in the yield exists for all crops in most of the states accounting for more than three-fourths of crop area. Emphasis must be given to the states in which current yield levels are below the national average yield. Bihar, Orissa, Assam, West Bengal and Uttar Pradesh are the priority states accounting for 66% of rice area which need emphasis on bridging yield gaps to attain target demand and yield growth. For wheat we must focus mainly on Uttar Pradsh, Madhya Pradesh, Bihar and Rajasthan accounting for 68% of

TABLE 4.14

Total Factor Productivity Trends for Crops in Selected States

Crop	*TFP trend*		
	Increasing	*No change*	*Declining*
Paddy	Andhra Pradesh, Orissa, Punjab, Tamil Nadu, Uttar Pradesh, West Bengal	Assam, Haryana	Bihar, Karnataka, Madhya Pradesh
Wheat	Haryana, Punjab, Rajasthan, Uttar Pradesh	Madhya Pradesh	
Sorghum	Andhra Pradesh, Maharashtra, Karnataka	Madhya Pradesh, Rajasthan	
Pear millets	Gujarat, Haryana,	Rajasthan,	
Maize	Rajasthan, Madhya Pradesh	Uttar Pradesh	
Barley	Uttar Pradesh	Rajasthan	
Chickpea	Haryana	Rajasthan, Uttar Pradesh	Madhya Pradesh
Black gram	Maharashtra	Andhra Pradesh, Madhya Pradesh, Uttar Pradesh	Orissa
Moong	Madhya Pradesh	Andhra Pradesh, Rajasthan	Orissa
Pigeon pea	Madhya Pradesh	Gujarat, Uttar Pradesh	
Groundnut	Andhra Pradesh, Karnataka, Maharashtra, Orissa	Gujarat, Tamil Nadu	
Rapeseed and Mustard	Rajasthan, Uttar Pradesh	Assam, Haryana	Punjab
Soyabean		Madhya Pradesh	
Sugarcane	Bihar	Andhra Pradesh, Haryana, Karnataka, Maharashtra, Uttar Pradesh	
Cotton	Gujarat, Haryana, Tamil Nadu	Andhra Pradesh, Karnataka, Madhya Pradesh, Maharashtra, Punjab	
Jute	Assam, Haryana, Tamil Nadu		Bihar
Onion	Maharashtra	Himachal Pradesh	
Potato	Uttar Pradesh	Himachal Pradesh	

Source: IARI-FAO/RAP study (2001) based on cost of cultivation data, DES, GOI.

wheat area. For coarse cereals, major emphasis must be given to Rajasthan, Maharashtra, Karnataka, Madhya Pradesh, Andhra Pradesh and Uttar Pradesh. To meet the demand for pulses greater emphasis is needed in almost all the states with particular focus on Madhya Pradesh, Maharashtra, Rajasthan, Gujarat, Andhra Pradesh, Karnataka and Uttar Pradesh which have three-fourths of total pulse area. The target growth in pulse yield from these states annually must be 6 per cent; otherwise the nation will experience shortage of pulses for all times to come. The task of attaining self-sufficient in pulses production looks difficult without area expansion and irrigation. In cases of oilseeds greater emphasis is needed on Andhra Pradesh, Madhya Pradesh, Rajasthan, Maharashtra, Karnataka, West Bengal and Uttar Pradesh to increase the yield by about 4 per cent. The possibilities of developing processing industry for extracting edible oils from non-oilseeds commodities, like rice bran, etc. needing to be explored. The introduction of palm cultivation for oil production may release pressure on traditional oilseeds crops to meet future edible oil demand. In case of sugarcane, research and development efforts are to be strengthened in Uttar Pradesh and Bihar to increase the yields per hectare by about 4% per annum. The demand for sugar can also be met by developing mini sugar mills so that substantial sugarcane production can be diverted from Khandsari to sugar production. This may also help release some sugarcane area to other crops. Cotton crop requires greater yield improvement emphasis on 81 per cent of the cotton area in Maharashtra, Gujarat and Andhra Pradesh.

(e) Water for Sustainable Food Security

India will be required to produce more and more from less and less land and water resources. Alarming rates of ground water depletion and serious environmental and social problems of some of the major irrigation projects on one hand, and the multiple benefits of irrigation water in enhancing production and productivity, food security, poverty alleviation, as mentioned earlier, are well known to be further elaborated here. In India, water availability per capita was over 5000 cubic metres (m^3) per annum in 1950. It now stands at around 2000 m^3 and is projected to decline to 1500 m^3 by 2025. Further, the quality of available water is deteriorating. Also, there are gross inequalities between basins and geographic regions. Agriculture is the biggest user of water, accounting for about 80 percent of the water withdrawals. There are pressures for diverting water from agriculture to other sectors. A study has warned that re-allocation of water out of agriculture can have a dramatic impact on global food markets. It is projected that availability of water for agricultural use in India may be reduced by 21 percent by 2020, resulting in drop of yields of irrigated crops, especially rice, thus price rise and withdrawal of food from poor masses. Policy reforms are needed from now to avoid the negative developments in the years to come. These reforms may include the establishment of secure water rights to users, the decentralization and privatization of water management functions to appropriate levels, pricing reforms, markets in tradable property rights, and the introduction of appropriate water-saving technologies. The needs of other sectors for water cannot be ignored. Therefore, it is necessary that an integrated water use policy is formulated and judiciously implemented. Several international initiatives on this aspect have been taken in recent years. India should critically examine these initiatives and develop its country-specific system for judicious and integrated use and management of water. A national institution should be established to assess the various issues, regulatory concerns, water laws and legislations, research and technology development and dissemination, social mobilization and participatory and community involvement, including gender and equity concerns and economic aspects. This institution should function in a trusteeship mode and seen as the flagship of a national system for sustainable water security.

(f) Emphasis on Rainfed Ecosystem

Resource-poor farmers in the rainfed ecosystems practice less-intensive agriculture, and since their incomes depend on local agriculture, they benefit little from increased food production in irrigated areas. To help them, efforts must be increased to disseminate available dry land technologies and to generate new ones. It will be necessary to enlarge the efforts for promoting available dry land technologies, increasing the stock of this knowledge, and removing pro-irrigation biases in public investment and expenditure, as well as credit flows, for technology-based agricultural growth. Watershed development for raising yields of rainfed crops and widening of seed revolution to cover oilseeds, pulses, fruits and vegetables. Farming system research to develop location specific technologies must be intensified in the rainfed areas. Strategy to make grey areas green will lead to second Green Revolution, which would demand three-pronged strategy—watershed management, hybrid technology and small farm mechanisation.

(g) Accent on Diversification of Agriculture and Value Addition

In the face of shrinking natural resources and ever increasing demand for larger food and agricultural production arising due to high population and income growths, agricultural intensification is the main course of future growth of agriculture in the region. Research for product diversification should be yet another important area.

Besides developing technologies for promoting intensification, the country must give greater attention to the development of technologies that will facilitate agricultural diversification particularly towards intensive production of fruits, vegetables, flowers and other high value crops that are expected to increase income growth and generate effective demand for food. The per capita availability of arable land is quite low and declining over time. Diversification towards these high value and labour intensive commodities can provide adequate income and employment to the farmers dependent on small size of farms. Due importance should be given to quality and nutritional aspects. High attention should be given to develop post-harvest handling and agro-processing and value addition technologies not only to reduce the heavy post-harvest losses and also improve quality through proper storage, packaging, handling and transport. The role of biotechnology in post-harvest management and value addition deserves to be enhanced.

(h) Accent on Post-Harvest Management, Value Addition and Cost-Effectiveness

Post-harvest losses generally range from 5 to 10 percent for non-perishables and about 30 percent for perishables. This loss could be and must be minimized. Let us remember, a grain saved is a grain produced. Emphasis should therefore be placed to develop post-harvest handling, agro-processing and value-addition technologies not only to prevent the high losses, but also to improve quality through proper storage, packaging, handling and transport. With the thrust on globalization and increasing competitiveness, this approach will improve the agricultural export contribution of India, which is proportionately extremely low. Cost-effectiveness in production and post-harvest handling through the application of latest technologies will be a necessity. The agro-processing facilities should preferably be located close to the points of production in rural areas, which will greatly promote off-farm employment. Such centers of processing and value addition will encourage production by masses against mass production in factories located in urban areas. Agricultural cooperatives and Gram Panchayats must play a leading role in this effort. In doing so, the needs of small farmers should be kept in mind.

(i) Increased Investment in Agriculture and Infrastructures

The public investment in agriculture has been declining and is one of the main reasons behind the declining productivity and low capital formation in the agriculture sector. With the burden on productivity-driven growth in the future, this worrisome trend must be reversed. Private investment in agriculture has also been slow and must be stimulated through appropriate policies. Considering that nearly 70 percent of India still lives in villages, agricultural growth will continue to be the engine of broad-based economic growth and development as well as of natural resource conservation, leave alone food security and poverty alleviation. Accelerated investment are needed to facilitate agricultural and rural development through:

- Productivity increasing varieties of crops, breeds of livestock, strains of microbes and efficient packages of technologies, particularly those for land and water management, for obviating biotic, a biotic, socio-economic and environmental constraints;
- Yield increasing and environmentally-friendly production and post-harvest and value-addition technologies;
- Reliable and timely availability of quality inputs at reasonable prices, institutional and credit supports, especially for small and resource-poor farmers, and support to land and water resources development;
- Effective and credible technology, procurement, assessment and transfer and extension system involving appropriate linkages and partnerships; again with an emphasis on reaching the small farmers;
- Improved institutional and credit support and increased rural employment opportunities, including those through creating agriculture-

based rural agro-processing and agro-industries, improved rural infrastructures, Including access to information, and effective markets, farm to market roads and related infrastructure;

- Particular attention to the needs and participation of women farmers; and
- Primary education, health care, clean drinking water, safe sanitation, adequate nutrition, particularly for children (including through mid-day meal at schools) and women.

The above investments will need to be supported through appropriate policies that do not discriminate against agriculture and the rural poor. Given the increasing role of small farmers in food security and poverty alleviation, development efforts must be geared to meet the needs and potential of such farmers through their active participation in the growth process. Government should facilitate and support community level action by private voluntary organizations, including farmers groups aimed at improving food security, reducing poverty, and assuring sustainability in the management of natural resources. In addition, governments should enhance efforts to ensure good nutrition and access to sufficient food for all through primary health care and education for all. Modern biotechnology tools, genetic engineering, as well as conventional breeding methods are all expected to play important roles in the generation of higher yielding, pest and stress resistant varieties of rice, wheat, maize and other cereal crops. The availability of genetic innovations in developing countries will depend on continued high levels of investments in agricultural research, both at the international and the national levels. Free and unhindered access to germ plasma to breeders worldwide is absolutely crucial to the rapid dissemination and adoption of improved germ plasm. This free movement and the dissemination of modern biotechnology innovations to developing countries are hampered by increased patent protection and private sector investments. There is an urgent need to address this problem of free access to technology in the future. Increased attention will also have to be given to development of sustainable systems that protect the natural resource base. Recent evidence of resource degradation and declining productivity in some intensively cropped areas is of particular concern. Also population driven intensification of agriculture without the use of external inputs, is leading to a serious problem of mining soil fertility sustaining global food supplies will depend on continued high levels of investments in research and technology development. It is essential that research capacity has to be increased substantially. In addition to investments in research, infrastructure investments, particularly in irrigation, transport and market infrastructure development are equally important for sustaining the productivity and profitability of food crop production. Mobilize the best of science and development efforts (including traditional knowledge and modern scientific approach) through partnerships involving national and international research institutions, NGOs, farmers' organizations and private sector in order to tackle the present and future problems of food security and production. Donors and Government must urgently increase funding for agricultural research targeted at the needs of the rural and urban poor, and every effort must be made to ensure the free flow of information, technology and germplasm so that a proper sustainable agriculture can be achieved.

(j) Accent on Empowering the Small Farmers

Contributions of small holders in securing food for growing population have increased considerably even though they are most insecure and vulnerable group in the society. The off-farm and non-farm employment opportunities can play an important role. Against expectation under the liberalized scenario, the non-agricultural employment in rural areas has not improved. Greater emphasis needs to be placed on non-farm employment and appropriate budgetary allocations and rural credit through banking systems should be in place to promote appropriate rural enterprises. Specific human resource and skill development programmes to train them will make them better decision-makers and highly productive. Human resource development for increasing productivity of these small holders should get high priority. Thus, knowledge and skill development of rural people both in agriculture and non-agriculture sectors is essential for achieving economic and social goals. A careful balance will therefore need to be maintained between the agricultural and non-agricultural employment and farm and non-farm economy, as the two sectors are closely inter-connected. Raising agricultural productivity requires continuing investments in human resource development, agricultural research and development, improved information and extension, market, roads and related infrastructure development and efficient small-scale, farmer-controlled irrigation technologies, and custom hiring services. Such investments would give small farmers the options and flexibility to adjust and respond to market conditions.

For poor farm-households whose major endowment is its labour force, economic growth with equity will give increased entitlement by offering favourable markets for its products and more employment opportunities. Economic growth if not managed suitably, can lead to growing inequalities. Agrarian reforms to alleviate unequal access to land, compounded by unequal access to water, credit, knowledge and markets, have not only rectified income distribution but also resulted in sharp increases in productivity and hence need to be adopted widely. Further, targeted measures that not only address the immediate food and health care requirements of disadvantaged groups, but also provide them with developmental means, like access to inputs, infrastructure, services and most important, education should be taken. Identification of need-based productive programs is very critical, which can be explored through characterisation of production environment. We have to develop demand-driven and location-specific programs to meet the requirements of different regions to meet the nutritional security of most vulnerable population in the rural areas. Improved agricultural technology, irrigation, livestock sector and literacy will be most important instruments for improving the nutritional security of the farm-households. Watershed development and water saving techniques will have far reaching implications in increasing agricultural production and raising calorie intake in the rainfed areas. Livestock sector should receive high priority with multiple objectives of diversifying agriculture, raising income and meeting the nutritional security of the poor farm households. Need-based and location-specific community programs, which promise to raise nutritional security, should be identified and effectively implemented. Expansion of micro-credit programmes for income-generation activities, innovative approaches to promote family planning and providing primary health services to people and livestock and education should enhance labour productivity and adoption of new technologies. Development of the post-harvest sector, co-operatives, roads, education, and research and development should be an investment priority. A congenial policy environment is needed to enable smaller holders to take the advantage of available techniques of production, which can generate more incomes and employment in villages. For this poor farmer needs the support of necessary services in the form of backward and forward linkages. Small-mechanised tools, which minimise drudgery and do not reduce employment, but only add value to the working hours are needed to enhance labour productivity. Special safety nets should be designed and implemented for them. Can agricultural co-operatives internalise and galvanize these marginal and excluded people? Off-farm employment provided through co-operatives will go a long way in pulling them out of the state where poverty breeds poverty. Therefore, investment in the empowerment of the small landholders will pay off handsomely. Let us create rural centres of production and processing by masses through co-operatives or empowerment of Gram Panchayats to promote co-operatives. This will improve efficiency of input and output marketing and give higher income. There is need to disseminate widely post-harvest handling and agro-processing and value addition technologies not only to reduce the heavy post-harvest losses but also improve quality through proper storage, packaging, handling and transport. Panchayati Raj institutions and co-operatives can play significant role in all these directions. Giving them power over the administration, as contemplated under the 73rd and 74th Amendment of the Constitution has not been implemented seriously so far in any of the states.

(k) Keeping Pace with Globalisation

The globalization of agricultural trade will bring to the fore access to markets; new opportunities for employment and income generation; productivity gains and increased flow of investments into sustainable agriculture and rural development. I believe that if managed well, the liberalization of agricultural markets will be beneficial to developing countries in the long-run. It will force the adoption of new technologies, shift production functions upwards and attract new capital into the deprived sector. However, this will only come to pass if we are mindful of the interests of billions of small and subsistence oriented farmers, fisher-folk and forest dwellers in the short and medium-term. So far the magic of globalization has not been felt in India. During the past one-decade of liberalization certain trends such as deceleration of the growth rate of agricultural GDP, declaration in yield growth rates, and low non-agricultural employment have emerged against expectations. As we globalize, however, it is imperative that we do not forget social aspirations for a more just, equitable and sustainable way of life. Trade agreements must be accompanied by operationally effective measures to ease the adjustment process for a small farmer in developing countries.

(l) Exploiting Cyberspace

Information is power and will underpin future progress and prosperity. Efforts must be made to strengthen the informatics in agriculture by developing new databases, linking databases with international databases and adding value to information to facilitate decision-making at various levels. Development of production models for various agro-ecological regimes to forecast the, production potential should assume greater importance. Using the remote sensing and GIS technologies, natural land other agricultural resource should be mapped at micro and macro-levels and effectively used for land and water use planning as well as agricultural forecasting, market intelligence and e-business, contingency planning

4.11: CONCLUSION

To sum up, it may be said that agriculture still employs two-thirds of India's labour force. There is enormous scope for increasing employment and production in agriculture through higher private and public investment, more and better infrastructure, faster dissemination of best-practice cropping techniques and improvements in water management. The bias against agriculture in the overall incentive framework has been greatly reduced in recent years and should be eliminated. Remaining restrictions on internal and external trade in agricultural commodities should be removed. The sector of agro-industry, still subject to licensing control should be delicensed so that competition between manufacturers can work to the benefit of farmers and rural workers. Irrigation is the life-blood of rural economy, but the funds allocated in the state budgets are usually insufficient for maintenance of irrigation canals and channels and the bureaucratic functioning of irrigation departments often impedes best use of water resources. Institutional innovations should be sought to make the provision and maintenance of irrigation services much more responsive to farmers' interests. Conversely, farmers must be prepared to shoulder a growing proportion of the costs of irrigation services.

Notes and References

1. Govt. of India, Planning Commission, "Working Group Report on Agriculture and Allied Sector.
2. Gupta, K.L., Harvinder Kaur, "New Indian Economy and Reforms," Deep & Deep Publishers, New Delhi, pp. 267-70.
3. *Economic Survey*, 1999-2000, p. 134.
4. *Economic* Survey, 2005-06, p. 156.
5. Ramesh Chand, "India's Agro Food Trade Policies and W.T.O. Negotiations," National Centre for Agriculture Economies and Policy Research, New Delhi,
6. Ramesh Chand, "India's Agro Food Trade Policies and W.T.O. Negotiations," National Centre for Agriculture Economies and Policy Research, New Delhi.
7. Govt. of India, Planning Commission: Tenth Plan, p. 524.
8. Mahesh V. Joshi, "Economic Reforms in India—A critical evaluation", A.P.H. Publishing Corporation, New Delhi, 1999.
9. "Towards Faster and More inclusive Growth," An approach to the 11th Five Year Plan, Planning Commission, Govt. of India
10. Vision 2020, "The Report of the Committee on India Vision 2020," Planning Commission, Govt. of India.

CHAPTER

5

Foreign Direct Investment

Analysis and Trends

5.1: INTRODUCTION

Economic development remains an urgent global need. The need for economic development is self-raised as an automatic consequence of the globalisation. Although many countries have achieved significant increases in income in the last few years, there still exist great international inequalities in the level of income. The lower class of nations is still far bigger. More than two-thirds of the people live in countries where the per capita income is only a tiny fraction of what it is in the highly developed countries. To raise the standard of living of the people in such countries and to enable them to use the fruits of scientific and technological miraculous advances in agriculture, industry, transport, communication, education, health services and other fields, it is almost essential that in such economies, capital formation should take place at a higher rate than before, so that the big developmental projects may be financed properly. Thus, for rapid economic development, the central problem is capital formation.

Developing countries have two options of raising capital. First, by creating capital surplus from internal sources of capital formation such as controlling consumption, reducing foreign imports and other measures such as taxation, public borrowing, budgetary savings from current revenue and profits of public enterprises. However, due to many rigidities in the internal economy, these measures cannot accumulate much capital and the rate of their accumulation will be more or less static and not flexible.

The second method of capital formation is taking foreign assistance for accelerating the rate of internal capital formation in the shortest period of time. Foreign capital helps the developing economies overcome their balance of payments crisis as well. When a developing country undertakes its development programmes in a planned way, it has to import a large amount of capital goods, such as big machines, tools, chemicals and many other similar things from the developed countries during this period. Export industries do not provide sufficient foreign currency for the purchase of these goods. Foreign investment not only brings in capital, but also carries with it managerial ability, technical knowledge, technical personnel, innovations in products and production techniques and hence the development of infrastructure and demand creation and in turn additional domestic investment.[1]

In a world of intensifying competition and accelerating technological change, the complementary and catalytic role of foreign capital can be very valuable. However, globalisation has it dangers. Therefore, countries need to prepare their own capabilities to harness its potential, including through foreign capital. The present chapter identifies the role of foreign capital in the context of globalisation process.

5.2: CONCEPTUAL FRAMEWORK[2]

Financial flows to developing countries can be put in four categories:

1. Private Debt Flows
2. Official Development Finance
3. Foreign Direct Investment
4. Portfolio Investment

1. Private Debt Flows

They are composed of bonds, bank loans and other credits issued or acquired by private sector enterprises in a country without any public guarantee.

2. Official Development Finance

It consists of official development assistance and other official flows.

(i) Official Development Assistance (ODA)

ODA consists of net disbursement of loans and grants made on concessional terms by official agencies of the members of DAC (Development Assistance Committee) and certain Arab Countries to promote economic development and welfare in recipient economies listed as developing by DAC. Loans with a grant element of more than 25% are included in ODA. ODA also includes technical co-operation and assistance.

(ii) Other Official Flows

These are transactions by the official sector whose main objective is other than development or whose grant element is less than 25% such as official export credits, official sector equity and portfolio investment and debt re-organisation undertaken by the official sector on non-concessional terms.

3. Foreign Direct Investment (FDI)

It is defined as an investment involving a long-term relationship and reflecting a lasting interest and control of a resident entity of one economy in an enterprise resident of another economy other than that of the foreign direct investor. FDI implies that the investor exerts a significant degree of influence on the management of the enterprise resident in the other economy. Such a transaction involves both the initial transaction between the two entities and all subsequent transactions between them. FDI may be undertaken by individuals as well as business entities. It takes the form of:

- (i) acquiring stock of the existing foreign enterprises to participate in the management of the concerned enterprise;
- (ii) establishing abroad new subsidiary with 100% ownership;
- (iii) participating in a joint venture through stock holdings; and
- (iv) establishing new branches or expanding existing ones. There are three components of FDI:

(1) Equity Capital

This is the foreign direct investor's purchase of shares of an enterprise in a country other than its own.

(2) Reinvested Earnings

Reinvested earnings comprise the direct investor's share (in proportion of direct equity participation) of the earnings not distributed as dividends by FDI enterprise or earnings not remitted to the direct investor. Such retained profits are reinvested.

(3) Intra-company Loans or Intra-company Transaction

These refer to short-term or long-term borrowing and lending of funds between direct investors and FDI enterprises.

4. Foreign Portfolio Investment (FPI)

This involves:

(i) Purchase of existing bonds and stocks with the sole objective of obtaining dividends or capital gains; and
(ii) Investment in new issues of international bonds and debentures by the financial institution or foreign government.

5.3: TRENDS OF FOREIGN DIRECT INVESTMENT AFTER 1991

During the early phase of planning era, the national policy towards foreign capital did recognize the need for foreign capital, but decided not to permit it a dominant position. Consequently, foreign collaborations had to keep their equity within the ceiling of 49% and allow the Indian counterpart a majority stake. Moreover, foreign collaborations were to be permitted in priority areas, more especially those in which we had not developed our capabilities. But in an overall sense, our policy towards foreign collaborations remained restrictive and selective. Consequently, during 1948 to 1960, a total of 1,080 foreign collaborations were approved and during the next decade (1961-70), a total of 2,475 foreign collaborations were approved. During (1971-80) and (1981-90) the collaborations were 3,041 and 7,436 respectively. The growth of foreign collaborations during pre-reform period is shown in Table 5.1.

Table 5.1 reveals that during the period of 43 years of pre-reform era there were 14,032 foreign collaboration agreements in total. The majority of these agreements, i.e. about 53 percent came into existence during 1981-90. It is also clear in the table that 78 percent agreements were technical collaboration agreement and only 22 percent were related to Direct Foreign Investment.

TABLE 5.1

Foreign Collaboration Approvals in Pre-Reform Period

Period	*Technical Collaboration Agreement*	*Foreign Collaboration Agreement*	*Total number of Foreign Collaborations*
1948-60	1,080	—	1,080
1961-70	1,675	800	2,475
1971-80	2,623	418	3,041
1981-90	5,595	1,841	7,436
Total	10,973	3,059	14,032

Source: Dutt and Sundharam: Indian Economy, 2002, p. 336.

After the announcement of New Industrial Policy, 1991, there has been an acceleration in the flow of foreign capital in India. The progress of Foreign Collaborations in post-reform period is shown in Table 5.2. The perusal of Table 5.2 shows an increasing trend in Foreign Technology and Foreign Direct Investment. Collaboration during post-reform period, although there is some slowdown in Foreign Technology agreements since 1997. It must be mentioned here that response to policies of liberalization in post-reform period has been very encouraging. It is clear from the fact that in 43 years of pre-reform period total of Foreign Technology and Foreign Direct Investment Collaboration was just 14,032 whereas in 12 years of post-reform period total agreement were 23,462. On an average basis in pre-reform period, the number of these agreements was 326 per year while in post-reform period these agreements were 1,955 per year.

It is worth mentioning that in post-reform period there has been remarkable increase in Foreign Direct Investment Collaboration. During 1948 to 1960 there were no 1990, there were total 3,059 Foreign Direct Investment Collaborations and their average was 102 agreements per year, whereas in post-reform period there were in total 15,998 Foreign Direct Investment Collaborations with an average of 1,333 agreements per year in the real assessment of Foreign Direct Investment, it is not only the number but amount that is also important. The year-wise amount of Foreign Direct Investment is shown in Table 5.3.

TABLE 5.2

Progress of Foreign Collaboration Approvals in Post-Reform Period

Year	*No. of FTAs Approved*	*No. of FDI Approved*	*Total Foreign Collaboration Approved*
1991	661	289	950
1992	828	692	1520
1993	691	785	1,476
1994	792	1,062	1,854
1995	982	1,355	2,337
1996	744	1,559	2,303
1997	660	1,665	2,325
1998	595	1,191	1,786
1999	498	1,726	2,224
2000	418	1,726	2,144
2001	288	1,982	2,270
2002	307	1,966	2,273
Total	7,464	15,998	23,462

FTA: Foreign Technology Agreement
FDI: Foreign Direct Investment
Source: Economic Survey, 2001-02, p. 167.

TABLE 5.3

Year-wise Total Foreign Direct Investment in Post-Reform Period

(Rs. in crores)

Year	*Amount of FDI Approved*	*Amount of FDI Inflows*
1991-92	1,345	408
1992-93	5,546	1,904
1993-94	7,469	2,018
1994-95	9,971	4,312
1995-96	36,608	6,916
1996-97	40,206	9,654
1997-98	40,033	13,548
1998-99	30,324	12,343
1999-00	17,976	10,311
2000-01	25,207	12,645
2001-02	14,465	19,361
2002-03	7,904	14,932
2003-04	6,,224	12,117
2004-05	6,784	11,726
Total (1991-2005)	2,50,062	1,31,385

Source: *Economic Survey*, 2004-05, p. 161.

Table 5.3 reveals following facts:

(i) The cumulative approval since 1991 has been Rs. 2,50,062 crores whereas actual FDI inflows has been Rs. 1,31,385 crores.
(ii) The amount of FDI approved has increased about 512 times over the period of 15 years, i.e. from 1991 to 2005.
(iii) The amount of FDI inflow has increased about 370 times over the period of 15 years.

Industry-wise approvals of FDI in Table 5.4 reveal that for the entire period August 1991 to March 2002, basic goods industries accounted for about 39 per cent of FDI. Out of this, the major share was appropriated by power (15.6%) and oil refineries (10.8%). Mining and metallurgy (ferrous and non-ferrous) accounted for 5.6% and chemicals only 4.6%. The next group in order of importance was that of services accounting for 37% of

TABLE 5.4

Share of Different Industries in Foreign Collaboration Approvals

(August 1991 to March 2002)

	No. of Approvals	*Approved FDI Investment (Rs. crores)*	*Percent of Total*
A. Basic Goods	2,459	1,07,576	38.8
(i) Power	353	43,359	15.6
(ii) Oil Refinery	373	30,008	10.8
(iii) Chemicals	1,713	12,734	4.6
(iv) Mining, Metallurgy and other metals	689	15,403	5.6
(v) Other Fertilizers, cement, etc.	331	6,072	2.2
B. Capital Goods	6,538	25,117	9
(i) Transportation Industry	1.172	9,456	3.4
(ii) Electrical Equipment	1,661	5,963	1.2
(iii) Electronics	485	3,228	1.2
(iv) Others	3,220	6,470	2.3
C. Intermediate Goods	811	4,993	1.8
D. Consumer Non-durables	4,363	27,623	10.1
E. Consumer Durables	159	9,357	3.4
F. Services	6,172	1,02,928	37.1
(i) Telecommunication	801	55,281	19.9
(ii) Computer Software	2,353	17,616	6.4
(iii) Financial Services	414	11,760	4.2
(iv) Other Services	2,604	18,271	6.6
Total	21,502	2,77,597	-100

Source: Compiled and computed from Ministry of Commerce and Industry, SIA Newsletter (various issues).

FDI. The share of telecommunications was about 20% and that of computer software was 6.4%. Financial services contributed barely 4.2%. Capital goods and intermediate goods accounted only 11% of FDI approvals. Consumer non-durables shared about 10% FDI.[3]

Analysis of FDI approvals underlines the fact that nearly 75 percent was accounted for by basic goods industries, capital good and telecommunication and computer software services which are high on our priority list. Since segregated data about actual flows industry-wise is not available, it is not possible to comment whether the intentions are being realised in practice, or are distorted in the process of implementation.

DIAGRAM 1

The Share of Different Industries in Foreign Collaboration Approvals

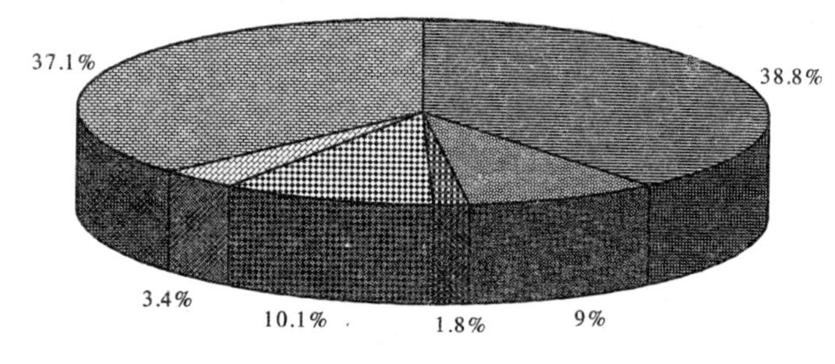

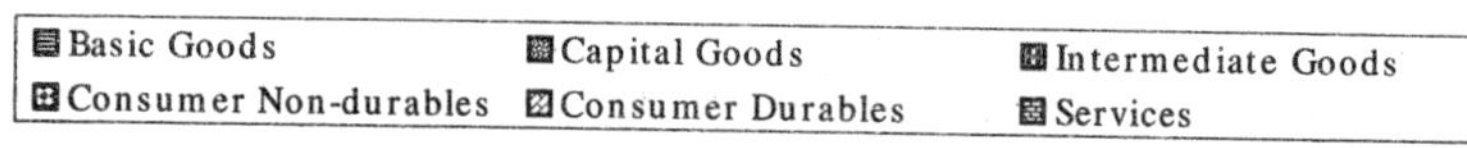

The country wise analysis of FDIs is also important. The country wise approvals and actual inflow of FDI is shown in Table 5.5.

Table 5.5 provides information about country-wise investment approvals and actual inflows. Although USA was at the top in approvals for the period 1991-2000 accounting for 20.4 per cent of total approvals, its share in actual inflows was only 10.9 per cent. As against it, Mauritius accounted for 11.9 per cent in approvals, but its share in actual flows was of the order of 17.5 per cent. This was due to the fact that Indian government accord special tax treatment to investments routed through Mauritius as such Mauritius is used as a tax shelter and investors belonging to several

TABLE 5.5

Country-wise Approvals and Actual Inflows of Foreign Direct Investment (1991-2002)

(Rs. Crores)

Country	*Approvals*		*Actual Inflows*		*Actual as %age of approval*
	Total	*(%)*	*Total*	*(%)*	
1. USA	50,379	20.4	9,697	10.9	19.2
2. Mauritius	29,432	11.9	15,596	17.5	53.0
3. UK	16,388	6.6	2,485	2.8	15.2
4. Japan	9,935	4.0	3,651	4.1	36.7
5. South Korea	9,731	3.9	2,168	2.4	22.3
6. Germany	8,497	3.4	2,685	3.0	31.6
7. Australia	6,617	2.7	290	0.3	4.4
8. Malaysia	5,576	2.3	197	0.2	3.5
9. France	5,238	2.1	1,265	1.4	24.1
10. Netherlands	4,700	1.9	2,498	2.8	31.9
11. Italy	4,555	1.8	1,504	1.7	33.0
12. Singapore	4,483	1.8	1,327	1.5	29.6
13. Israel	4,236	1.7	138	0.1	3.3
14. Belgium	3,998	1.6	282	0.3	7.1
15. Cayman Island	3,733	1.5	20	0.0	0.5
16. NRIs	9,534	3.9	8,656	9.7	90.8
Total of all Countries	2,46,798	100.00	89,287	100.00	36.2

Note: Top 15 countries have been ranked according to cumulative total of approvals from 1991 to 2002 (upto December).

Source: Compiled and computed from Annual Report of Ministry of Commerce and Industry, (2001-02).

countries use it as a conduit to avoid payment of taxes. Next largest contributor of actual inflows was Non-Resident Indians (NRIs) who accounted for 9.7 per cent of total inflows.

The other contributors to actual inflows of some significance were Japan, Germany, UK, Netherlands, South Korea, France and Singapore. The country-wise actual inflows of foreign direct investment is also shown in Pie Diagram 2.

DIAGRAM 2

Country-wise Actual Inflows of Foreign Direct Investment (2002)

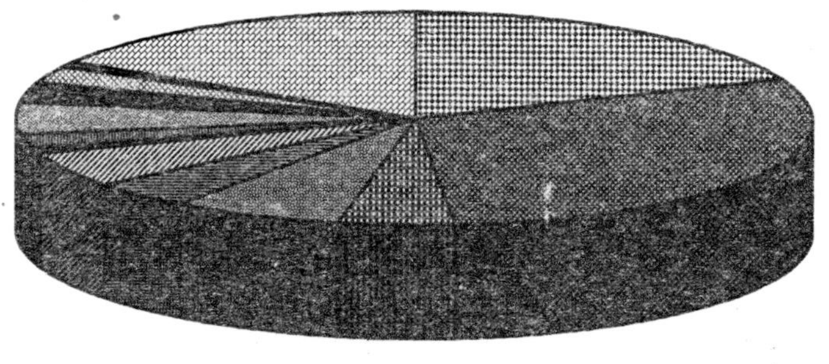

Pie-diagram shows country-wise actual inflows of foreign direct investments in the year 2002.

Table 5.5 also brings out the proportion of actual inflows to approvals. In this respect, NRIs record stands out distinctly superior to all countries accounting for about 91 per cent. Mauritius comes next and actual inflows were 53 percent of approvals. Next in order was Japan, Italy, Netherlands, Germany, France and South Korea. In case of USA, the situation showed a wide gap and actual inflows were barely 19.2 per cent of approvals. It is vitally necessary to reduce the gap between approvals and actual inflows.

The entire situation of foreign capital investment in India can be shown through foreign investment flow which is presented in Table 5.6.

Table 5.6 shows that after the announcement of new industrial policy (1991), there has been an acceleration in the flow of foreign capital in India. As per data provided in the Government of India, Economic Survey (2002-03) during 1990-91 to 2001-02, total foreign investment flow were of the order of US $ 45,122 million, out of which $ 21,823 million (48.38 percent) were in the form of foreign direct investment and the remaining $ 23,279 million (51.62 percent) were in the form of portfolio investment. This clearly shows that the preference of foreign firms was more in favour of portfolio investment and much less in the form of direct investment. Moreover, out of total direct foreign investment of the order of $ 45,122 million, nearly 5.9 percent ($ 2,663 million) was contributed by Non-resident Indians. Thus, the net contribution of foreign firms in direct investment was merely 42 percent of total foreign investment flows.

As a response to the policies of liberalization the foreign investors were very keen to undertake portfolio investment (including GDR, investment by foreign institutional investors, offshore funds and others). It rose sharply from $ 6 million in 1990-91 to $ 3,312 million in 1996-97 and then declined to $ 2,021 million in 2001-02. It stood at $ 8909 million in 2004-05.

5.4: USE-PATTERN OF FOREIGN DIRECT INVESTMENT IN INDIA: INDUSTRIAL SECTORS[4]

The sectoral distribution of foreign direct investment inflows approved between August 1991 and December 2002 is given in Table 5.7. It shows that telecommunication and power and refinery industries

TABLE 5.6

Foreign Investment Flows by Different Categories

(US$ million)

	1990-91	*1991-92*	*1992-93*	*1993-94*	*1994-95*	*1995-96*	*1996-97*	*1997-98*	*1998-99*	*1999-00*	*2000-01*	*2001-02*	*2004-05*	*%age to Total*
A. Direct Investment	97	129	315	586	1314	2144	2821	3557	2462	2155	2339	3904	5536	48.38
(a) RBI automatic route	—	—	42	89	171	169	135	202	179	171	454	767	1259	5.27
(b) SIA/FIPB route	50	66	222	280	701	1249	1922	2754	1821	1410	1456	2221	1062	31.38
(c) NRIs (40% and 100%)	47	63	51	217	442	715	639	241	62	84	67	35	—	5.90
(d) Acquisition of shares	—	—	—	—	—	11	125	360	400	490	362	881	930	5.83
B. Portfolio investment	6	4	244	3567	3824	2748	3312	1828	-61	3026	2760	2021	8909	51.62
(a) FIIs#	—	—	1	1665	1503	2009	1926	979	-390	2135	1847	1505	8282	29.22
(b) GDRs/ADRs @	—	—	240	1520	2082	683	1366	645	270	768	831	477	613	19.70
(c) Offshore funds and others	6	4	3	382	239	56	20	204	59	123	82	39	16	2.70
Total (A+B)	103	133	559	4153	5138	4892	6133	5385	2401	5181	5099	5925	14425	100.00

Source: *Economic Survey*, 2002-03, p. 119. *RBI Annual Report*, 2004-05.

TABLE 5.7

Industrial Break-up of Foreign Direct Investment Approved (August 1991 to December 2002)

(Amount Rupees in million)

Sr. No.	*Industry*	*Foreign Technology Approvals (No.)*	*Foreign Investment Approvals (No.)*	*Amount of FDI Approvals*	*Share in Total Approvals (%)*	*Actual Inflow of FDI*	*Share in Actual Approvals*	*Actual Inflow as % of Inflow*
1.	Power and Oil Refinery	196	448	421567.40	17.1	41359.94	4.6	9.8
2.	Telecommunication	119	579	458845.03	18.6	47232.24	5.3	10.3
3.	Transportation Industry	538	722	184467.61	7.5	63780.45	7.1	34.6
4.	Service Sector	47	790	152389.00	6.2	42304.99	4.7	27.8
5.	Metallurgical Industries	339	304	143796.77	5.8	6987.43	0.8	4.9
6.	Chemicals	780	809	123016.21	5.0	45241.94	5.13	36.8
7.	Electrical Equipment	1108	2491	245791.54	10.0	58436.99	6.5	23.8
8.	Food Processing Industries	150	648	87574.92	3.5	25901.37	2.9	29.6
9.	Hotel and Tourism	147	302	46501.08	1.9	3567.49	0.4	7.7
10.	Textile	135	548	33617.86	1.4	8374.48	0.9	24.9
11.	Industrial Machinery	807	530	22438.52	0.9	3927.57	0.4	17.5
12.	Other Industries	2267	3794	547019.38	22.2	548343.21	61.2	100.2
	Total	6633	11965	2467025.30	100.00	8954581.21	100.00	36.3

Source: Annual Report, Department of Industrial Policy and Promotion, Ministry of Commerce and Industry, 2000-01, 2001-02.

are the largest beneficiaries of FDI approvals with shares of 18.6% and 17.1% in the total FDI approved during August 1991 and December 2002. Electrical equipment is the third largest recipient of FDI approved with the share of 10%. Transportation industry received 7.5% of the FDI approved during this period and occupied the fourth rank. Service sector just received 6.2% of FDI approved. Metallurgical Industries, Chemicals, Food processing industries and hotel and

TABLE 5.8

Industry-wise Distribution of the Stock of Foreign Direct Investment in Indian Corporate Sector

(Percentage)

Sr. No.	*Industry*	*End March*				
		1980	*1986*	*1992*	*1996*	*2002*
1.	Plantations	4.1	8.9	8.5	1.7	1.2
2.	Mining	0.8	0.3	0.6	0.2	0.1
3.	Petroleum	3.9	0.1	2.0	1.2	0.9
4.	Manufacturing	86.9	85.7	83.2	47.1	48.0
	(a) Food and Beverages	48.8	6.4	4.9	5.2	6.7
	(b) Textile products	3.9	5.5	2.9	3.1	2.8
	(c) Transport equipment	6.3	10.1	12.4	6.7	6.7
	(d) Machinery and Machine tools	8.8	11.8	12.6	6.0	5.3
	(e) Metal and Metal products	14.6	4.9	5.1	2.5	2.1
	(f) Electrical Goods and Machinery	12	11.5	11	5.2	8.1
	(g) Chemicals and Allied products	29.1	29.6	28.0	10.9	8.9
5.	Trading	2.5	0.3	1.1	0.5	1.6
6.	Construction and turnkey projects	-0.6	0.9	0.5	0.4	0.5
7.	Transport	0	0.6	0.1	0.0	0
8.	Utilities	0	0.6	0.5	1.6	4.9
9.	Services	1.31	—	—	8.5	8.0
10.	Others	-0.6	2.6	3.3	38.8	34.8
	TOTAL	100.0	100.0	100.0	100.0	100.0

Source: Reserve Bank of India, "India's International Investment Position", *Bulletin*, April 1985, "India's Foreign Liabilities and Assets", *Bulletin*, August 1993, October 2002.

touring were other industries, which received 6% to 2% of FDI approved during this period. The reclassification of data to get the sectoral distribution of FDI comparable to the pattern of FDI stock before liberalisation policy has revealed striking differences.

The industry-wise distribution of the stock of foreign direct investment in Indian Corporate Sector is shown in Table 5.8.

The Table 5.8 reveals that in particular, the relative importance of manufacturing sector has declined with the opening up of infrastructure and service sectors including telecommunications to foreign direct investment under the liberalisation policy. And within the manufacturing itself the preference pattern of FDI is shifting away from heavy capital goods industries to light industries.

However, the stock of portfolio investment in India shows the increasing importance of manufacturing sector till 1995. Its share was 62.8% of the total stock of portfolio investment in 1979. It went upto 82.5% in 1991 and 89.3% in 1995. Within the manufacturing sector, there is a similar trend of shifting away from heavy capital goods to light industries. Textile industry has the largest share in the manufacturing sector. There is seen increasing importance of chemicals and allied products. Metal and metal products, transport equipment and electrical goods are other important industries attracting large portfolio flows.[5]

The proportion of agreements with foreign ownership range of more than 51% during the period 1988-90 was just 4.9%. The proportion increased to 53.9% during 1991-2002.

The relatively large proportion of firms with foreign majority ownership after the liberalisation policy is not a revealing finding. It shows that a number of TNCs taking full advantage of the new rules under the liberalisation policy, increased their stake in their existing associates and liberalisation policy, and also bargained and secured government's approval for majority ownership stake in their new associates in

TABLE 5.9

Foreign Equity Range in Foreign Collaboration Agreement Approved

(Percentage)

Percentage of Range	*1988-90*	*1991-2002*
Upto 24%	27.2	15
More than 24% to 51%	67.8	31.1
More than 51% to 74%	3.3	11.6
More than 74% to 100%	1.6	8.5
Equal to 100%	—	33.8
Total	100.00	100.00

Source: 1. SIA, Newsletter, Annual Issue, 2002.

India. In 1990, just 469 foreign companies were at work in India. Their number increased to 1141 in March 2001. Thus, foreign majority ownership is now being widely found in Indian Industry.

5.5: FII FLOWS TO INDIA: AN INCREASING TREND[6]

Foreign investment flows into India, comprising foreign direct investment (FDI) and foreign portfolio investment (FPI), have risen sharply during the 1990s reflecting the policies to attract non-debt creating flows. Foreign investment flows have increased from negligible levels during 1980s to reach US $ 20 billion by 2005-06 (see Chart on next page).

Cumulative foreign investment flows have amounted to US $ 106 billion since 1990-91 and almost evenly balanced between direct investment flows (US $ 49 billion) and portfolio flows (US $ 57 billion). Since 1993-94, FDI flows have exceeded portfolio flows in five years while portfolio flows have exceeded FDI flows in the remaining eight years. As a proportion to FDI flows

DIAGRAM 3

Foreign Investment into India

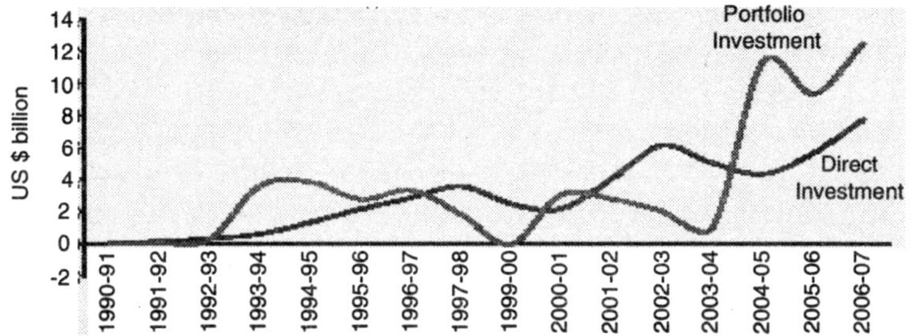

to emerging market and developing countries, FDI flows to India have shown a consistent rise from 1.6 per cent in 1998 to 3.7 per cent in 2005. The share of net FDI flows to India as a proportion to total flows to emerging market and developing countries is higher and remained in the range of 12-15 per cent during 2004 and 2005.

The sharp rise in portfolio investment into India since 2003-04 reflects both global and domestic factors. Search for yield in view of very low real long-term rates in advanced economies have been an important factor driving portfolio flows to emerging market economies as a group and India has also attracted such flows. Domestic factors such as strong macro-economic fundamentals, resilient financial sector, deep and liquid capital market, improved financial performance of the corporate sector and attractive valuations also attracted large portfolio flows between 2003-04 and 2005-06.[7]

Recognising the macro-economic implications of volatility associated with capital flows, India has adopted a policy of managing the capital account with a preference for non-debt flows (Mohan, 2005). Consistent with the principle of hierarchy of capital flows, India has been making efforts towards encouraging more inflows through FDI and enhancing the quality of portfolio flows by strict adherence to 'Know Your Investor' principle (Reddy, 2005). The Government has also taken steps to enhance the FDI sectoral caps in infrastructure in recent years (e.g. telecom, civil aviation). FDI up to 100 per cent through the Reserve Bank's automatic route was permitted for a number of new sectors in 2005-06 such as greenfield airport projects, laying of pipelines, export trading. FDI caps under the automatic route were enhanced to 100 per cent for coal and lignite mining for captive consumption and setting up infrastructure relating to marketing in petroleum and natural gas sector. All these measures have been contributing towards increasing direct investment. With the FDI inflows to developing world still in a stage of recovery to the pre-East Asian crisis level, India's FDI growth of above 30 per cent during past two years is encouraging. Although the FDI inflows into India are small as compared to other emerging markets, their size is growing on the back of growing interest by many of the world's leading multinationals. India has improved its rank from fifteenth (in 2002) to become the second most likely FDI destination after China in 2005 (A.T. Kearney). In the context of encouraging FII flows, sufficient attention needs to be given to address the macro-economic implications of volatility of capital flows. There is a need to examine the likely implications of excessive inflows and outflows on macro-economic management. Furthermore, in order to maintain the financial integrity of the Indian markets, there is a need to take suitable measures to address the growing international concerns regarding origin and source of investment funds flowing into the country. Such measures would enhance the confidence of the foreign investors and regulators alike in the Indian financial system, given the fact that adherence to best practices and standards are important determinants for assessment of the quality of regulation.

5.6: FDI IN RETAILING IN INDIA: RECENT TRENDS AND DEVELOPMENTS

India is sometimes referred to as the nation of shopkeepers. This is because the country has the highest density of retail outlets—over 15 million[8] in the world. Comparatively, the US has only 0.9 Million catering to more than 13 times the total retail market of India.[9] Since most outlets in India are located in the organised sector, the average size of these is much smaller than that of other countries. Only four per cent of Indian retail outlets are longer than 500 square feet.[10] Retailing is the largest industry in India and second largest employer after agriculture. Presently, the sector contributes around 10 percent of GDP and 6-7 percent of employment.[11] However, unlike most developed and developing countries, Indian retail sector is highly fragmented and bulk of the business is in the unorganized sector. This makes it difficult to obtain reliable data an India's retail trade. The available information shows that retail sales, which amounted to Rs. 7,400 billion in 2002, expended at an average annual rate of 7 per cent during 1999-2002.[12]

A. Growth of Organised Retailing in India

About 98 per cent of the retail trade in India is in the unorganized sector. Retail outlets in this segment are in the form of Mom-and-Pop stores offering limited choice to the consumers. These are low profit outlets which survive on unpaid/cheap labour and free land use. Seventy-eight percent of these are small family business utilizing only household labour. Even those that hire, often pay below the minimum wage. The initial setup/cost/investment is low and largely financed by the unorganized sector. There is no organised system of evaluating the turnover of such outlets or tax purposes and hence, many of them avoid paying taxes. Even though these formats do not employ modern retail technique and know-how, they have significant competitive advantage over organised sector in terms of low overheads and local market knowledge. Many of them offer services such as home delivery or sales on credit that would be uneconomical for the organised sector. The other advantages of these stores is convenience, that is, consumers do not incur additional costs in terms of transport costs and time since they can just walk over to these stores.

It is only the past 10 years that modern retail formats in the India are developing. The slow growth of organised formats in the past is due to significant restrictions on consumer goods and consumerism that existed prior to the liberalisation of the 1990s. During that period, rigid licensing policies and high tariffs on imported goods discouraged manufacturers from investing in consumer good industry. In the absence of wide range of products, marketers found it difficult to reap the benefits of economies of scale in sourcing. Restrictions on inter-state movements of goods and stocks and the highly fragmented supply chain also limited the development of scale. Low levels of income of Indian consumers together with high tax regime and saving-biased government programmes prevented the development of large scale outlets. Moreover, owing to strict control on radio and television media, Indian consumers were less aware of the growing consumerism in the West and other parts of Asia.

With the liberalization is the 1990's, modern distribution services sectors started evolving. On the supply side, consumer goods industry saw significant growth with the reduction in custom duties and a shift from quota to tariff-based system. Entry barriers on multinationals were largely removed and multinationals such as Sony, Kelloggs, and Samsung entered the Indian market. A survey by the research group ORG found that in 19 consumer goods categories, 1,378 brands and 2579 individual products entered the Indian market between 1990 and 1996.[13] With increase in product base, chain retailers now have better sourcing options and average margins.

Economic liberalization, competition and foreign investment in manufacturing led to proliferation of brands with both foreign and Indian companies acquiring strong brand equity for their products. This led to emergence of franchising. Sale of franchises grew at a rapid pace of 14 per cent per annum since 1997 and in 2002 there were 5,000 franchised outlets.[14]

Different studies have made different projections about the size of organised retailing and its future growth potential. *The Economic Times* Report "Changing gears—Retailing in India (2003)" estimated the size of organised retailing at Rs.16,000 crore in 2001-02. It pointed out that organised retailing is growing at the rate about 18-20 percent per annum and would continue to grow at the some rate since GDP growth is predicted at 6-7 percent and private consumption which comprises about two-third of GDP would simultaneously grow. Based on these estimates, organised retailing is expected to cross Rs. 37,000 crores sales mark by the year 2007. The predicted growth of different segment of retailing is shown in Table 5.10.

This table shows that food and groceries and clothing are two major segments of organised retailing. A recent Price Water House Coopers study[15] projected that organised retailing will be US$ 6.7 billion by 2005, representing per central the total retail market.

Growth of organised retailing is not evenly spread across the country. Organised formats have developed much faster in the southern part of the country with cities like Chennai, Bangalore and Hyderabad taking the lead. Several factors have contributed towards this uneven pattern of development—the primary being the lower real estate prices in the southern cities. Apart from south, organised retailing is rapidly expanding in other metros such as Mumbai, Delhi and Kolkata and in some smaller cities like Pune, Lucknow, Jaipur and Ahmedabad. The top 10 cities account for 96 percent of total organised retailing while top 6 cities account for 86 percent.[16] It is predicted that the spread of organised retailing world increase in year 2005 the share of the

TABLE 5.10

Size of Organized Retail Market

(in Rs. Crore)

	2001-02	*2007*	*CAGR (%)*
Large Segments	8,850	23,109	21
Other Segments	6,050	12,169	15
Non-store Retailing	1,100	1,939	12
Total Organised Retail	**16,000**	**37,217**	**18**
The 4 Large Segments			
FOOD			
Chain Stores	1,500	6,726	35
Single Large Stores and Others	300	746	20
	1800	**7,472**	**33**
CLOTHING			
Manufacturer Retailer	1,350	2,715	15
Chain Stores	1,450	3,919	22
Single, Large Stores	2,150	3,789	12
	4,950	**10,423**	**16**
CONSUMER DURABLES			
Manufacturer Retailer	650	1,307	15
Chain Stores	450	1,373	25
Single Large Stores	550	1,106	15
	1,650	**3,786**	**18**
BOOKS and MUSIC			
Chain Stores	250	928	30
Single Large Stores	200	498	20
	450	**1,426**	**26**

Source: *The Economic Times*, Changing Gears—Retailing in India (2003).

top 6 cities would reduce to 66 percent. The choice of retail destination is dependent on factors such as availability of high income and brand conscious consumers, conducive laws and regulations and infrastructure facilities. Most organised retailers tend to start their operations in larger cities. They prefer to remain regional or local until they have saturated the market and then they move to other cities/areas.

B. FDI in Retailing in India: Policy and Entry Routes

In India, till recently, FDI is not allowed in retailing but the union cabinet on January 24, 2006 nationalized and simplified the FDI policy and allowed the contentious issue of foreign investment in retail sector by allowing FDI upto 51 percent with prior government approval for retail trade in single brand products. This world imply that foreign companies would be allowed to sell goods sold internationally under a single brand viz. Reebok, Nokia, Adidas, retailing of goods of multiple brands, even if such products are produced by same manufactures would not be allowed.[17]

Although FDI is not allowed in retailing, many international players are operating in the country. Some of these entry routes are discussed in detail below.[18]

(a) Manufacturing and Local Sourcing

Companies that set-up manufacturing facilities are allowed to sell the products in the domestic market. Consumer durable companies such as Sony and Samsung have entered the retail sector through this route. Due to high labour cost in their domestic market, many international brands are setting up manufacturing bases in developing countries such as India and China and/or are sourcing products from local manufacturers. For example, Levi's and Tommy Hilfiger are sourcing products from Indian manufacturer like Arvind Mills. Benetton has a manufacturing unit in India. Other international brands like GIVO from Italy have set-up export-oriented manufacturing facilities. These companies are allowed to sell products to Indian consumers through franchising, local distributors, existing Indian retailers, own outlets, etc.

(b) Franchising[19]

Franchising is the most preferred mode through which foreign players have entered the Indian market. Franchising is often used as a mode to expand the market of a particular retail enterprise outside domestic economy since it allows firms to expand without investing their own capital, is based on local expertise and endless firms to curb local oppositions and regulations. This is the most common mode for entry of fast food chains across the world. Apart from fast food chains like Pizza Hut, players such as Lacoste, Mango, Nike and Marks and Spencer, have entered the Indian market through this route.

For setting up franchising operations, the foreign players are required to take permission from the Reserve Bank of India (RBI). RBI often imposes the condition that franchisers have to bring in foreign investment and set-up a base for carrying on operational activities. A foreign franchiser not wishing to make a direct investment would have to render technical assistance to the franchisee. Some franchises such as Pizza Hot have made significant investment in the supply chain.

The arrangements between franchisee and franchiser are found to be extremely flexible and are based as negotiation between the two. Some Indian franchisees have complained about high franchising fees together with high real estate costs, high import duties and other costs escalate the prices. For instance, the cost of a Marks and Spencer product is higher than not only the brands produced domestically but also in comparison to the price of the product in the UK. The high prices restrict the ability of the foreign players to penetrate the market but they have entered the country to make their brands visible to the huge Indian Market.

If FDI is allowed in retailing, franchisees are not very sure whether they would hold the retailing rights for the brands. According to industry representatives, since franchisees largely constitute of domestic traders who have made significant investment in infrastructure, government through legislation must ensure that they do not loose cut their franchising rights if FDI is allowed in retailing and the franchisers decide to change the mode of operation. The existing franchises have also expressed an interest in entering into joint venture with the franchisers if FDI is allowed in retailing.

(c) Test Marketing[20]

Test marketing is another route which many foreign players have entered the Indian market. Foreign Investment Promotion Boards (FIPB) allows foreign companies to test market products for a two-period by the end of which they are required to set-up manufacturing facilities in India. Direct selling companies like Amway and Oriflame entered the Indian Market through this route. Initially, Amway got an approval for test marketing for a period of two years but they managed to secure an extension of one more year. At the end of the third year, they set-up contract manufacturing facilities and brought in foreign investment and technical know-how. Oriflame too extended its test marketing licence for a third year and at the end of which had set-up a manufacturing facility in Noida (UP) for producing certain specific products. Other products are imported and would continue to be imported from abroad.

Nokia came to India through the test marketing route in Mid-1990s. Initially they got a license for two years to test their products in the Mumbai circle. After three months of their entry they tied up with the service providers to provide integrated services to their customers. Due to pressure from the FIPB, Nokia had tied up with the HCL Infotech as a strategic partner for all India distribution of Nokia products. After the success of its products in the country, Nokia had opened up an office but had not set-up a manufacturing facility and continued to import all products. After another two years they divided the country into four zones and entered into a strategic alliance for distribution with Supreme for East and West India while HCL continued with North and Southern Zone. Nokia had also applied for the cash and carry license from the FIPB and has recently got the license. Nokia is aggressively targeting the Indian consumers and plan to capture 75 percent of the mobile market in the next seven years. The company, which currently operates as a wholesale cash-and-carry, recently announced that it would set-up manufacturing facilities by 2006.

The test marketing route allows foreign players to test the demand for their products in Indian market before undertaking investment. Even if FDI is allowed in retailing, many foreign players would like to enter the Indian market through this route.

(d) Wholesale Cash-and-Carry Operations

This is the route through which large international retailers such as Germany's Metro cash-and-carry GMGH and Shoprite Checkers of South Africa have entered the Indian Market. The wholesale cash-and-carry operation is defined as any trading outlets where goods are sold at the wholesale rate for retailers and businesses to buy. The transactions are only for business purposes and not for personal consumption as in the case of retailing.

(e) Distributor

Companies such as Swarovski and Hugo Boss have set-up distribution offices in India and these offices supply the products to local Indian retailers. All products of Hugo Boss are imported and distributed through the company's distributor.

(f) Special Cases

The Sri Lankan retailers have entered the Indian market through the initiatives of Export Development Board of Sri Lanka (EDB) which obtained special permission from the RBI to set-up retail operations in India. The EDB has leased 17 retail outlets in Spencer Plaza in Chennai in which Sri Lankan retailers are showcasing and selling their products. The Sri Lankan products showcased in these stores are mostly at the higher end of the quality spectrum and can be brought into the country free duty. This gives an advantage to large Sri Lankan retailers like Hameedia not only to establish a global presence but also to access the large customer base of India at competitive prices. The EDB is also exploring the possibilities of setting up similar trade centres in other cities like Delhi and Mumbai. Although this mode has allowed retailers from Sri Lanka to enter the Indian market without domestic manufacturing and sourcing conditions and some products sold by these traders are similar to those sold by Indian retailers, EDB did not face any opposition from chambers, retailers and the trading houses.

Although the official policy is that as yet FDI is not allowed in retailing, but it has not acted as any entry barrier. Foreign players have a substantial presence in the country and have used different routes to enter Indian Trading Sector. Some of the existing foreign players and prospecting entrants are listed in Table 5.11.

C. Present FDI Policy of Government of India in Retail Sector

FDI in retail sector is currently allowed up to 51% in single brand stores like Reebok, Gucci, Lovis vuitton and Hugo Boss, etc. single brand stores here refer to such retail stores as sell products of one brand only. For example, Reebok store set-up with FDI participation can sell items of Reebok brand only. In this regard

TABLE 5.11

Some Existing Foreign Players and Prospective Entrants

Retailers	*Type*	*Status*
7-Eleven	Supermarket	Evaluating
Amway	Direct Selling	Already in
Auchan	Hypermarket	Evaluating
Carrefour	Multi-format retailer	Postponed entry
Dairy Farm	Multi-format retailer	Tied up with RPG
JC Penny	Product sourcing	Already in
Landmark	Department store	Already in
Lee Cooper	Product sourcing	Already in
Levi's	Product sourcing	Already in
Mango	Apparel retailer	Already in
Marks and Spencer	Department store	Already in
Metro	Cash-and-carry	Already in
Oriflame	Direct selling	Already in
Reebok	Joint venture	Already in
Shoprite	Wholesale cash-and-carry and franchising	Already in
Sony	Manufacturer retailer	Already in
Wal-Mart	Hypermarket	Wait and watch (has a distribution centre)

Source: "FDI in Retail Sector", Department of Consumer Affairs, Government of India, p. 115.

Government took the decision on 24th January 2006. Pressure has been building on government from World Bank, US and other developed nations to open retail sector in multi-brand stores and to increase FDI limit up to 100%. But taking note of present Indian retail profile, the government has decided to go slow on its plans to open the retail sector for FDI. Left parties are opposing the opening of retail sector to FDI. They view that FDI in retail sector would harm the local unorganized retail sector.

There are many controversies on the issue of FDI in retail sector. In the present scenario the basic questions involved are—

1. Should FDI be opened in multi-brand retail sector?
2. Should FDI limit be increased to 100%?
3. Is the current decision of the government regarding 51% participation in single brand retail stores justified?

These controversies are discussed below:

- FDI should not be opened for multi-brand stores, as Indian retailers will not be able to face competition with these stores. The entry of big stores like Wall Mart will have bull-dozing effect on retail market. The vast number of small retail shops will be perished and lakhs of people will become jobless. Allowing FDI in multi brand sector will be a suicidal step, which will be the beginning of another dark chapter of economic sovereignty.
- A present, it is not desirable to increase FDI ceiling to 100% even for single premium brand stores. It will help us to ensure check and control on business operations of foreign investors and protect the domestic interest. Moreover, the equity participation limit can be increased in the due course of time as we did in telecom banking and insurance sectors. So it is not desirable to allow 100% FDI in retail business.
- The current decision of the government regarding 51% FDI participation is justified keeping in view the following:
  (a) Luxury single brand stores don't pose any threat to our domestic small retail outlets. Commerce Minister Sh. Kamal Nath assured that government is formulating a policy to ensure that luxury single brand stores do not displace the neighbourhood Kirana (Grocery) stores.

(b) Experiences of China, Thailand, Hong Kong and Malaysia in opening their retail sector for FDI have been encouraging.

(c) At present approximately three million Indian customers shop abroad. By allowing FDI in premium brand stores, these Indian customers will shop in India only. So we can retain such customers. Moreover, it will also attract the customers from neighbouring countries.

(d) By allowing FDI in luxury products India could create more jobs through indigenously designed luxury products like footwear, handicraft, handlooms, etc. cheap and skilled labour force gives India a natural advantage in becoming an important hub for production of such luxury products. FICCI president Sajoj K. Paddar said, "We can create millions of jobs in luxury goods by adopting conducive policies."

(e) By allowing FDI in single premium brand stores India has given positive message to foreign investors that India is not against FDI in retail sector. It has increased confidence of foreign investors.

Now foreign investors are looking for more investment opportunities in India besides China so as to spread out their risk wider. Buoyed by its success in China, Wall Mart is now trying to enter India. In December 2005 its high officials came to India for lobbying for FDI in retail in India. Recently speaking at Word Economic Forum 2006, our Honorable Finance Minister P. Chidambaram said, "Japan, for instance is looking at diversifying its investment basket and we expect the bulk of the fresh investment to come to India." As per Food Processing Industries Minister Sh. Subodh Kant Sahai, "It is estimated that retail sector will grow to rupees 1,50,000 crores in next 10 years.

But if we get in FDI, then this will be achieved in five years only." But for attracting more FDI, government should improve infrastructure and electricity sector where India lags behind its Key Asian Competitors China, Malaysia and Thailand.

D. Emerging Growth of Foreign Retailers after New Policy

Despite the liberalizing of FDI policies in January 2006, retailers and consumer products companies can still expect a highly calibrated approach to FDI. The new policy permits FDI of up to 51% in retail trading, but companies can trade only in a single brand. Approval of the Foreign Investment Promotion Board (FIPB) is also required. The retailing of multiple brands—even when the same manufacturer produces them—is not allowed.[21]

Until now, Government approval was required for FDI in wholesale cash-and-carry trading and for FDI of more than 51% in export trading. To facilitate easier FDI inflow, up to 100% now will be allowed automatically for cash-and-carry wholesale trading and export trading.

Total relaxation of restrictions is expected to take one to five years. This type of calibrated approach may deter some, but most retailers and consumer products companies recognize the long-term promise of this market. Returns on FDI are expected to even higher than in China because even the largest Indian retailers are much smaller than their Chinese counterparts, offering retailers a less competitive environment and the promise of healthy market share.

The most common channels for entry of multi-brand foreign retailers are Strategic License Agreements (e.g. partnering with Indian promoter-owned companies in the Middle East (UAE) or Far East, franchising and cash-and-carry wholesale trading).

FDI restrictions have not deterred prominent international players from entering India. Many U.S. and other international retailers and consumer goods companies consider India a top-priority market with the potential for breakthrough growth:

- Wal-Mart CEO, John Menzar, visited India in 2005 and met with Prime Minister Dr. Manmohan Singh to lobby for FDI.[22] At the same time, Wal-Mart's sourcing from India, which was U.S. $300 million in 2004, has gone up to U.S. $1.2 billion in 2005.[23]
- Tommy Hilfiger, international fashion icon, says, "The Indian economy is soaring. I think Indian people love brands. There isn't another American designer on this soil, may be because they don't know it, maybe because they don't understand it, may be because they don't care. I understand it, I care about it, I am excited about it and I feel very positive that we are going to build a wonderful lifestyle business here."[24]
- Fashion brand DKNY is also set to foray into the Indian fashion industry through a franchisee agreement with Indian company, S. Kumar's.[25]
- Calvin Klein visited India last year and was quoted by United Press International as saying that he is enormously inspired by the unique work of Indian textiles, fashion, and the vibrant hues the country has to offer, and that he was in the country to make connections.[26]

E. Emerging Foreign Retailing in Consumer Goods

- Phillip Morris is also ready to unveil its plans for Kraft in India. The company plans to storm the Indian processed foods market through Kraft Jacob Suchard (KJS) India, a wholly owned arm of Philip Morris India. Brands such as Toblerone from their international portfolio, and salad oils, dips and spreads will be introduced. The company plans to import and begin cash-and-carry wholesale trading of a range of agro-based processed food products and has firmed up a distribution agreement with a local company.[27]

- Strabucks[28] recently expressed its interest in entering India through the franchise route, as did Pizza Hut, Subway and McDonalds.
- In the next three years, McDonalds plans to open another 100 outlets in cities across India.[29]
- BMW AG announced in December that it would establish a production and sales unit in India, offering its 3-series and 5-series sedans to the local market.[30]
- Motorola announced in December that it is debuting three locally assembled products, including a handset priced under $40. Motorola employs 3,000 people at a software-development facility in Bangalore.[31]

The four major organized retail segments are Food and Grocery, Clothing, Consumer Durables, and Books and Music. Food and Grocery ($154 billion) constitutes 41% of private consumption expenditure and 77% of total retail sales. However, 99% of this segment is unorganised. The segment is defined by low gross margins but there appears to be tremendous growth potential in the form of supermarkets, hard discount chains, and hypermarkets.

There currently are only 25 hypermarkets in India, which are operated by four retail companies. The largest hypermarket is Pantaloon's Big Bazaar hypermarket at Phoenix Mills, Mumbai, which has sales of $20 million per year. India has the potential to absorb more than 1,000 hypermarkets by 2010, according to industry sources. Three out of India's top five retailers have aggressive hypermarket strategies; international retailers are likely to make this a focus as well.

Footwear is the most organized retail sector and is driven by dominance of domestic players, such as Liberty and multinational retailer Bata. Foreign companies, such as Adidas,[32] Reebok[33] and Nike,[34] have entered India through the franchise route. Franchisee activity in this segment is expected to rise, particularly in Tier II cities. Apparel is the second most organized sector and growth is expected here as well, due to the high level of branding activities by apparel retailers and increased formats such as department stores. The same is true for Books and Music. Consumer durables are likely to grow in preparation to increases in urban incomes.

During the next few decades, India is likely to surpass China as the world's most populous country. Multinational consumer goods companies seeking faster growth have always been attracted by India's consumer potential and are now beginning to look at relatively uncluttered segments such as luxury goods.

The Indian Fast Moving Consumer Goods sector is the fourth largest sector in the economy. Penetration levels as well as per capita consumption in most product categories (e.g. jams, toothpaste, skin care and hair wash) in India are low, indicating the untapped market potential. Growth is likely to come from consumer "upgrading" in the matured product categories. With 200 million people expected to shift to processed and packaged food by 2010, India will need approximately U.S. $28 billion of investment in the food-processing industry. The current foreign retail scenario is shown in pie chart.

F. Risk Management and Foreign Retailers[35]

The opportunities and international retailers and consumer products companies entering India are great, but not without risks, according to Daniel Lentz with the Fraud Investigation and Dispute Services group of Ernst and Young LLP. India is a unique and complex risk environment. A company entering India should conduct a comprehensive risk assessment based on its business plan objectives and develop a framework of sustainable processes for ongoing risk management.

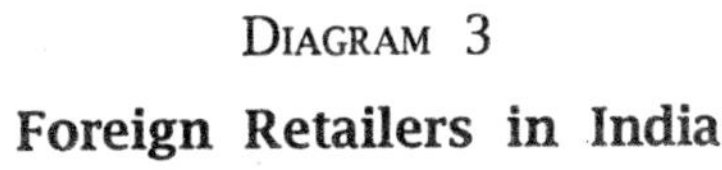
DIAGRAM 3

Foreign Retailers in India

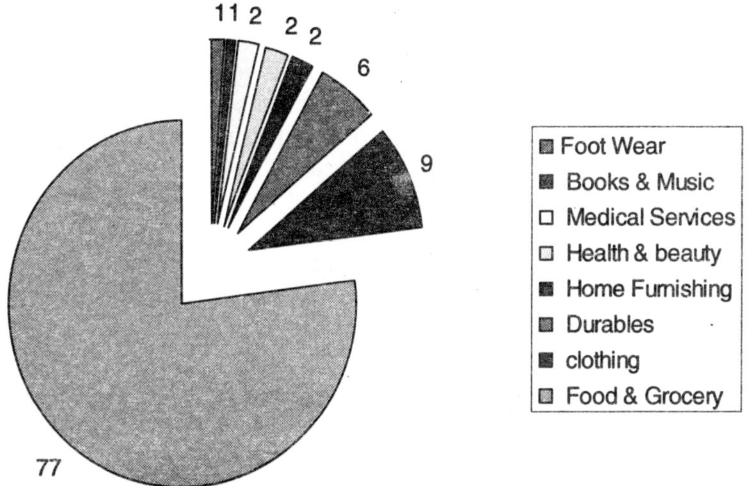

Fraud and theft—including employee pilferage, shoplifting, vendor frauds, and simple inaccuracies—already cost the India retail sector about U.S. $120 million every year. This is despite the fact that most large retailers use standard security.

Insuring against this type of exposure is difficult and expensive. Companies must anticipate spending more time not only securing good coverage but also working with insurance providers when problems arise.

Companies should be aware of the nuances in the different regions where they operate. India, with 35 states and union territories—each with its own language, culture, habits, risks, and challenges—is actually very similar to the European Union. Companies must understand the unique risks in the regions here they operate. A leading U.S. software manufacturer, for example, ran into problems recently when police failed to register a case against a former company official for alleged theft of software. The region's chief minister ultimately intervened, admitting that the police had failed to understand the nuances of IT and intellectual property rights.

"As companies expand into new markets, they have to be sure that they have coverage tailored to address the new location and the unique exposures there," says Lent. "In addition, there is some transition in the risk market-place from traditional exposures to types that insurance products are not well-suited to handle, at least at the moment—for example, the unauthorized flow or loss of data, or corruption or misuse of confidential information. The theft of a customer list can have significant economic impact. Unless you buy insurance tailored to those types of exposures, you may not be protected."

George P. Farragher, with the Fraud Investigation and Dispute Services Group of Ernst and Young LLP, agrees that companies must aggressively protect their intellectual property in India. "Any company going to India must be prepared so that they can protect the assets and reputation of the company."

Farragher says that companies must maintained control of trade secrets and have controls in place to identify other issues that could potentially cause problems. "One control is adequate training of the people on the ground and the people responsible for activities in that environment. The second is frequent and variable internal audits to ensure compliance with policies and procedures. Companies must routinely designate people to observe operations and check for corruption. They should be familiar with the types and indicators of corruption so they can identify risks early on."

A "special" sales representative may often be involved in "special" deals that may represent a violation of the Foreign Corrupt Practices Act. Companies also must know—and be able to take some responsibility for—the vendors and subcontractors with whom they do business. Companies benefit from connecting with knowledgeable people in the regions where they operate. Among other things, those contacts help companies identify reputable vendors and sub-contractors to avoid short- and long-term problems. Companies also should establish adequate qualification programs for vendors and sub-contractors.

Retailers and consumer products companies also must be prepared for a crowded retail environment characterized by rapidly changing consumer preferences and logistical challenges, which can impede development of efficient and adaptable supply chains. India has limited highways and deteriorating railways. Not only does this impede the overall transportation of goods, but it also limits the size of the loads that trucks can carry. However, the government is investing heavily in highway systems. The Indian government plans to spend U.S. $150 billion over the next few years to develop a world-class infrastructure. This should lead to a decline in logistics costs, which are currently 10-12% of the GDP. This also should lead to more timely distribution, which will help retailers improve operational performance.

There is also a severe shortage of talented professionals. This is true in almost every area of retail sector—technology, supply chain, business development, marketing, product development and research. Successful retailers hire aggressively, but this problem is likely to escalate as the demand for workers increases over the next several years. The retail sector will generate two million jobs between now and 2010. The growing need for people also will put increased pressure on wage costs and operating margins, especially for mid-sized retailers.

"India is phenomenal opportunity," says Farragher. "But like any other business opportunity, you have to recognize and determine how to deal with the risks. You have to have controls in place to be able to manage the risks and the challenges."

G. FDI in Retailing in China: A Case Study

FDI in retail sector of China was permitted in 1992. At that time 40 foreign retailers had got approval to enter retail sector. FDI in retail sector in China was initially allowed in 6 major cities including Beijing, Shanghai and Guangzhon. The important point here is that foreign ownership in China was restricted to 49%. It was decided that the current restrictions of FDI in retail sector will be phased out over 5 years as condition to entry into WTO. As a result of FDI the retailing in China has increased at 15% compound as shown below:

DIAGRAM 4

Retailing in China

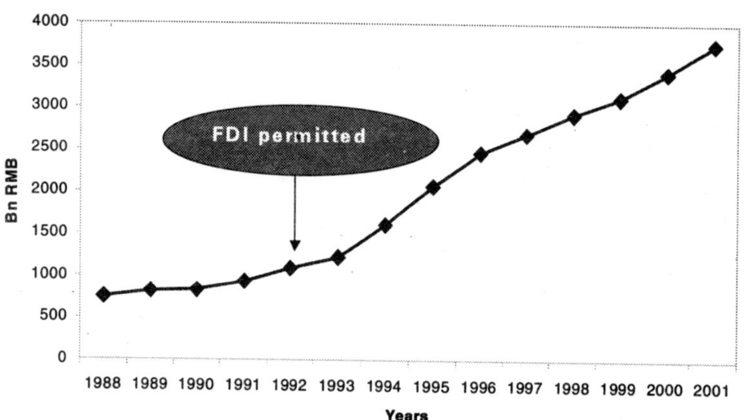

The following Table 5.12 shows the impact of FDI in the retail sector in China.

The Table 5.12 also shows that whereas modern formats of retailing has grown at a fast speed in China after FDI, the traditional formats also grew in the said period. Interestingly, the employment in retail sector in China after FDI also increased from 4% of total labour force to about 8% during this period.

TABLE 5.12

China: The Effect of FDI

Type	*No. of Stores in 1996*	*No. of Stores in 2004*
Traditional	19,20,604	29,65,027
Supermarkets	13,079	2,74,196
Convenience	—	26,889
Hyper markets	—	987

DIAGRAM 5

Employment in Retailing in China

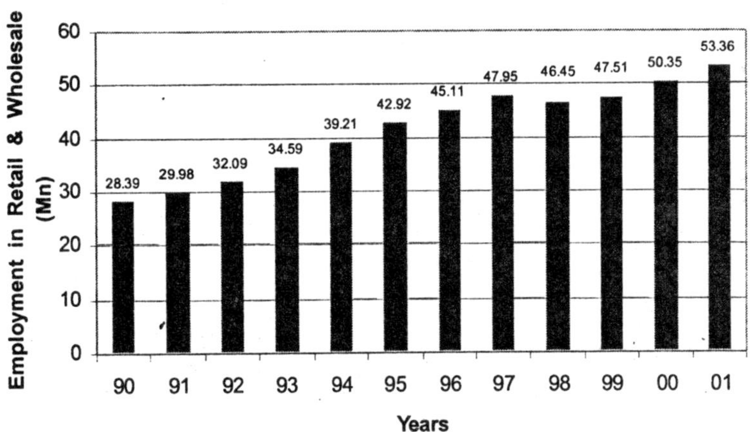

The biggest surprise of FDI in retailing in China is that even after permission of FDI in retailing, the majority of retailers are Chinese owned as shown in Table 5.13.

The Table 5.13 clearly reveals that Chinese owned retailers lead not only in terms of turnover but also in terms of No. of stores. The Wal-Mart owns only 22 stores in China with turnover of just $422 million.

TABLE 5.13

Chinese and Foreign Retailers

Top 10 Retailers	*Turnover $ m*	*No. of Stores*
1. Lianhua	6981	225
2. Hualian	27	818
3. Beijing Hualian	966	42
4. Shanghai Nong Gong Shang	903	325
5. Carrefour	823	28
6. Suguo	638	663
7. Trustmart	607	43
8. Metro	598	15
9. China Resources Vanguard	561	343
10. Wallmart	422	22

Source: Retail Census 2001 AC-Nielsen.

H. China: A Better Destination for FDI

The above analysis clearly indicates that China is much more successful in attracting FDI in retail sector. Let us analyze some facts which prove China, a better destination for FDI than India:

- China is characterized by setting new regulations to permit joint-ventures like setting up of Special Economic Zones, Open Cities, etc. since late 1970's and early 1980's whereas in India liberalization process started after 1990. Some firms already had deep roots in China.
- In China wholly foreign-owned enterprises were allowed after 1986, whereas in India, till date it is allowed only in very few sectors. So, in case of 100% foreign ownership, future lies with China.
- Investors favour China over India for its market size, access to export markets, government incentives, favourable cost

structure, infrastructure and macro-economic climate. So with regard to these factors, India is in danger zone.

- Problems in India such as poor public administration, political instability often force investors to choose China rather than India.
- China's FDI policy is proactive while in case of India it is reactive. If we desire a higher FDI, there is a need of being proactive.
- India's policies towards FDI in some areas such as agriculture, telecommunications are still far from satisfaction of foreign investors. China is much ahead of us in this case.
- Hong Kong has so far been the most important source of China's FDI inflow due to set-up of SEZ in Shenzhen in 1970. It is a conscious implementation of FDI policy. India lacks such planned implementations. Decisions regarding set-up of SEZ and other facilities should be taken keeping in view investor's convenience.
- The Chinese Government has committed itself to invest over $ 800 billion in infrastructure projects over the next ten years, which will improve the nation's poor highway system, so China may be a better option than India.

I. Lessons for China

- It seems surprising that a communist country like China is more favourite of the capitalist investment companies. When China has become successful in attracting huge FDI, India has not. In fact, china, in terms of attracting FDI, has set standards for India. In 2004, FDI in China was $54 billion while in India it was only $ 1 billion. Anyhow China has proved that:
- FDI in retail sector had improved the entire size of industry. Retailing in China has grown

at a compound growth of 15% per annum after FDI inflow.

- FDI has led to increase in employment in retail sector.
- Local players can survive and even beat foreign competition, if a country can make its retailing industry strong. In fact, sale is the key to success for local retailers.
- There can be greater level of exports due to increased sourcing by major players. Sourcing by Wal-Mart from China improved multifold after FDI was permitted in China.
- FDI has resulted in manpower and skill development through retail trading and greater managerial talent inflow from other countries.
- FDI in technology leads to better operations in production cycle and distribution.
- The life style of the retail workers has become better due to greater level of wages

It is important to note that economic growth is closely related to the growth of retailing. Economic growth depends crucially on the growth of private consumption as it comprises about two thirds of GDP. The growth of private consumption, on the other hand, depends on the development of retail industry. This linkage makes it imperative for the retail sector to experience high growth in order to have sustainable growth. The evolution of organized formats would enable the retail sector to grow. Hence, the government through appropriate reform measures should support the growth of organized formats.

5.7: INDIA: AN IDEAL DESTINATION FOR FOREIGN DIRECT INVESTMENT[36]

P. Chidambaram Ex-Finance and Commerce Minister presented following four reasons which makes India an ideal destination for foreign direct investment.

First, India remains perhaps the world's pre-eminent development frontier. India is among the handful of countries which simply have to expand at a furious pace. India is not just an expanding consumer market. It is a place where infrastructure has to be built to meet the needs and aspirations of over a billion people, and that is where there is an unprecedented opportunity for American business and industry.

Second, India is not just a low-wage country. It is a country that produces technicians, scientists, engineers and technical personnel of world-class. A survey of expatriate managers reported in the *London Economist* had placed India at the very top on the availability of skilled manpower at competitive rates. Jack Welch of GE has described India as a developing country with the intellectual infrastructure of a developed country.

Third, India has a preponderance of entrepreneurial skills and entrepreneurs who are taking on multinationals and global brands and are competing effectively. With the increasing availability of venture capital and the freeing of licensing restrictions, there has been a mushrooming of new small and medium-sized companies, started and managed by professionals. American companies will find them enthusiastic partners.

Fourth, a market economy is founded on a system of honouring contracts, enforcing property rights and respecting legal obligations. India has a well-developed judicial infrastructure that has time and again demonstrated its independence, as in the Enron case. A number of independent regulatory authorities are also being set-up in sectors that are being restructured.

5.8: CONCLUSION

The advantages of India as an investment destination rest on strong fundamentals which include a large and growing market; world-class scientific, technical and managerial manpower; abundance of labour and natural resource; independent judiciary, etc. This is now recognized by a number of global investors who have either already established a base in India or are in the process of doing so. Ongoing initiatives such as further simplification of legislation, de-licensing, setting up regulatory authorities such as Central/State Electricity Regulatory Commissions, etc. is expected to provide necessary impetus to accommodate enlarged FDI inflows in future.

In the final analysis, large volume inflows of FDI would depend on domestic economic conditions and the FDI policy, world economic trends, and strategies of global investors. Government, on its part is fully committed to create strong economic fundamentals and an increasingly pro-active FDI policy regime.

Notes and References

1. Chanchal Chopra, "Foreign Investment in India", pp. 13-14; Deep & Deep Publishers, New Delhi.
2. Chanchal Chopra, "Foreign Investment in India", pp. 13-14; Deep & Deep Publishers, New Delhi.
3. Ruddar Datt and KPM Sundharam, "Indian Economy", S. Chand Publication, pp. 344-45.
4. Chanchal Chopra, "Foreign Investment in India", pp. 161-64., Deep & Deep Publishers, 2004, New Delhi.
5. Department of Company Affairs, Annual Report, Ministry of Law, Justice and Company Affairs, 1999-2000.
6. Mohan, Rakesh (2005), "Indian Economy in the Global Setting", *Reserve Bank of India Bulletin*, October.
   (i) Planning Commission (2002), Foreign Investment: India, Government of India, August.
   (ii) Reddy, Y.V. (2005), "Overcoming Challenges in a Globalising Economy: Managing India's External Sector", *Reserve Bank of India Bulletin*, July.
   (iii) A.T. Kearney (2005), FDI Confidence Index Survey.
7. P. Chidambaram: Seminar on India, Organised by the *Washington Post*, October 28th, 1997.
8. Price Water House Coopers Report (2004-2005).
9. www.euromonitor.com
10. Assocham (2000).
11. Bajpai, N. and N. Das Gupta (2004).
12. www. euromonitor.com

13. McKinsey and Company (2003), New Horizons: Multinational Company Investment in Development Economies, Presentation by McKinsey Global Institute, 2003. Website:http://www.mckinsey.com/mgi/publications/newhorizons/index.asp.
14. Mukherjee, A. (2002), "Distribution Services: India and the GATS 2000 Negotiations", ICRIER Working Paper No. 80.
15. Price Water House Coopers Report (2004-2005).
16. *Ibid.*
17. *The Tribune*, Chandigarh, Jan. 25, 2006
18. FDI in Retail Sector in India, Department of Consumers Affairs, Ministry of Consumer Affairs, Public and Food Department, Government of India, pp. 107-11.
19. Mandeep singh, "Globalization in Retailing: Causes, Impact and Trends in India", Research paper presented in national Seminar "FDI in retail business", G.N. Khalsa College, Karnal, Feb. 18, 2006
20. Mandeep Singh, "Globalization in Retailing: Causes, Impact and Trends in India", Research paper presented in National Seminar, "FDI in Retail Business", G.N. Khalsa College, Karnal, Feb. 18, 2006
21. NASSCOM.
22. India Resource Centre/CNN, June 2006.
23. Fibre 2 Fashion, January 2005.
24. "Tommy Unplugged", *The Hindu Business Line*, May 2004.
25. *Economic Times*, January 2006.
26. *Asia Times Online*, November 2004.
27. *Economic Times*, November 2005.
28. www.frnachiseindia.com
29. www.franchiseindia.com
30. *Hindustan Times*, November 2005.
31. Indian Express, December 2005.
32. March 2006, *Reuter's News.*
33. *Business Standard*, February 2006.
34. *RetailBiz*, February 2006.
35. *Financial Express*, October 2005.

CHAPTER

6

Financial Sector Reforms

6.1: INTRODUCTION

Reforms in the financial sector play an important role in the process of overall economic development of the country. Liberalisation of this sector is one of the significant strategies of structural adjustment programmes. Major stability in monetary and fiscal mechanism is supposed as a basic prerequisite for financial sector reforms. Before opening the door of our economy to global competition, it is indispensable to have our domestic economy restructured and the financial sector reform is a forward step in this direction.

The main objective of the financial sector reforms in India initiated in the early 1990s was to create an efficient, competitive and stable financial sector that could then contribute in greater measure to stimulate growth. Concomitantly, the monetary policy framework made a phased shift from direct instruments of monetary management to an increasing reliance on indirect instruments. However, as appropriate monetary transmission cannot take place without efficient price discovery of interest rates and exchange rates in the overall functioning of financial markets, the corresponding development of the money market, Government securities market and the foreign exchange market became necessary. Reforms in the various segments, therefore, had to be coordinated. In this process, growing integration of the Indian economy with the rest of the world also had to be recognized and provided for. Against this backdrop, the coverage of this study is three-fold:

First, a synoptic account of the reforms in financial sector and monetary policy, exchange rate policy is undertaken.

Second, this is followed by an assessment of these reforms in terms of outcomes and the health of the financial sector.

Finally, lessons emerging from the Indian experience for issues of topical relevance for monetary authorities are considered in the final Section.

6.2: FINANCIAL SECTOR AND MONETARY POLICY: OBJECTIVES AND REFORMS[1]

Till the early 1990s the Indian financial sector could be described as a classic example of "financial repression." The financial system was characterized by extensive regulations such as administered interest rates, directed credit programmes, weak banking structure, lack of proper accounting and risk management systems and lack of transparency in operations of major financial market participants. Such a system hindered efficient allocation of resources. Financial sector reforms initiated in the early 1990s have attempted to overcome these weaknesses in order to enhance efficiency of resource allocation in the economy. Simultaneously, the Reserve Bank took a keen interest in the development of financial markets, especially the money, government securities and forex markets in view of their critical role in the transmission mechanism of monetary policy. As for other central banks, the money market is the focal point for intervention by the Reserve Bank to equilibrate short-term liquidity flows on account of its linkages with the foreign exchange market. Similarly, the Government securities market is important for the entire debt market as it serves as a benchmark for pricing other debt market instruments, thereby aiding the monetary transmission process across the yield curve. The Reserve Bank had, in fact, been making efforts since 1986 to develop institutions and infrastructure for these markets to facilitate price discovery. These efforts by the Reserve Bank to develop efficient, stable and healthy financial markets accelerated after 1991. There has been close co-ordination between the Central Government and the Reserve Bank, as also between different regulators, which helped in orderly and smooth development of the financial markets in India. The major contours of the financial sector reforms were:

- Removal of the erstwhile existing financial repression.
- Creation of an efficient, productive and profitable financial sector.
- Enabling the process of price discovery by the market determination of interest rates that improves allocative efficiency of resources.
- Providing operational and functional autonomy to institutions.
- Preparing the financial system for increasing international competition.
- Opening the external sector in a calibrated manner.
- Promoting financial stability in the wake of domestic and external shocks.

The financial sector reforms since the early 1990s could be analytically classified into two phases.[2]

1. The First Phase, or the First Generation of Reforms was aimed at creating an efficient, productive and profitable financial sector which would function in an environment of operational flexibility and functional autonomy.

2. **The Second phase, or the Second Generation Reforms**, which started in the mid-1990s, the emphasis of reforms has been on strengthening the financial system and introducing structural improvements. Against this background reforms in various sectors and segments of the financial sector were following:

6.2:1 Banking Sector Reforms

The main objective of banking sector reforms was to promote a diversified, efficient and competitive financial system with the ultimate goal of improving the allocative efficiency of resources through operational flexibility, improved financial viability and institutional strengthening. The reforms have focused on removing financial repression through reductions in statutory pre-emptions, while stepping up prudential regulations at the same time. Furthermore, interest rates on both deposits and lending of banks have been progressively deregulated. Y.V. Reddy noted that the approach towards financial sector reforms in India has been based on five principles:

(i) cautious and appropriate sequencing of reform measures;
(ii) introduction of mutually reinforcing norms;
(iii) introduction of complementary reforms across monetary, fiscal and external;
(iv) development of financial institutions; and
(v) development of financial markets.

Reforms in banking sector can be classified into six parts which are as follows:[3]

(A) Competition Enhancing Measures

- Granting of operational autonomy to public

sector banks, reduction of public ownership in public sector banks by allowing them to raise capital from equity market up to 49 per cent of paid-up capital.

- Transparent norms for entry of Indian private sector, foreign and joint-venture banks and insurance companies, permission for foreign investment in the financial sector in the form of Foreign Direct Investment (FDI) as well as portfolio investment, permission to banks to diversify product portfolio and business activities.
- Roadmap for presence of foreign banks and guidelines for mergers and amalgamation of private sector banks and banks and NBFCs.
- Guidelines on ownership and governance in private sector banks.

(B) Measures Enhancing Role of Market Forces

- Sharp reduction in pre-emption through reserve requirement, market determined pricing for government securities, disbanding of administered interest rates with a few exceptions and enhanced transparency and disclosure norms to facilitate market discipline.
- Introduction of pure inter-bank call money market, auction-based repos-reverse repos for short-term liquidity management, facilitation of improved payments and settlement mechanism.
- Significant advancement in dematerialization and markets for securitized assets are being developed.

(C) Prudential Measures

- Introduction and phased implementation of international best practices and norms on risk weighted capital adequacy requirement, accounting, income recognition, provisioning and exposure.

- Measures to strengthen risk management through recognition of different components of risk, assignment of risk-weights to various asset classes, norms on connected lending, risk concentration, application of marked-to-market principle for investment portfolio and limits on deployment of fund in sensitive activities.
- 'Know Your Customer' and 'Anti-Money Laundering' guidelines, roadmap for Basel II, introduction of capital charge for market risk, higher graded provisioning for NPAs, guidelines for ownership and governance, securitisation and debt restructuring mechanisms norms, etc.

(D) Institutional and Legal Measures

- Setting up of Lok Adalats (people's courts), debt recovery tribunals, asset reconstruction companies, settlement advisory committees, corporate debt restructuring mechanism, etc. for quicker recovery/restructuring.
- Promulgation of Securitisation and Reconstruction of Financial Assets and Enforcement of Securities Interest (SARFAESI) Act, 2002 and its subsequent amendment to ensure creditor rights.
- Setting up of Credit Information Bureau of India Limited (CIBIL) for information sharing on defaulters as also other borrowers.
- Setting up of Clearing Corporation of India Limited (CCIL) to act as central counter party for facilitating payments and settlement system relating to fixed income securities and money market instruments.

(E) Supervisory Measures

- Establishment of the Board for Financial Supervision as the apex supervisory authority for commercial banks, financial institutions and non-banking financial companies.
- Introduction of CAMELS supervisory rating system, move towards risk-based supervision, consolidated supervision of financial conglomerates, strengthening of off-site surveillance through control returns.
- Recasting of the role of statutory auditors, increased internal control through strengthening of internal audit.
- Strengthening corporate governance, enhanced due diligence on important shareholders, fit and proper tests for directors.

(F) Technology Related Measures

- Setting up of INFINET as the communication backbone for the financial sector, introduction of Negotiated Dealing System (NDS) for screen-based trading in government securities and Real Time Gross Settlement (RTGS) System.

As the Indian banking system had become predominantly government owned by the early 1990s, banking sector reforms essentially took a two pronged approach:

First, the level of competition was gradually increased within the banking system while simultaneously introducing international best practices in prudential regulation and supervision tailored to Indian requirements. In particular, special emphasis was placed on building up the risk management capabilities of Indian banks while measures were initiated to ensure flexibility, operational autonomy and competition in the banking sector.

Second, active steps were taken to improve the institutional arrangements including the legal framework and technological system. The supervisory system was revamped in view of the crucial role of supervision in the creation of an efficient banking system. Measures to improve the health of the banking system have included:

(i) restoration of public sector banks net worth through recapitalisation where needed;
(ii) streamlining of the supervision process with combination of on-site and off-site surveillance along with external auditing;
(iii) introduction of risk based supervision;
(iv) introduction of the process of structured and discretionary intervention for problem banks through a prompt corrective action (PCA) mechanism;
(v) institutionalisation of a mechanism facilitating greater coordination for regulation and supervision of financial conglomerates;
(vi) strengthening creditor rights (still in process); and
(vii) increased emphasis on corporate governance. Consistent with the policy approach to benchmark the banking system to the best international standards with emphasis on gradual harmonization, all commercial banks in India are expected to start implementing Basel II with effect from March 31, 2007—though a marginal stretching beyond this date should not be ruled out in view of the latest indications on the state of preparedness.

Recognizing the differences in degrees of sophistication and development of the banking system, it has been decided that the banks will initially adopt the Standardized Approach for credit risk and the Basic Indicator Approach for operational risk. After adequate skills are developed, both by the banks and also by the supervisors, some of the banks may be allowed to migrate to the Internal Rating Based (IRB) Approach. Although implementation of Basel II will require more capital for banks in India, the cushion available in the system--at present, the Capital to Risk Assets Ratio (CRAR) is over 12 per cent—provides some comfort. In order to provide banks greater flexibility and avenues for meeting the capital requirements, the Reserve Bank has issued policy guidelines enabling issuance of several instruments by the banks viz., innovative perpetual debt instruments, perpetual non-cumulative preference shares, redeemable cumulative preference shares and hybrid debt instruments.

6.2:2 Ownership and Governance of Banks—Recent Guidelines of R.B.I.

In recent years, the Reserve Bank has initiated several measures to enhance transparency and strengthen corporate governance practices in the banking sector in India in order to ensure financial sector stability. In this context, issues of ownership and governance in private sector banks assumed importance in 2004-05. The BFS formulated a draft comprehensive policy framework with regard to ownership of and governance in private sector banks and placed it in the public domain on July 2, 2004. Based on the feedback and inputs received from the public, and in consultation with Government, the Reserve Bank released detailed guidelines on February 28, 2005. Some of the major guidelines were following:

(a) Guidelines on Ownership and Governance in Private Sector Banks[4]

The broad principle underlying the guidelines on ownership and governance in private sector banks is to ensure that the control of private sector banks is well diversified to minimise the risk of misuse or imprudent use of leveraged funds. The guidelines require that:

(i) important shareholders (i.e., with shareholding of five per cent and above) are 'fit and proper' as per the Reserve Bank's guidelines on acknowledgement for allotment and transfer of shares;
(ii) the directors and the Chief Executive Officer who manage the affairs of the bank are 'fit and proper' and observe sound corporate governance principles;
(iii) banks have minimum capital/net worth for optimal operations and systemic stability; and
(iv) policy and processes are transparent and fair.

Some additional requirements are that:

(a) banks maintain a net worth of Rs. 300 crore at all times;
(b) shareholding or control in any bank in excess of 10 per cent of the paid up capital by any single entity or group of related entities requires the Reserve Bank's prior approval;
(c) banks (including foreign banks having branch presence in India)/financial institutions are not allowed to exceed equity holding of five per cent of the equity capital of the investee bank;
(d) large industrial houses are allowed to acquire shares not exceeding 10 per cent of the paid-up capital of the bank subject to the Reserve Bank's prior approval;
(e) the Reserve Bank would permit a higher level of shareholding on a case-by-case basis for restructuring of problem/weak banks or in the interest of consolidation in the banking sector; and
(f) if the shareholding exceeds the prescribed limit or if the net worth is below Rs. 300 crore in any bank, a time-bound programme to reduce the stake or to augment the capital should be submitted to the Reserve Bank.

On the issue of aggregate foreign investment in private banks from all sources (FDI, FII, NRI), the guidelines stipulate that it cannot exceed 74 per cent of the paid-up capital of a bank. If FDI (other than by foreign banks or foreign bank groups) in private banks exceeds 5 per cent, the entity acquiring such stake would have to meet the 'fit and proper' criteria indicated in the share transfer guidelines and get the Reserve Bank's acknowledgement for transfer of the shares. The aggregate limit for all FII investments is restricted to 24 per cent which can be raised to 49 per cent with the approval of the board/shareholders. The current aggregate limit for all NRI investments is 24 per cent, with the individual NRI limit being five per cent, subject to the approval of the board/shareholders.

(b) Road Map for Presence of Foreign Banks[5]

Under the road map, during the first phase, between March 2005 and March 2009, foreign banks satisfying the eligibility criteria prescribed by the Reserve Bank will be permitted to establish presence by way of setting up a wholly owned banking subsidiary (WOS) or converting the existing branches into a WOS following the one mode presence criterion. The WOS should have a minimum capital of Rs. 300 crore and sound corporate governance. The WOS will be treated on par with the existing branches of foreign banks for branch expansion with flexibility to go beyond the existing WTO commitments of 12 branches in a year and preference for branch expansion in underbanked areas. The Reserve Bank would also prescribe market access and national treatment limitation consistent with WTO commitments as also other appropriate limitations consistent with international practices and the country's requirements. Permission for acquisition of shareholding in Indian private sector banks by eligible foreign banks will be limited to banks identified by the Reserve Bank for restructuring. The Reserve Bank would consider permitting such acquisition if it is satisfied that such investment by the foreign bank concerned will be in the long-term interest of all the stakeholders in the investee bank. Where such acquisition is by a foreign bank having presence in India, a maximum period of six months will be given for conforming to the 'one form of presence' concept. The second phase will commence in April 2009 after a review of the experience gained and after due consultation with all the stakeholders in the banking sector. Extension of national treatment to WOS, dilution of stake and permitting mergers/acquisitions of any private sector banks in India by a foreign bank would be considered, subject to the overall investment limit of 74 per cent.

(c) Growth of ATMs and Demand for Higher Denomination Banknotes[6]

Ever since the first automated teller machine (ATM) was introduced in the late 1960s, the usage of ATM has grown exponentially. The cash dispenser and the ATMs have gradually become the electronic face of banking. It is estimated that there are 49 billion cash withdrawals worldwide through ATMs in a year. Foreign banks in India were the first to introduce experimental ATMs in 1988. Usage picked up in the 1990s. Although a number of services are offered through fully functional ATMs, about 98 per cent people use the ATM primarily for withdrawing cash. Banks have devised competitive strategies around the ATMs, recognising that ATMs can be a potent source of value added service to consumers through access to banking services at any time and at a large number of outlets, thereby increasing customer convenience as well as cost effectiveness in banking functions. With the increase in the usage of ATMs, a shift has taken place towards stocking higher denomination banknotes—particularly Rs. 100 and Rs. 500 denominations—as banks do not find it commercially viable to stock the machines with all denominations of banknotes. Lower denomination banknotes run out sooner and increase both capital cost and operating costs. The Reserve Bank has accordingly been facing an increasing demand for fresh banknotes in Rs. 500 and Rs. 100 denominations. In the context of the increased demand for ATM-fit banknotes, emphasis has been laid on banks using desktop sorters to salvage good quality banknotes for use in ATMs.

(d) Working Group on Regulatory Mechanism for Cards[7]

Plastic cards (credit, debit and smart cards) have increasingly become an important mode of payment in the country in recent years. The number of cards issued by banks increased from 2.69 crore as on December 31, 2003 to 4.33 crore as on December 31, 2004. Accordingly, issues relating to the regulation of this mode of payment as well as those relating to customer protection have assumed considerable importance. The Reserve Bank's Working Group on Regulatory Mechanism for Cards recommended that the present eligibility criteria for issue of credit cards are appropriate and do not warrant allowing access to non-banking entities in this business. On issues relating to customer services, the Group made the following recommendations.

Transparency and Disclosure

(i) Communication of terms and conditions by card issuing banks to customers should be in simple language;
(ii) Separate communication of Most Important Terms and Conditions (MITC);
(iii) Card issuing banks should mention interest charges on an annual basis;
(iv) Persons entrusted with product marketing to have high degree of professionalism and integrity;
(v) Direct Selling Agents (DSA)/Direct Marketing Agents (DMA) work to be entrusted to well known firms on whom due diligence has been carried out and in case of cards issued

through DSAs/DMAs, KYC norms laid down by the Reserve Bank to be scrupulously followed; and

(vi) DSA/DMA staff should be properly trained and briefed and card issuing banks should formulate a code of conduct for them.

Customer Rights Protection

(i) Card issuing banks should take specific approval of card-holders before releasing customer information;

(ii) Customer information can be released in compliance with court order, statutory compliance or to Credit Information Bureau. In case of default, only required information to be released to collection/recovery agent;

(iii) 'Do Not Call' registry to be maintained by card issuing banks and the IBA for telephone and cell phone number of customers and non-customers who do not wish to be disturbed by marketing calls;

(iv) Banking Ombudsman should arbitrate in disputes between card issuing banks and card-holders;

(v) Unsolicited cards activated without approval of recipient would lead to payment of penalty by the bank concerned; and

(vi) Insurance cover for card outstanding to be introduced to cover dues in case of demise of the card-holder.

Code of Conduct

Card issuing banks should set-up a self-regulatory body to deliberate on important issues and card issuing banks should adopt and conform to the IBA's Code of Conduct for card issuing banks.

(e) Enterprise Knowledge Management System[8]

The Reserve Bank has information—both structured as well as unstructured - in different forms. The Reserve Bank is moving towards an information accumulation mechanism to systematically leverage this scattered knowledge for efficient and effective use. Focusing on creating, gathering, organising and disseminating an organisation's 'knowledge' in knowledge repository is the key idea behind the Enterprise Knowledge Management System (EKMS). The proposed EKMS for the Reserve Bank has been initiated for designing a system to enable the users to reach to the knowledge base, whenever and wherever required, for the purpose of decision-making. Various applications could form an integral part of the EKMS. Of these, following have been identified as building blocks for the Knowledge Management System:

- Document and Content Management System—to help organise the document and content for faster retrieval whenever required;
- Workflow Automation System—to automate the organisational processes for faster action, better management and for reducing paper;
- Collaboration Techniques - to help exchange ideas and important information among all;
- Intranet—to help departments display the information for specific purpose of the users within the department/LAN; and
- Knowledge Portal—front-end to display information in the form of customisable portals, keeping in view the specific requirement of the users.

The challenge for the Reserve Bank is to put in a place a culture of sharing individuals' knowledge assets within the organisation.

(f) Drivers of Credit Growth[9]

Sustained demand for bank credit has characterised the Indian banking system in the past four years in consonance with the upturn in economic activity. Non-food credit extended by Scheduled Commercial Banks (SCBs) recorded an average annual growth of 26.1 per cent between 2002-03 and 2005-06, notably higher than that of 14.5 per cent recorded during the preceding four-year period (1998-99 to 2001-02) as well as the long-run average of 17.8 per cent (1970-2006). The recent acceleration in credit growth could be partly attributed to the step-up in real GDP growth from 5.7 per cent between 1998-99 and 2001-02 to 7.1 per cent between 2002-03 and 2005-06.

Empirical evidence indicates that credit demand is strongly influenced by economic activity. For the period since mid-1970s, income elasticity of (real) credit demand is estimated to be 1.61. In recent years, growth in credit demand has outpaced the growth that would have emanated from the historical relationship between credit and economic activity decline in interest rates in the recent years could have also boosted demand for credit. The stagnation in credit flow observed during the late 1990s, in retrospect, was partly caused by reduction in demand on account of increase in real interest rates, turn down in the business cycle, and the significant business restructuring that occurred during that period.[10] The sharp expansion in credit in recent years also reflects, in part, policy initiatives to improve flow of credit to sectors like agriculture. Thus, growth of credit to agriculture accelerated from 10.7 per cent during 1990s to 24.9 per cent between 2002-03 and 2004-05. Similarly, demand for credit by industry has shown a recovery in the current cyclical upturn. Growth of credit to the industrial sector accelerated from 15.6 per cent during 1990s to 18.5 per cent between 2002-03 and 2004-05. Increasingly, retail credit led by demand for housing loans has emerged as a driver of growth in bank credit. Credit to housing sector recorded an increase of 57.3 per cent during 2002-05, well above the growth recorded in the overall non-food credit over the same period. As a result, the share of housing credit in overall credit extended by SCBs has increased from 2.4 per cent at end-March 1990 to 11.0 per cent at end-March 2005. Retail credit growth has also emanated from increased use of credit cards, loans for consumer durables and demand for education loans. The share of non-housing retail credit has increased from four per cent at end-March 1990 to around 11 per cent at end-March 2005. Thus, the share of total retail credit in bank credit has increased from 6.4 per cent to over 22 per cent in the past 15 years. The share of agriculture in total credit, which had declined from 15.9 per cent at end-March 1990 to 9.6 per cent at end-March 2001 has since recovered to 10.8 per cent by end-March 2005. The share of industry in total credit has continued to decline, falling to 38.8 per cent by March 2005 from its recent peak of 49.1 per cent in March 1999. Demand for bank credit is expected to remain buoyant. With their investments in SLR securities fast approaching the statutory requirement, banks will need to intensify efforts to mobilise higher deposits through stable sources in order to be able to finance higher credit requirements. At the same time, in the light of high credit growth, a need is recognized to ensure that asset quality is maintained.

(g) Banking Ombudsman Scheme[11]

The Banking Ombudsman scheme in operation since 1995 provides for a system of redressal of grievances against banks in an expeditious and inexpensive manner. In India, any person whose grievance against a bank is not resolved to his satisfaction by that bank within a period of one month can approach the Banking Ombudsman if his complaint pertains to any of the matters specified in the Scheme. Banking Ombudsmen have been authorised to look into complaints concerning—

(a) deficiency in banking service;
(b) sanction of loans and advances as they relate to non-observance of the Reserve Bank directives on interest rates, delay in sanction or non-observance of prescribed time schedule for disposal of loan applications or non-observance of any other directions or instructions of the Reserve Bank as may be specified for this purpose, from time to time; and
(c) such other matters as may be specified by the Reserve Bank.

The Banking Ombudsman on receipt of any complaint endeavours to promote a settlement of the complaint by agreement between the complainant and the bank named in the complaint through conciliation or mediation. If a complaint is not settled by agreement within a period of one month from the date of receipt of the complaint or such further period as the Banking Ombudsman may consider necessary, he may pass an Award after affording the parties reasonable opportunity to present their case. He shall be guided by the evidence placed before him by the parties, the principles of banking law and practice, directions, instructions and guidelines issued by the Reserve Bank from time to time and such other factors, which in his opinion are necessary in the interest of justice. The Banking Ombudsman Scheme, 1995 covered all commercial banks and scheduled primary co-operative banks. The Banking Ombudsman Scheme, 2002 which came into effect on 14th June 2002 also included RRBs within its ambit. It additionally provided for the institution of a "Review Authority" to review the Banking Ombudsman's Award, when warranted. A bank against whom an Award has been passed, may with the approval of its Chief Executive, file an application to the Deputy Governor-in-charge of Rural Planning and Credit Department, Reserve Bank to seek a review of the Award, only when the Award appears to be patently in conflict with the Reserve Bank's instructions and/or the law and practice relating to banking. The Banking Ombudsman was also authorised to function as an Arbitrator on reference to him of disputes (value of subject matter not exceeding Rs. ten lakh) either between banks and their customers or between banks. The various reviews of the Scheme during the year 2005 indicated that though the complaints received at the Banking Ombudsman Offices have been increasing, the Scheme was not addressing some areas of the customer complaints of the customers. Furthermore, the functioning of the Scheme needed to be facilitated by streamlining the process of settlement of customer complaints. As the formulator and monitoring authority of the Scheme, the Reserve Bank needed to have more control over functioning of the Scheme. These issues have been addressed in the Banking Ombudsman Scheme, 2006 which came into effect from January 1, 2006. The following are the major changes in the revised Scheme:

(i) New grounds of complaints such as credit card issues, failure in providing the promised facilities, non-adherence to fair practices code and levying of excessive charges without prior notice have been included.

(ii) In order to facilitate complaint submission, the prescribed application format is not mandatory for filing the complaint. Complaints can be filed online as well as by sending an email.

(iii) Only serving senior officers of the Reserve Bank are appointed as Banking Ombudsmen.

(iv) The cost of running the Scheme, which was shared by all the participant banks, shall be borne by the Reserve Bank.

(v) The secretariat of the office of the Banking Ombudsman, which earlier also consisted of officers from SLBC Convenor banks, will consist of officers deputed from the Reserve Bank only.

(vi) The banks are required to appoint Nodal Officers in their Zonal Offices/Regional Offices for the Scheme.

(vii) The complainants can also appeal against the Award of Banking Ombudsman.

(viii) In order to enable the Banking Ombudsmen concentrate on the complaints, rather than on arbitration of inter-bank disputes, the arbitration option rested with the Banking Ombudsman has been removed in the Banking Ombudsman Scheme, 2006 to strengthen them, sponsor banks were encouraged to merge, State-wise, the RRBs sponsored by them.

In this context, the Government of India, after consultation with NABARD, the concerned State Governments and the concerned sponsor banks initiated the process of amalgamation of the RRBs in September 2005. As a result of these initiatives, 132 RRBs have been amalgamated till August 2, 2006 to form 41 new RRBs (sponsored by 19 banks in 15 States). This has brought down the total number of RRBs from 196 at end-March 2005 and 133 at end-March 2006 to 105 as on August 2, 2006. Some more amalgamation proposals are under consideration of the Government of India.

6.2:3 Banking Sector Reforms an Assessment

An assessment of the banking sector shows that banks have experienced strong balance sheet growth in the post-reform period in an environment of operational flexibility. Improvement in the financial health of banks, reflected in significant improvement in capital adequacy and improved asset quality, is distinctly visible. It is noteworthy that this progress has been achieved despite the adoption of international best practices in prudential norms. Competitiveness and productivity gains have also been enabled by proactive technological deepening and flexible human resource management.

These significant gains have been achieved even while renewing our goals of social banking viz., maintaining the wide reach of the banking system and directing credit towards important but disadvantaged sectors of society. A brief discussion on the performance of the banking sector under the reform process is given below.

(a) Spread of banking

The banking system's wide reach, judged in terms of expansion of branches and the growth of credit and deposits indicates continued financial deepening (Table 6.1). The population per bank branch has not changed much since the 1980s, and has remained at around 16,000.

TABLE 6.1

Progress of Commercial Banking in India

	1969	*1980*	*1991*	*1995*	*2000*	*2005*
1. No. of Commercial Banks	73	154	272	284	298	288
2. No. of Bank Offices	8262	34594	60570	64234	67868	68339
Of which: Rural and Semi-urban Bank Ofices	5172	23227	46550	46602	47693	47491
3. Population per Office ('000s)	64	16	14	15	15	16
4. Per Capita Deposit (Rs.)	88	738	2368	4242	8542	16699
5. Per Capita Credit (Rs.)	68	457	1434	2320	4555	10135
6. Priority Sector Advances (per cent)	15	37	39	34	35	40
7. Deposits (per cent of National Income)	16	36	48	48	54	65

Source: Reserve Bank of India.

In the post-reform period, banks have consistently maintained high rates of growth in their assets and liabilities. On the liability side, deposits continue to account for about 80 per cent of the total liabilities. On the asset side, the shares of loans and advances on the one hand and investments on the other hand have seen marked cycles, reflecting banks' portfolio preferences as well as growth cycles in the economy. The share of loans and advances declined in the second half of 1990s responding to slowdown in investment demand as well as tightening of prudential norms. With investment demand again picking up in the past 3-4 years, banks' credit portfolio has witnessed sharp growth. Banks' investment in gilts have accordingly seen a significant decline in the past one year, although it still remains above the minimum statutory requirement. Thus, while in the 1990s, greater investments and aversion to credit risk exposure may have deterred banks from undertaking their 'core function' of financial intermediation viz., accepting deposits and extending credit, they seem to have struck a greater balance in recent years between investments and loans and advances. The improved atmosphere for recovery created in the recent years seems to have induced banks to put greater efforts in extending loans.

(b) Capital position and asset quality

Since the beginning of reforms, a set of micro-prudential measures have been stipulated aimed at imparting strength to the banking system as well as ensuring safety. With regard to prudential requirements, income recognition and asset classification (IRAC) norms have been strengthened to approach international best practice. Initially, while it was deemed to attain a CRAR of 8 per cent in a phased manner, it was subsequently raised to 9 per cent with effect from 1999-2000. The overall capital position of commercial banks has witnessed a marked improvement during the reform period (Table 6.2). Illustratively, as at end-March 2005, 86 out of the 88 commercial banks operating in India maintained CRAR at or above 9 per cent. The corresponding figure for 1995-96 was 54 out of 92 banks. Improved capitalisation of public sector banks was initially brought through substantial infusion of funds by government to recapitalise these banks. Subsequently, in order to mitigate the budgetary impact and to introduce market discipline, public sector banks were allowed to raise funds from the market through equity issuance subject to the maintenance of 51 per cent public ownership. Ownership in public sector banks is now well diversified. As at end-March 2005, the holding by the general public in six banks ranged between 40 and 49 per cent and in 12 banks between 30 and 49 per cent. It was only in four banks that the Government holding was more than 90 per cent.

TABLE 6.2

Distribution of Commercial Banks According to Risk-Weighted Capital Adequacy

Year	*Below 4 per cent*	*Between 4-9 per cent**	*Between 9-10 per cent@*	*Above 10 per cent*	*Total*
1995-96	8	9	33	42	6
2000-01	3	2	11	84	100
2004-05	1	1	8	78	88

* Relates to 4-8 per cent before 1999-2000.
@ Relates to 8-10 per cent before 1999-2000.
Source: Reserve Bank of India.

Despite tightening norms, there has been considerable improvement in the asset quality of banks. India transited to a 90-day NPL recognition norm (from 180-day norm) in 2004. Nonetheless, nonperforming loans (NPLs), as ratios of both total advances and assets, have declined substantially and consistently since the mid-1990s (Table 6.3). Improvement in the credit appraisal process, upturn of the business cycle, new initiatives for resolution of NPLs (including promulgation of the Securitisation and Reconstruction of Financial Assets and Enforcement of Security Interest

TABLE 6.3

Non-Performing Loans (NPL) of Scheduled Commercial Banks

	Gross NPL/ Advances	*Gross NPL/ Assets*	*Net NPL/ Advances*	*Net NPL/ Assets*
1996-97	15.7	7	8.1	3.3
1997-98	14.4	6.4	7.3	3.0
1998-99	14.7	6.2	7.6	2.9
1999-00	12.7	5.5	6.8	2.7
2000-01	11.4	4.9	6.2	2.5
2001-02	10.4	4.6	5.5	2.3
2002-03	8.8	4	4.4	1.9
2003-04	7.2	3.3	2.9	1.2
2004-05	5.2	2.6	2	0.9

(SARFAESI) Act), and greater provisioning and write-off of NPLs enabled by greater profitability, have kept incremental NPLs low.

(c) Competition and efficiency

In consonance with the objective of enhancing efficiency and productivity of banks through greater competition—from new private sector banks and entry and expansion of several foreign banks—there has been a consistent decline in the share of public sector banks in total assets of commercial banks. Notwithstanding such transformation, the public sector banks still account for nearly three-fourths of assets and income. Public sector banks have also responded to the new challenges of competition, as reflected in their increased share in the overall profit of the banking sector. This suggests that, with operational flexibility, public sector banks are competing relatively effectively with private sector and foreign banks. Public sector bank managements are now probably more attuned to the market consequences of their activities (Mohan, 2006a).

Shares of Indian private sector banks, especially new private sector banks established in the 1990s, in the total income and assets of the banking system have improved considerably since the mid-1990s (Table 6.4). The reduction in the asset share of foreign banks, however, is partially due to their increased focus on off-balance sheet non-fund based business.

TABLE 6.4

Bank Group-wise Shares: Select Indicators

(Per cent)

	1995-96	*2000-01*	*2004-05*
Public Sector Banks			
Income	82.5	78.4	75.6
Expenditure	84.2	78.9	75.8
Total Assets	84.4	79.5	74.4
Net Profit	-39.1	67.4	73.3
Gross Profit	74.3	69.9	75.9
New Private Sector Banks			
Income	1.5	5.7	11.8
Expenditure	1.3	5.5	11.4
Total Assets	1.5	6.1	12.9
Net Profit	17.8	10.0	15.0
Gross Profit	2.5	6.9	10.7
Foreign Banks			
Income	9.4	9.1	7.0
Expenditure	8.3	8.8	6.6
Total Assets	7.9	7.9	6.8
Net Profit	79.8	14.8	9.7
Gross Profit	15.6	15.7	9.0

Source: Reserve Bank of India.

Efficiency gains are also reflected in containment of the operating expenditure as a proportion of total assets (Table 6.5). This has been achieved in spite of

TABLE 6.5

Earnings and Expenses of Scheduled Commercial Banks

Year	*Total Assets*	*Total Earnings*	*Interest Earnings*	*Total Expenses*	*Interest Expenses*	*Establishment Expenses*	*Net Interest Earning*
1969	68	4	4	4	2	1	2
		(6.2)	(5.3)	(5.5)	2.8)	(2.1)	(2.5)
1980	582	42	38	42	27	10	10
		(7.3)	(6.4)	(7.2)	(4.7)	(1.7)	(1.8)
1991	3275	304	275	297	190	76	86
		(9.3)	(8.4)	(9.1)	(5.8)	(2.3)	(2.6)
2000	11055	1149	992	1077	690	276	301
		(10.4)	(9.0)	(9.7)	(6.2)	(2.5)	(2.7)
2005	22746	1867	1531	1660	866	491	665
		(8.2)	(6.7)	(7.3)	(3.8)	(2.2)	(2.9)

Note: Figures in brackets are ratios to total assets.
Source: Reserve Bank of India.

TABLE 6.6

Intermediation Cost of Scheduled Commercial Banks: 1996-2005

(as percentage to total asset)

Year (end-March)	*Public Sector Banks*	*New Private Banks*	*Foreign Banks*	*All Scheduled Commercial Banks*
1996	2.99	1.82	2.78	2.94
1997	2.88	1.94	3.04	2.85
1998	2.66	1.76	2.99	2.63
1999	2.65	1.74	3.40	2.65
2000	2.52	1.42	3.12	2.48
2001	2.72	1.75	3.05	2.64
2002	2.29	1.12	3.03	2.19
2003	2.25	1.95	2.79	2.24
2004	2.20	2.02	2.76	2.20
2005	2.03	2.06	2.85	2.09

Note: Figures in brackets are ratios to total assets.
Source: Reserve Bank of India.

large expenditures incurred by Indian banks in installation and upgradation of information technology and, in the case of public sector banks, large expenditures under voluntary pre-mature retirement of nearly 12 per cent of their total staff strength.

Improvements in efficiency of the banking system are also reflected, *inter alia*, in costs of intermediation. which, defined as the ratio of operating expense to total assets, witnessed a gradual reduction in the post-reform period across various bank groups barring foreign banks (Table 6.6). However, intermediation costs of banks in India still tend to be higher than those in developed countries. Similarly, the cost-income-ratio (defined as the ratio of operating expenses to total income less interest expense) of Indian banks has shown a declining trend during the post-reform period. For example, Indian banks paid roughly 45 per cent of their net income towards managing labour and physical capital in 2004 as against nearly 72 per cent in 1993. Indian banks thus recorded a net cost saving of nearly 27 per cent of their net income during the post-reform period.

(d) Productivity

What is most encouraging is the very significant improvement in the productivity of the Indian banking system, in terms of various productivity indicators. The business per employee of Indian banks increased over three-fold in real terms from Rs. 5.4 million in 1992 to Rs.17.3 million in 2005, exhibiting an annual compound growth rate of more than 9 per cent (Table 6.7). The profit per employee increased from Rs. 20,000 to Rs. 130,000 over the same period, implying a compound growth of around 15.5 per cent. Branch productivity also recorded concomitant improvements. These improvements could be driven by two factors: *technological improvement*, which expands the range of production possibilities and a *catching up effect*, as peer pressure amongst banks compels them to raise productivity levels. Here, the role of new business practices, new approaches and expansion of the business that was introduced by the new private banks has been of the utmost importance.

TABLE 6.7

Select Productivity Indicators of Scheduled Commercial Banks

Year	*Business per employee*	*Profit per employee*	*Business per branch*
1992	5.4	0.02	109.9
1996	6.0	0.01	119.6
2000	9.7	0.05	179.4
2005	17.3	0.13	267.0

Source: Statistical Tables relating to Banks in India.

6.2:4 Looking at Future

The next point of debate is the future of banks of India. As long as the overriding mantra for banks is capital adequacy and capital adequacy alone, not just at any point of time, but on an ongoing basis, it is difficult to visualise that banks that exist as of now will all continue to do so in the next five years or so. A few will; most won't. Recapitalising weak banks is no longer possible. On the other hand, prudential norms will only get tighter. Therefore, banks should prepare themselves to meet the challenge. Following assertions are noteworthy in this regard:

1. Apart from the State Bank of India, there are just about four or five other large PSU banks that can be expected to hold their own in the years ahead. They need to get their act together on two fronts, take their level of provisions for bad debts to 70 percent from their current levels of 40-60 percent and put in place appropriate technology of world class standards that will make them be seen more as virtual banks rather than of the brick and mortar stuff. This by itself will lead to consolidation of their respective network which may stand reduced to 40 percent or 50 percent. They must be given autonomy, operational and administrative, and be completely Board driven including the selection of the CEO.
2. There are two or three PSU banks that are sound in the financials but not big enough to carry the day on their own. In fact, they are pretty targets for take-over even as of now with potential suitors prowling around. Who should decide their future, the State or the Market?
3. There is the third rung of PSU banks where the problem is a lot more serious to handle.

There will be political compulsions to keep them going but the markets may not allow for that beyond a point. It is best that they tidy themselves up in the time they have at their disposal: raise their provisioning for bad debt up to say 50 percent of their loan losses, reduce their network considerably, shed unproductive business practices of the past. In fact, for the vulnerable category of banks, it might make eminent sense to segregate the assets and liabilities of different business segments and re-integrate them in a manner that will appeal to different players in the market, other Indian banks, financial institutions and foreign banks.

The problems specific to each Public Sector Banks have to be left to be tackled by a board specifically selected and manned by persons who can combine professionalism with a flair for democratic accountability; with operational freedom and flexibility insulated from interference from bureaucratic and political establishments. No outside authority, statutory or otherwise, can be a proxy for it.

4. There are two types of private sector banks, the old and the new. As far as the old (mostly regional banks) are concerned, fatigue and inadequacy of capital will lead to their mergers sooner than later. And as far as the new banks are concerned, it is true that they started on a clean slate, became technology savvy and offered attractive products and services. But it is still too early to assert that their corporate governance and risk management are far superior to what obtains in the PSBs. Already their shake-out is imminent as evidenced by a couple of mergers. The rest will follow the same fate. The only exception is the HDFC Bank which is a classic role model of banking in the private

sector with a promising future. Even here, it will be compelled to shift from organic growth to acquisitions to reach critical mass to stand alone.

5. There have been quite a few foreign banks operating in the country, and there are at least five of them who have completed a hundred years of operation each. For the most part, they all had to rest content with muted growth over the years on grounds of policy that they had to operate within. However, with the opening up of the economy, their prospects for growth and expansion had brightened. This is not to mean that all of them will do so. In fact, in the recent past, at least three banks have taken the exit route in keeping with the corporate policies in their host countries.
   As of now, there is evidence to suggest that at least 3 major international banks will get aggressive on the Indian banking scene—Citibank, ABN-AMRO and HSBC. But in the foreseeable future, one can expect three to four banks from the U.S.; two from Europe and two from the Eastern hemisphere, to make their presence in India increasingly felt. The global franchise that these institutions enjoy worldwide, coupled with their financial muscle, will facilitate this taking place[12]
6. There are two sectors in the Indian economy that received special focus—small scale industries in view of their vast employment potential, and agriculture which was the backbone of post-Independence India. Perhaps, it would be worthwhile to strengthen SIDBI to address the problems and growth of the SSI sector more comprehensively than hitherto. Likewise, NABARD might be commissioned with complete responsibility over the agriculture sector, even if necessary by taking

over the agricultural portfolios along with the infrastructure spread across banks, both in the public and private sector. Even the RRB's (Regional Rural Banks) can be brought under the exclusive coverage of NABARD.

In other words, commercial banks may be freed of the responsibility towards agriculture which cannot all the time be run on a commercial basis. Such an arrangement would necessary entail additional infusion of capital in NABARD to sustain concentrated attention and promote growth in agriculture. In due course, it is hoped that with the introduction of high tech, in agriculture, and with the certainty of agricultural produce entering the export market, NABARD should be in a position to manage agriculture on commercial terms.

7. As the economy evolved over the years, several multi-sectoral specific financial institutions emerged over time and they are all in the business of lending to their specific sector. However, such an arrangement runs two risks: one of overlapping or duplicatingeach other's function at their respective peripheries, and the other, which is a bit more serious, their not being able to manage road-blocks caused by trade cycles which hit each sector by turn. The possible way out is to consolidate these institutions with two major power houses, one to cater to the needs of core infrastructure and the other to earmark for non-core developmental activities. Treasury management of such an arrangement could become more efficient and yet meet the needs of all sectors more scientifically.

   Conclusively, it can be said that in any banking system, no bank, howsoever owned, can survive unless it continuously strives to transform its organization as a self-governing, self-correcting and self-adjusting entity. For banks to grapple with these problems and manage the future, structural and institutional rigidities need to be eased in two critical areas: comprehensive legal support for recovery of bad debts and a fundamental change in the pattern of governance for the PSB's. While the recent ordinance for recovery of bad debts and securitisation of assets is a godsend, it remains to be seen whether dilutions to it take place when the bill is finally passed.

6.3: REFORMS IN THE MONETARY POLICY FRAMEWORK[13]

The basic emphasis of monetary policy since the initiation of reforms has been to reduce market segmentation in the financial sector through increased inter-linkages between various segments of the financial market including money, government security and forex market. The key policy development that has enabled a more independent monetary policy environment as well as the development of Government securities market was the discontinuation of automatic monetisation of the government's fiscal deficit since April 1997 through an agreement between the Government and the Reserve Bank of India in September 1994. In order to meet the challenges thrown by financial liberalisation and the growing complexities of monetary management, the Reserve Bank switched from a monetary targeting framework to a multiple indicator approach from 1998-99. Short-term interest rates have emerged as the key indicators of the monetary policy stance. A significant shift is the move towards market-based instruments away from direct instruments of monetary management. In line with international trends, the Reserve Bank has put in place a liquidity management framework in which market liquidity is managed through a mix of open market (including repo) operations (OMOs), changes in reserve requirements and standing facilities, reinforced by changes in the policy rates, including the Bank Rate and the short-term (overnight) policy rate. In order to carry out these market operations effectively, the Reserve Bank has initiated several measures to strengthen the health of its balance sheet. Over the past few years, the process of monetary policy formulation has become relatively more articulate, consultative and participative with external orientation, while the internal work processes have also been re-engineered. A recent notable step in this direction is the constitution of a Technical Advisory Committee on Monetary Policy comprising external experts to advise the Reserve Bank on the stance of monetary policy

6.3:1 Objectives of Monetary Policy Framework

- Twin objectives of "maintaining price stability" and "ensuring availability of adequate credit to productive sectors of the economy to support growth" continue to govern the stance of monetary policy, though the relative emphasis on these objectives has varied depending on the importance of maintaining an appropriate balance.
- Reflecting the increasing development of financial market and greater liberalisation, use of broad money as an intermediate target has been de-emphasised and a multiple indicator approach has been adopted.
- Emphasis has been put on development of multiple instruments to transmit liquidity and interest rate signals in the short-term in a flexible and bi-directional manner.
- Increase of the interlinkage between various segments of the financial market including money, government security and forex markets.

6.3:2 Instruments

- Move from direct instruments (such as, administered interest rates, reserve requirements, selective credit control) to indirect instruments (such as, open market operations, purchase and repurchase of government securities) for the conduct of monetary policy.
- Introduction of Liquidity Adjustment Facility (LAF), which operates through repo and reverse repo auctions, effectively provide a corridor for short-term interest rate. LAF has emerged as the tool for both liquidity management and also as a signalling devise for interest rate in the overnight market.
- Use of open market operations to deal with overall market liquidity situation those emanating from capital flows.
- Introduction of Market Stabilisation Scheme (MSS) as an additional instrument to deal with enduring capital inflows without affecting short-term liquidity management role of LAF.

6.3:3 Developmental Measures

- Discontinuation of automatic monetization through an agreement between the Government and the Reserve Bank. Rationalization of Treasury Bill market. Introduction of delivery versus payment system and deepening of inter-bank repo market.
- Introduction of Primary Dealers in the government securities market to play the role of market maker.
- Amendment of Securities Contracts Regulation Act (SCRA), to create the regulatory framework.

- Deepening of government securities market by making the interest rates on such securities market-related.
- Introduction of auction of government securities.
- Development of a risk-free credible yield curve in the government securities market as a benchmark for related markets.
- Development of pure inter-bank call money market. Non-bank participants to participate in other money market instruments.
- Introduction of automated screen-based trading in government securities through Negotiated Dealing System (NDS). Setting up of risk-free payments and system in government securities through Clearing Corporation of India Limited (CCIL).
- Deepening of forex market and increased autonomy of Authorized Dealers.

6.3:4 Institutional Measures

- Setting up of Technical Advisory Committee on Monetary Policy with outside experts to review macro-economic and monetary developments and advise the Reserve Bank on the stance of monetary policy.
- Creation of a separate Financial Market Department within the RBI.
- Following the reforms, the financial markets have now grown in size, depth and activity paving the way for flexible use of indirect instruments by the Reserve Bank to pursue its objectives. It is recognized that stability in financial markets is critical for efficient price discovery. Excessive volatility in exchange rates and interest rates masks the underlying value of these variables and gives rise to confusing signals. Since both the exchange rate and interest rate are the key prices

reflecting the cost of money, it is particularly important for the efficient functioning of the economy that they be market determined and be easily observed. The Reserve Bank has, therefore, put in place a liquidity management framework in the form of a liquidity adjustment facility (LAF) for the facilitation of forex and money market transactions that result in price discovery sans excessive volatility. The LAF coupled with OMOs and the Market Stabilisation Scheme (MSS) has provided the Reserve Bank greater flexibility to manage market liquidity in consonance with its policy stance. The introduction of LAF had several advantages. First and foremost, it helped the transition from direct instruments of monetary control to indirect and, in the process, certain dead weight loss for the system was saved.

- Second, it has provided monetary authorities with greater flexibility in determining both the quantum of adjustment as well as the rates by responding to the needs of the system on a daily basis.
- Third, it enabled the Reserve Bank to modulate the supply of funds on a daily basis to meet day-to-day liquidity mismatches.
- Fourth, it enabled the Reserve Bank to affect demand for funds through policy rate changes.
- Fifth and most important, it helped stabilise short-term money market rates.
- LAF has now emerged as the principal operating instrument of monetary policy. Although there is no formal targeting of a point overnight interest rate, the LAF is designed to nudge overnight interest rates within a specified corridor, the difference between the fixed repo and reverse repo rates currently being 100 basis points. The evidence

suggests that this effort has been largely successful with the overnight interest rate moving out of this corridor for only a few brief periods. The LAF has enabled the Reserve Bank to de-emphasise targeting of bank reserves and focus increasingly on interest rates. This has helped in reducing the cash reserve ratio (CRR) without loss of monetary control. Given the growing role played by expectations, the stance of monetary policy and its rationale are communicated to the public in a variety of ways. The enactment of the Fiscal Responsibility and Budget Management Act, 2003 has strengthened the institutional mechanism further: from April 2006 onwards, the Reserve Bank is no longer permitted to subscribe to government securities in the primary market. The development of the monetary policy framework has also involved a great deal of institutional initiatives to enable efficient functioning of the money market: development of appropriate trading, payments and settlement systems along with technological infrastructure.

6.3:5 Liquidity Management by the Reserve Bank[14]

Following the initiation of reforms in India in the early 1990s, the monetary policy framework also witnessed a significant transformation. While the conduct of monetary policy continues to be guided by the twin objectives of maintaining price stability and to provide appropriate liquidity to meet genuine credit needs of the economy, maintenance of financial stability has also emerged as a key consideration in the conduct of monetary policy. Concomitantly, with the growing market-orientation of the economy, there has been a shift from direct instruments of monetary management to an increasing reliance on indirect instruments. In the context of this shift towards indirect instruments and in line with international trends, the Reserve Bank has put in place a liquidity management framework. Liquidity management is carried out through open market operations (OMO) in the form of outright purchases/ sales of Government securities and reverse repo/repo operations, supplemented by the Market Stabilisation Scheme (MSS). The Liquidity Adjustment Facility (LAF), introduced in June 2000, enables the Reserve Bank to manage day-to-day liquidity or short-term mismatches under varied financial market conditions in order to ensure stable conditions in the overnight money market. The LAF operates through reverse repo and repo auctions, thereby setting a corridor for the short-term interest rate consistent with the policy objectives. The introduction of LAF had several advantages. First, it helped the transition from direct instruments of monetary control to indirect instruments. Second, it enabled the Reserve Bank to modulate the supply of funds on a daily basis to meet day-to-day liquidity mismatches. Third, it enabled the Reserve Bank to affect demand for funds through policy rate changes. Finally, it helped stabilise short-term money market rates. Open market operations (OMOs) through outright sale and purchase of securities are also an important array of tools of the Reserve Bank's monetary management. Apart from being directed at influencing enduring liquidity, OMOs can also be undertaken as 'switch' operations through purchase of gilts of a particular maturity against the sale of another to provide liquidity. In view of the large stock of Government securities in its portfolio, the OMOs were used effectively by the Reserve Bank from the second half of the 1990s to 2003-04 to manage the impact of capital flows. However, in the context of sustained large capital flows, large-scale OMOs led to a decline in the Reserve Bank's holdings of Government securities. The finite stock of Government securities held by the Reserve Bank as well as the legal restrictions on the Reserve Bank on issuing its own paper were seen as placing constraints on future sterilization operations. Accordingly, an innovative scheme in the form of MSS was introduced in April 2004 wherein Government of India dated securities/Treasury Bills are being issued to absorb enduring surplus liquidity. These dated securities/ Treasury Bills are the same as those issued for normal market borrowings and this avoids segmentation of the market. With the introduction of MSS, the pressure of sterilisation on LAF has declined considerably and the LAF operations have been able to fine-tune liquidity on a day-to-day basis more effectively. The MSS has provided the flexibility to the Reserve Bank to not only absorb liquidity but also to inject liquidity in case of need. The efficacy of various liquidity management tools was reflected clearly in the Reserve Bank's market operations during 2005-06. Liquidity surpluses declined during October-November 2005 due to sustained demand for bank credit and currency demand during the festival season. Ahead of the redemption of the IMDs in December 2005, the Reserve Bank, making a forward looking assessment, began to unwind sterilised liquidity in a calibrated manner from September 2005. As part of this unwinding, fresh issuances under the MSS were suspended between November 2005 and April 2006. Redemptions of securities/Treasury Bills issued earlier along with active management of liquidity through repo/reverse repo operations under LAF during January-March 2006 provided liquidity to the market. Some private placement during March 2006 and purchases of foreign exchange from the market also injected liquidity. The various tools of liquidity management, thus, provided the flexibility to Reserve Bank to maintain liquidity conditions and conduct monetary policy in accordance with the stated objectives.

6.4: FINANCIAL MARKETS REFORMS[15]

The success of a framework that relies on indirect instruments of monetary management such as interest rates, is contingent upon the extent and speed with which changes in the central bank's policy rate are transmitted to the spectrum of market interest rates and exchange rate in the economy and onward to the real sector. Given the critical role played by financial markets in this transmission mechanism, the Reserve Bank has taken a number of initiatives to develop a pure inter-bank money market. A noteworthy and desirable development has been the substantial migration of money market activity from the un-collateralized call money segment to the collateralized market repo and collateralized borrowing and lending obligations (CBLO) markets. The shift of activity from uncollateralized to collateralized segments of the market has largely resulted from measures relating to limiting the call market transactions to banks and primary dealers only. This policy-induced shift is in the interest of financial stability and is yielding results. Concomitantly, efforts have been made to broaden and deepen the Government securities market and foreign exchange market so as to enable the process of efficient price discovery in respect of interest rates and the exchange rate. It is pertinent to note that the phased approach to development of financial markets has enabled RBI's withdrawal from the primary market since April 1, 2006. This step completes the transition to a fully market-based system in the G-sec. market. Looking ahead, as per the recommendations of the Twelfth Finance Commission, the Central Government would cease to raise resources on behalf of State Governments, who, henceforth, have to access the market directly. Thus, State Government's capability in raising resources will be market determined and based on their own financial health. In order to ensure a smooth transition to the new regime, restructuring of current institutional processes has already been initiated. These steps are helping to achieve the desired integration in the conduct of monetary operations.

6.4:1 Reforms in the Government Securities Market

(A) Institutional Measures

- Administered interest rates on government securities were replaced by an auction system for price discovery.
- Automatic monetisation of fiscal deficit through the issue of *ad hoc* Treasury Bills was phased out.
- Primary Dealers (PD) were introduced as market-makers in the government securities market.
- For ensuring transparency in the trading of government securities, Delivery *versus* Payment (D *v.* P) settlement system was introduced.
- Repurchase agreement (repo) was introduced as a tool of short-term liquidity adjustment. Subsequently, the Liquidity Adjustment Facility (LAF) was introduced.
- LAF operates through repo and reverse repo auctions and provide a corridor for short-term interest rate. LAF has emerged as the tool for both liquidity management and also signaling device for interest rates in the overnight market. The Second LAF (SLAF) was introduced in November 2005.
- Market Stabilisation Scheme (MSS) has been introduced, which has expanded the instruments available to the Reserve Bank for managing the enduring surplus liquidity in the system.
- Effective April 1, 2006, RBI has withdrawn from participating in primary market auctions of Government paper.

- Banks have been permitted to undertake primary dealer business while primary dealers are being allowed to diversify their business.
- Short sales in Government securities is being permitted in a calibrated manner while guidelines for 'when issued' market have been issued recently.

(B) Increase in Instruments in the Government Securities Market

- 91-day Treasury bill was introduced for managing liquidity and benchmarking. Zero Coupon Bonds, Floating Rate Bonds, Capital Indexed Bonds were issued and exchange traded interest rate futures were introduced. OTC interest rate derivatives like IRS/FRAs were introduced.
- Outright sale of Central Government dated security that are not owned have been permitted, subject to the same being covered by outright purchase from the secondary market within the same trading day subject to certain conditions.
- Repo status has been granted to State Government securities in order to improve secondary market liquidity.

(C) Enabling Measures

- Foreign Institutional Investors (FIIs) were allowed to invest in government securities subject to certain limits.
- Introduction of automated screen-based trading in government securities through Negotiated Dealing System (NDS).
- Setting up of risk-free payments and settlement system in government securities

through Clearing Corporation of India Limited (CCIL).

- Phased introduction of Real Time Gross Settlement System (RTGS).
- Introduction of trading in government securities on stock exchanges for promoting retailing in such securities, permitting non-banks to participate in repo market.
- Recent measures include introduction of NDS-OM and T+1 settlement norms.
- As regards the foreign exchange market, reforms focused on market development with inbuilt prudential safeguards so that the market would not be destabilised in the process (Reddy, 2002). The move towards a market-based exchange rate regime in 1993 and the subsequent adoption of current account convertibility were the key measures in reforming the Indian foreign exchange market. Banks are increasingly being given greater autonomy to undertake foreign exchange operations. In order to deepen the foreign exchange market, a large number of products have been introduced and entry of new players has been allowed in the market.

Summing up, reforms were designed to enable the process of efficient price discovery and induce greater internal efficiency in resource allocation within the banking system. While the policy measures in the pre-1990s period were essentially devoted to financial deepening, the focus of reforms in the last decade and a half has been engendering greater efficiency and productivity in the banking system. Reforms in the monetary policy framework were aimed at providing operational flexibility to the Reserve Bank in its conduct of monetary policy by relaxing the constraint imposed by passive monetisation of the fisc.

6.5: REFORMS IN FOREIGN EXCHANGE MARKET

(A) Exchange Rate Regime

- Evolution of exchange rate regime from a single-currency fixed-exchange rate system to fixing the value of rupee against a basket of currencies and further to market-determined floating exchange rate regime.
- Adoption of convertibility of rupee for current account transactions with acceptance of Article VIII of the Articles of Agreement of the IMF. *De facto* full capital account convertibility for non-residents and calibrated liberalisation of transactions undertaken for capital account purposes in the case of residents.

(B) Institutional Framework

- Replacement of the earlier Foreign Exchange Regulation Act (FERA), 1973 by the market-friendly Foreign Exchange Management Act, 1999. Delegation of considerable powers by RBI to Authorised Dealers to release foreign exchange for a variety of purposes.

(C) Increase in Instruments in the Foreign Exchange Market

- Development of rupee-foreign currency swap market.
- Introduction of additional hedging instruments, such as, foreign currency-rupee options.
- Authorised dealers permitted to use innovative products like cross-currency options, interest rate swaps (IRS) and currency swaps, caps/collars and forward rate agreements (FRAs) in the international forex market.

(D) Liberalisation Measures

- Authorised dealers permitted to initiate trading positions, borrow and invest in overseas market subject to certain specifications and ratification by respective Banks' Boards. Banks are also permitted to fix interest rates on non-resident deposits, subject to certain specifications, use derivative products for asset-liability management and fix overnight open position limits and gap limits in the foreign exchange market, subject to ratification by RBI.
- Permission to various participants in the foreign exchange market, including exporters, Indians investing abroad, FIIs, to avail forward cover and enter into swap transactions without any limit subject to genuine underlying exposure.
- FIIs and NRIs permitted to trade in exchange-traded derivative contracts subject to certain conditions.
- Foreign exchange earners permitted to maintain foreign currency accounts. Residents are permitted to open such accounts within the general limit of US $ 25,000 per year.

6.6: IMPACT OF MONETARY POLICY

What has been the impact of the monetary policy? From the innumerable dimensions of impact of monetary policy, let me focus on some select elements.

(A) Inflation

Turning to an assessment of monetary policy, it would be reasonable to assert that monetary policy has been largely successful in meeting its key objectives in the post-reforms period. Just as the late 1990s witnessed a fall in inflation worldwide, so too has India.

Inflation has averaged close to five per cent per annum in the decade gone by, notably lower than that of eight per cent in the previous four decades (Chart 1).

CHART 1

Whoesale Price Inflation in India

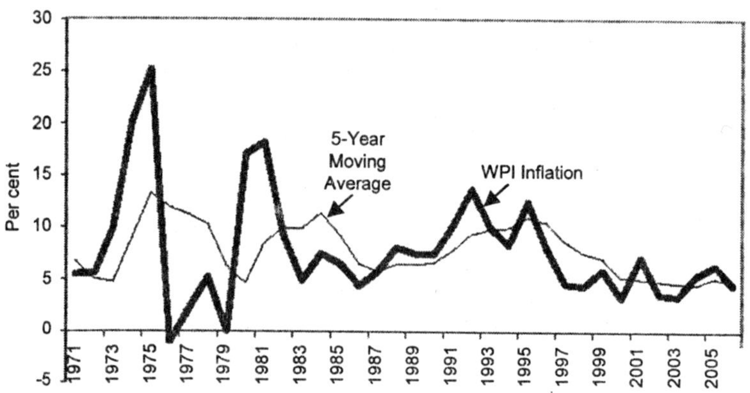

Structural reforms since the early 1990s coupled with improved monetary-fiscal interface and reforms in the Government securities market enabled better monetary management from the second half of the 1990s onwards. More importantly, the regime of low and stable inflation has, in turn, stabilised inflation expectations and inflation tolerance in the economy has come down. It is encouraging to note that despite record high international crude oil prices, inflation remains low and inflation expectations also remain stable. Since inflation expectations are a key determinant of the actual inflation outcome, and given the lags in monetary transmission, we have been taking preemptive measures to keep inflation expectations stable. As discussed further below, a number of instruments, both existing as well as new, were employed to modulate liquidity conditions to achieve the desired objectives. A number of other factors such as increased competition, productivity gains and strong corporate balance sheets have also contributed to this low and stable inflation environment, but it appears that calibrated monetary measures had a substantial role to play as well.

(B) Challenges Posed by Large Capital Inflows

It is pertinent to note that inflation could be contained since the mid-1990s, despite challenges posed by large capital flows. Following the reforms in the external sector, foreign investment flows have been encouraged. Reflecting the strong growth prospects of the Indian economy, the country has received large investment inflows, both direct and portfolio, since 1993-94 as compared with negligible levels till the early 1990s. Total foreign investment flows (direct and portfolio) increased from US$ 111 million in 1990-91 to US$ 17,496 million in 2005-06 (April-February). Over the same period, current account deficits remained modest —averaging one per cent of GDP since 1991-92 and in fact recorded small surpluses during 2001-04. With capital flows remaining in excess of the current financing requirements, the overall balance of payments recorded persistent surpluses leading to an increase in reserves. Despite such large accretion to reserves, inflation could be contained reflecting appropriate policy responses by the Reserve Bank and the Government. The emergence of foreign exchange surplus lending to continuing and large accretion to reserves since the mid-1990s has been a novel experience for India after experiencing chronic balance of payment problems for almost four decades. These surpluses began to arise after the opening of the current account, reduction in trade protection, and partial opening of the capital account from the early to mid 1990s. The exchange rate flexibility practiced since 1992-93 has been an important part of the policy response needed to manage capital flows. The composition of India's balance of payments has undergone significant change since the mid-1990s. (Table 6.8)

TABLE 6.8

Trends in India's Balance of Payment in Post-Reform Period

(As percent of GDP)

Year	*Exports*	*Imports*	*Net Invisibles*	*Trade Balance*	*Current Account balance*
1990-91	6.2	9.4	-0.1	-3.2	-3.2
1991-92	7.3	8.3	0.7	-1.1	-0.4
1992-93	7.8	10.2	0.6	-2.4	-1.8
1993-94	8.8	10.3	1.1	-1.6	-0.4
1994-95	8.3	11.1	1.8	-2.8	-1.0
1995-96	9.1	12.3	1.6	-3.2	-1.7
1996-97	8.9	12.7	2.7	-3.8	-1.2
1997-98	8.7	12.5	2.4	-3.8	-1.4
1998-99	8.3	11.5	2.2	-3.2	-1.0
1999-00	8.4	12.4	3.0	-4.0	-1.1
2000-01	9.8	13.0	2.6	-3.1	-0.5
2001-02	9.4	12.0	2.9	-2.6	0.3

Source: *Economic Survey,* 1997-98, 2002-03, p. 101.

In the current account, the growth of software exports and, more recently, of business process outsourcing, has increased the share of service exports on a continuing basis. Even more significant is the growth in remittances from non-resident Indians (NRIs), now amounting to about 3 per cent of GDP. The latter exhibit a great deal of stability. The remittances appear to consist mainly of maintenance flows that do not seem to be affected by exchange rate, inflation, or growth rate changes. Thus, the Indian current account exhibits only a small deficit, or a surplus, despite the existence of merchandise trade deficit that has grown from 3.2 per cent of GDP in the mid-1990s to 5.3 per cent in 2004-05. On the capital account, unlike other emerging markets, portfolio flows have far exceeded foreign direct investment in India in recent years.

Coupled with other capital flows consisting of official and commercial debt, NRI deposits, and other banking capital, net capital flows now amount to about 4.4 per cent of GDP. The downturn in the Indian business cycle during the early part of this decade led to the emergence of a current account surplus, particularly because the existence of the relative exchange rate insensitive remittance flows. Consequently, foreign exchange reserves grew by more than US $ 120 billion between April 2000 and April 2006.

The management of these flows involved a mix of policy responses that had to keep an eye on the level of reserves, monetary policy objectives related to the interest rate, liquidity management, and maintenance of healthy financial market conditions with financial stability. Decisions to do with sterilisation involve judgements on the character of the excess forex flows: are they durable, semi-durable or transitory. This judgements itself depends on assessments about both the real economy and of financial sector developments. Moreover, at any given time, some flows could be of an enduring nature whereas others could be of short-term, and hence reversible. On an operational basis, sterilisation operations through open market operations (OMOs) should take care of durable flows, whereas transitory flows can be managed through the normal daily operations of the LAF. By 2003-04, sterilisation operations, however, started appearing to be constrained by the finite stock of Government securities held by the Reserve Bank. The legal restrictions on the Reserve Bank on issuing its own paper also placed constraints on future sterilisation operations. Accordingly, an innovative scheme in the form of Market Stabilisation Scheme (MSS) was introduced in April 2004 wherein Government of India dated securities/Treasury Bills are being issued to absorb enduring surplus liquidity. These dated securities/Treasury Bills are the same as those issued for normal market borrowings and this avoids segmentation of the market. Moreover, the MSS scheme brings transparency in regard to costs associated with sterilisation operations. Hitherto, the costs of sterilisation were fully borne by the Reserve Bank in the first instance and its impact was transmitted to the Government in the form of lower profit transfers. With the introduction of the MSS, the cost in terms of interest payments would be borne by the Government itself in a transparent manner. It is relevant to note that the MSS has provided the Reserve Bank the flexibility to not only absorb liquidity but also to inject liquidity in case of need. This was evident during the second half of 2005-06 when liquidity conditions became tight in view of strong credit demand, increase in Government's surplus with the Reserve Bank and outflows on account of bullet redemption of India Millennium Deposits (about US $ 7 billion). In view of these circumstances, fresh issuances under the MSS were suspended between November 2005 and April 2006. Redemptions of securities/Treasury Bills issued earlier—along with active management of liquidity through repo/reverse repo operations under Liquidity Adjustment Facility—provided liquidity to the market and imparted stability to financial markets (Chart 2).

CHART 2

Liquidity Management

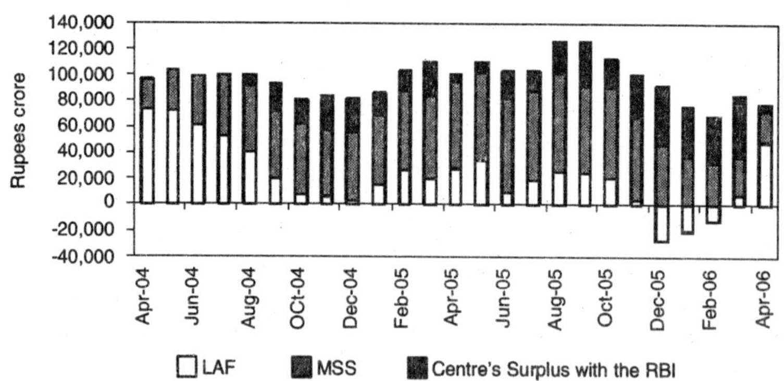

With liquidity conditions improving, it was decided to again start issuing securities under the MSS from

May 2006 onwards. The issuance of securities under the MSS has thus enabled the Reserve Bank to improve liquidity management in the system, to maintain stability in the foreign exchange market and to conduct monetary policy in accordance with the stated objectives.

The Indian experience highlights the need for emerging market economies to allow greater flexibility in exchange rates but the authorities can also benefit from having the capacity to intervene in foreign exchange markets in view of the volatility observed in international capital flows. A key lesson is that flexibility and pragmatism are required in the management of the exchange rate and monetary policy in developing countries, rather than adherence to strict theoretical rules. Three overarching features marked the transition of India to an open economy. First, the administered exchange rate became market determined and ensuring orderly conditions in the foreign exchange market became an objective of exchange rate management. Second, as already indicated, vicissitudes in capital flows came to influence the conduct of

CHART 3

Exchange Rate

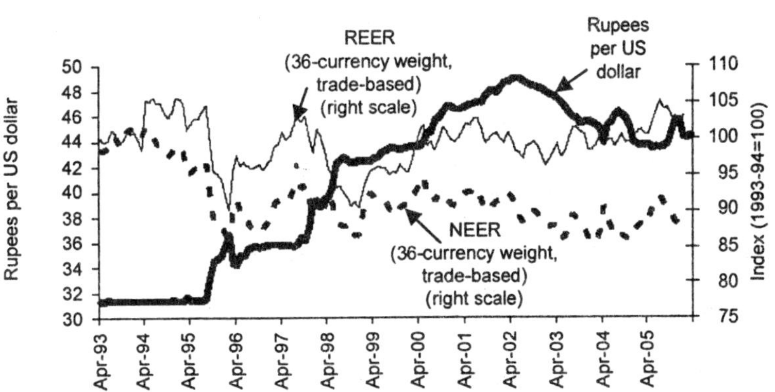

monetary policy. Third, lessons of the balance of payments crisis highlighted the need to maintain an adequate level of foreign exchange reserves and this in turn both enabled and constrained the conduct of monetary policy. From hindsight, it appears that the strategy paid-off with the exchange rate exhibiting reasonable two-way

6.7: SOME EMERGING ISSUES

This review of financial sector reforms and monetary policy has documented the calibrated and coordinated reforms that have been undertaken in India since the 1990s. In terms of outcomes, this strategy has achieved the broad objectives of price stability along with reduced medium and long-term inflation expectations; the installation of an institutional framework and policy reform promoting relatively efficient price discovery of interest rates and the exchange rate; phased introduction of competition in banking along with corresponding improvements in regulation and supervision approaching international best practice, which has led to notable improvement in banking performance and financials. The implementation of these reforms has also involved the setting up or improvement of key financial infrastructure such as payment and settlement systems, and clearing and settlement systems for debt and forex market functioning. All of this financial development has been achieved with the maintenance of a great degree of financial stability, along with overall movement of the economy towards a higher growth path. With increased deregulation of financial markets and increased integration of the global economy, the 1990s were turbulent for global financial markets: 63 countries suffered from systemic banking crises in that decade, much higher than 45 in the 1980s. Among countries that experienced such crises, the direct cost of reconstructing the financial system was typically very high: for example, recapitalization of banks had cost 55 per cent of GDP in Argentina, 42 per cent in Thailand, 35 per cent in Korea and 10 per cent in Turkey. There were high indirect costs of lost opportunities and slow economic growth in addition. It is therefore particularly noteworthy that India could pursue its process of financial deregulation and opening of the economy without suffering financial crises during this turbulent period in world financial markets. The cost of recapitalisation of public sector banks at less than 1 per cent of GDP is therefore low in comparison. Whereas we can be legitimately gratified with this performance record, we now need to focus on the new issues that need to be addressed for the next phase of financial development. That current annual GDP growth of around 8 per cent can be achieved in India at an about 30 per cent rate of gross domestic investment suggests that the economy is functioning quite efficiently. We need to ensure that we maintain this level of efficiency and attempt to improve on it further. As the Indian economy continues on such a growth path and attempts to accelerate it, new demands are being placed on the financial system.

6.8: CONCLUDING OBSERVATIONS

To conclude, the financial system in India, through a measured, gradual, cautious, and steady process, has undergone substantial transformation. It has been transformed into a reasonably sophisticated, diverse and resilient system through well-sequenced and coordinated policy measures aimed at making the Indian financial sector more competitive, efficient, and stable. Concomitantly, effective monetary management has enabled price stability while ensuring availability of credit to support investment demand and growth in the economy. Finally, the multi-pronged approach towards managing capital account in conjunction with prudential and cautious approach to financial liberalisation has ensured financial stability in contrast to the experience of many developing and emerging economies. This is despite the fact that we faced a large number of shocks, both global and domestic. Monetary policy and financial sector reforms in India had to be fine tuned to meet the challenges emanating from all these shocks. Viewed in this light, the success in maintaining price and financial stability is all the more creditworthy. As the economy ascends a higher growth path, and as it is subjected to greater opening and financial integration with the rest of the world, the financial sector in all its aspects will need further considerable development, along with corresponding measures to continue regulatory modernization and strengthening. The overall objective of maintaining price stability in the context of economic growth and financial stability will remain.

Notes and References

1. "Financial Sector Reforms and Monetary Policy—The Indian Experience," Paper presented by Mr Rakesh Mohan, Deputy Governor of the Reserve Bank of India, at the Conference on Economic Policy in Asia, organised by Stanford Center for International Development and Stanford Institute for Economic Policy Research, Stanford, 2 June 2006.
2. Y.V. Reddy (2002) noted that the approach towards financial sector reforms in India has been based on five principles:
   (i) cautious and appropriate sequencing of reform measures;
   (ii) introduction of mutually reinforcing norms;
   (iii) introduction of complementary reforms across monetary, fiscal and external sectors;
   (iv) development of financial institutions; and
   (v) development of financial markets.
3. Mohan Rakesh (2006), "Financial Sector Reforms and Monetary Policy: The Indian Experience", *Reserve Bank of India Bulletin*, July.
4. Reserve Bank of India, *Annual Report*, 2004-05
5. *Ibid.*
6. *Ibid.*
7. Reserve Bank of India (2005), 'Working Group on Regulatory Mechanism for Cards', March 2005.
8. Reserve Bank Of India, *Annual Report*, 2005-06.
9. Reserve Bank of India, *Annual Report*, 2004-05.
10. Mohan, Rakesh (2006), "Financial Sector Reforms and Monetary Policy: The Indian Experience", *Reserve Bank of India Bulletin*, July.

11. Reserve bank of India, *Annual Report*, 2005-06.
12. A.T. Pannir Selram "The Future of Indian Financial Sector—Foundation paper for National Debate", *Journal of Indian Institute of Bankers*, Platinum Jublee Special.
13. Mohan Rakesh (2006), "Financial Sector Reforms and Monetary Policy: The Indian Experience", *Reserve Bank of India Bulletin*, July.
14. Reserve Bank of India, *Annual Report*, 2005-06, p. 134.
15. Mohan Rakesh (2006), "Financial Sector Reforms and Monetary Policy: The Indian Experience", *Reserve Bank of India Bulletin*, July.

CHAPTER

7

The Path Ahead

The Indian economy at present is in a much stronger position than it was a few years ago. After slowing down to an average growth rate of about 5.5% in the Ninth Plan period (1997-98 to 2001-02), it has accelerated in recent years and the average growth rate in the Tenth Plan period (2002-03 to 2006-07) is likely to be about 7%. This is below the Tenth Plan target of 8%, but it is the highest growth rate achieved in any plan period. While this performance reflects the strength of the economy in many areas, it is also true that large parts of our population are still to experience a decisive improvement in their standard of living. The percentage of the population below the poverty line is declining, but only at a modest pace. Far too many people still lack access to basic services such as health, education, clean drinking water and sanitation facilities without which they cannot be empowered to claim their share in the benefits of growth. These problems are more severe in some states than in others, and in general they are especially severe in rural areas.

7.1: A VISION FOR THE FUTURE

Rapid growth has to be an essential part of the strategy since it is only in a rapidly rowing economy that we can expect to raise the incomes of the mass of the population sufficiently to bring about a general improvement in living conditions. Fortunately, the growth objective is now more achievable than it has ever been. Work done in the Planning Commission and elsewhere suggests that the economy can grow between 8% and 9% per year on a sustained basis provided appropriate policies are put in place. With population growing at 1.5% per year, this would ensure that the real income of the average Indian would double in ten years. It is also possible to adopt policies that will ensure that this growth is broad-based, benefiting all parts of the country, and especially the rural areas. This must be accompanied by a major effort to provide access to basic facilities such as health, education, clean drinking water, etc., to large parts of population which do not have such access at present. These essential public services not only impact directly on welfare in the short-run, they also determine economic opportunities for the future. Access to these services is not necessarily assured even when growth leads to rising income levels. Governments at different levels must ensure provision of these services. Improved levels of health and education are in fact critical inputs that determine the growth potential in the longer term.

Even if we succeed in achieving broad based and inclusive growth, there are many groups that may still be marginalized. These include primitive tribal groups, adolescent girls, children in the age group 0 to 3, and others who do not have strong lobbies to ensure that their rights are guaranteed. The future Reform Programme must pay special attention to the needs of these groups.

The private sector, including farming, small scale enterprises and the corporate sector, has a critical role to play in achieving the objective of faster and more inclusive growth. This sector accounts for 70% of the total investment in the economy and our policies must aim at creating an environment in which entrepreneurship can flourish. However, it will also call for a substantial increase in the allocation of public resources for plan programmes in critical areas. These resources will be easier to mobilise if the economy grows rapidly. The growth component of the strategy is therefore important for two reasons: it will contribute directly by raising income levels and employment for the population in general and it will also help to finance programmes that are necessary to ensure that growth is more broad-based and inclusive. All this is feasible but it is by no means inevitable. Converting potential into reality is a formidable task and cannot be achieved if we simply continue on a business as usual basis. There is need for a self-critical look at our programmes and policies to see what is working and what is not. Programmes designed to achieve particular objectives often fail to do so even though substantial expenditure may be incurred on them. We need to move away from a focus on outlays to a hard look at outcomes.

7.2. CHALLENGES AHEAD

Weaknesses and the strengths enumerated above are real and represent above a base on which we must build in the years ahead. However, there are some important challenges to be faced:

(a) Providing Essential Public Services for the Poor

The most important challenge is how to provide essential public services such as education and health to large parts of our population who are denied these services at present. Education is the critical factor that will empower the poor to participate in the growth process and our performance in this area has been disappointing. Literacy is still less than 70% and while the *Sarva Shiksha Abhiyan* [Education for all programme] has expanded access to primary schools in terms of enrolment, it has yet to provide quality education. Looking ahead, we need to move as rapidly as possible towards universalisation of secondary education which is an essential requirement in a knowledge driven world. In the matter of health also there are large gaps in the availability of health care and in related services such as maternal and child care, clean drinking water and access to basic sanitation facilities for the mass of our population especially the poor who do not have even minimum access. Some of these services, e.g. education and curative health, are available in the market to those who can afford to pay. However, quality sources of supply are costly and beyond the reach of the common man, and other privately provided services are of highly variable quality. In our situation, access for the mass of our people can only be assured through a substantial effort at public financing of these services. In most cases, this also means public provision though there is obviously room for partnership with private entities, including especially non-profit bodies and civil society involvement. A major institutional challenge is that even where service providers exist, the quality of delivery is poor and those responsible for delivering the services cannot be held accountable. Unless such accountability is established, it will be difficult to ensure significant improvement in delivery even if additional resources are made available. This is a major challenge of governance that must be faced.

(b) Regaining Agricultural Dynamism

One of the major challenges in the coming years must be to reverse the deceleration in agricultural growth from 3.2% observed between 1980 and 1996-97 to a trend average of only 1.5% subsequently. This deceleration is undoubtedly at the root of the problem of rural distress that has surfaced in many parts of the country. What is more, the problem is also not a purely distributional one, arising out of the special problems of small and marginal farmers and landless labour. In fact, the deceleration is general affecting all farm size classes. To reverse this trend, corrective policies adopted must focus not only on the small and marginal farmers, who continue to deserve special attention, but also on middle and large farmers who too suffer from productivity stagnation arising from a variety of constraints. A second green revolution is urgently needed to raise the growth rate of agricultural GDP to around 4%. This is not an easy task since actual growth of agricultural GDP, including forestry and fishing, was only 1% per annum in the first three years of 10th Plan and even the most rosy projections for 2005-06 and 2006-07 would limit this below 2% for the full five year period. The challenge posed is to at least double the rate of agricultural growth. This calls for action on both the demand side and the supply side.

(c) Increasing Manufacturing Competitiveness

Manufacturing sector has also not grown as rapidly as might have been expected. The average growth rate of this sector has accelerated compared to the nineties but is unlikely to exceed 8%. It should be targeted to grow at around 12% or so if we want to achieve a GDP growth of between 8 and 9% India's remarkable success in IT enabled services has prompted some observers to conclude that China has a comparative advantage in manufacturing whereas India has an advantage in services and we should therefore concentrate on growth of high value services. This approach is simplistic. India's performance in IT enabled services and other high end services is clearly a source of strength that we must build upon. However, India cannot afford to neglect manufacturing. India meets most of the requirements for attaining double digit growth in manufacturing. We have a dynamic entrepreneurial class that has gained confidence in its ability to compete. We have skilled labour and excellent management capability. However there are other constraints that limit our competitiveness, especially in labour intensive manufacturing, and the future must address, these on a priority basis. The most important constraint in achieving a faster growth of manufacturing is the fact that infrastructure, consisting of roads, railways, ports, airports, communication and electric power, is not up to the standards prevalent in our competitor countries. This must be substantially rectified within the next 5-10 years if our enterprises are to compete effectively. In the increasingly open trading environment that we face today, our producers must compete aggressively not only to win export market share but even to retain domestic market share against competition from imports. Indian industry recognises this and no longer expects to survive because of protection. But they do expect a level playing field in terms of quality of infrastructure. This should have high priority in the coming years. Shortage of electric power and the unreliability of power supply are universally recognised as a drag on the pace of India's development. Our competitors benefit from round the clock supply of power at stable voltage and frequency, but this remains elusive in most parts of India. The management of power systems, especially distribution, is the responsibility of state governments and a decisive improvement in this area is a critical challenge.

(d) Developing Human Resources

The emphasis we had put on quality higher education decades ago, setting up IITs and other premier educational institutions, has paid us rich dividends. However, expansion of such institutes has slackened in the past two decades, and there are clear signs of an emerging shortage of the high quality skills that are needed in the knowledge-intensive industries. This could quickly erode our competitive advantage in this area. To ensure a continuous and growing supply of quality manpower we need large investments in public sector institutions of higher learning, combined with fundamental reforms of the curriculum and also service conditions to attract high quality faculty. The scope for expanding capacity through private sector initiatives in higher learning must also be fully exploited, while also ensuring that quality standards are not diluted. Unless this is done on an urgent basis, we will fail to attain global standards. No society, certainly not at India's stage of economic development, can give everyone high-end skills to make them doctors, engineers, software specialists, financial analysts or even provide university level education to all. Industry also requires persons skilled in many specific trades and the situation in this area is not comforting. India has historically lagged behind in the area of technical/vocational training and even today enrolment rates in ITIs and other vocational institutes, including nursing and computer training schools, is only about a third of that in higher education. This is quite the opposite of other Asian countries which have outperformed us in labour intensive manufactures. Our ITIs will have to be substantially expanded not only in terms of the persons they train but also in the number of different skills and trades they teach. The quality and range of their training should keep pace with the changing needs of the economy.

(e) Protecting the Environment

Environmental concerns are growing globally as well as within the country. While there may appear to be a trade-off between environmental sustainability and economic growth in the short-run, it has to be recognised, that in the longer-run environmental sustainability and human well-being are not necessarily in conflict. Neglect of environmental considerations, as for example, in profligate use of water or deforestation can lead to adverse effects very quickly. The threat of climate change also poses real challenge to the well being of future generations which we can ill-afford to ignore. Our development strategy has to be sensitive to these growing concerns and should ensure that these threats and trade-offs are appropriately evaluated.

(f) Improving Rehabilitation and Resettlement Practices

Our practices regarding rehabilitation of those displaced from their land because of development projects are seriously deficient and are responsible for a growing perception of exclusion and marginalization. The costs of displacement borne by our tribal population have been unduly high, and compensation has been tardy and inadequate, leading to serious unrest in many tribal regions. This discontent is likely to grow exponentially if the benefits from enforced land acquisition are seen accruing to private interests, or even to the state, at the cost of those displaced. To prevent even greater conflict, and threat to peace and development, it is necessary to frame a transparent set of policy rules that address compensation, and make the affected persons beneficiaries of the projects, and to give these rules a legal format in terms of the rights of the displaced. In addition to those displaced by development projects, those displaced by social upheavals should also be properly resettled.

(g) Improving Governance

All our efforts to achieve rapid and inclusive development will come to naught, if we cannot ensure good governance both in the manner public programmes are implemented and, equally important, in the way the government interacts with the ordinary citizen. Corruption is now seen to be endemic in all spheres and this problem needs to be addressed urgently. Better design of projects and implementation mechanisms and procedures can reduce the scope for corruption. Much more needs to be done by both the Centre and the States to reduce the discretionary power of the government, ensure greater transparency and accountability, and create awareness among citizens. The Right to Information Act empowers the people to demand improved governance, and we must be ready to respond. Quick and inexpensive dispensation of justice is an aspect of good governance which is of fundamental importance in a successful civil society. The legal system in India is respected for its independence and fairness but it suffers from notorious delays in dispensing justice. Delays result in denial of justice. Delays cost money and therefore it is difficult for the poor in India to afford justice. Fundamental reforms are needed to give justice two attributes: speed and affordability.

7.3: DISPARITIES AND DIVIDE

Even as we address the specific challenges listed above, we must also deal with broader perceptions that development has not only failed to bridge the divides that afflict our country, it may even have sharpened some of them. Some of these perceptions may be exaggerated, but they are real nonetheless. The future Plan must seek to bridge these divides as an overarching priority. There are many divides, all demanding equal attention. Foremost among these is the divide between the rich and the poor. As explained in Table 7.1 poverty is declining, but only at a modest pace which is no longer acceptable given the minimalist level at which the poverty line is fixed. The pace of poverty reduction must be accelerated. There is also a divide between those who have access to essential services and those who do not, which leads to large disparities in health and nutritional status, in education and skills, as also in availability of clean water and sanitation. There are also excluded groups in our society such as SCs [schedule castes], STs [schedule tribes], and OBCs [other backward castes] and some minorities who continue to lag behind the rest.

Another important divide which compels immediate attention is gender discrimination. It begins

TABLE 7.1

Status of Some Socio-Economic Indicators in India

Average All India		*Best State*	*Worst State*	
	1991	*2005*	*2005*	*2005*
Per capita National Product [Rs. per person at 1993 prices]	7321	11799	16679	3557
Consumption Poverty:				
Head Count Ratio (%)	36	27.8	6.16	47.15
Literacy (age 7+) Male	64.1	75.3	94.2	59.7
Literacy (age 7+) Female	39.3	53.7	87.7	33.1
Attending elementary Schools (6-14 Years)	55.3	71.1	103.1	55.8
Sex Ratio (Females per 1000 Males)	92.7	93.3	1058	709
Infant Mortality (per 1000 Live Births)	80	80	11	83
Maternal Mortality Rate (per 1000 Live Births)		4		
Under Nourished Children:				
Weight for age		47	20.6	55.7
Height for Age		45.5	18.1	55.5
Weight for Height		15.5	4.8	24.3

Source: An Approach to 11th Five Year Plan, Government of India, p. 8.

with declining sex ratio and goes on to literacy differential between girls and boys plus the high rate of maternal mortality. The extent of bias is self-evident. The statistics given in table are reflective of the trend but do not tell the whole story. Differences in educational status and economic empowerment are heavily biased against women. Special, focused efforts must be made to purge society of this malaise by creating an enabling environment for women to become economically empowered. Measures for societal recognition of women's economic and societal worth will be a concomitant of this. The divide between urban and rural India has become a truism of our times. The Central Government has adopted a multi-pronged strategy to reduce this divide in its various dimensions. The *Bharat Nirman Programme* [India Building Programme] addresses gaps in rural infrastructure and covers irrigation, road connectivity, housing, water supply, electrification and telephony. The National Rural Employment Guarantee Act has elements of a social safety net as it provides guaranteed employment in rural areas, but can also help in building rural infrastructure especially if resources from other programmes are also pooled in. *The Sarva Shiksha Abhiyan* [Education For all] and National Rural Health Mission are ambitious programmes for providing primary education and primary health services universally. All these programmes are meant to give a new deal to rural India. To succeed, these Central Government initiatives have to be owned by states and local authorities, within whose constitutional responsibility most of them lie. Regional backwardness is another issue of concern. The differences across states have long been a cause of concern but increasingly there is recognition of the problem of severe imbalances within states. Backward districts of otherwise well performing states, present a dismal picture of intra-state imbalance and neglect. The Centre and the States together must deal with this problem on a priority basis. We cannot let large parts of the country be trapped in a prison of discontent, injustice and frustration that will only breed extremism. The spread of Naxalism in more than 100 districts in the country is a warning sign. Pockets of despair where communalism has left scars are also festering with anger. In all areas despair is the result of visible failures of the state apparatus to ensure good governance and create an environment where the bulk of the people experience the benefit of development. Special efforts must be made to remove the discontent, dispense justice, instill a sense of fairness among the people and give them dignity and hope. Otherwise, not only will the growth momentum in the rest of the country be disrupted, but we will not attain the dignity and pride of a good society.

In conclusion, it may be said that the Indian economy responded to the economic reform of the 1990s with a higher growth performance than in previous decades. The economy has shown that it is capable of achieving high growth rates in response to the implementation of appropriate economic reform polices. Consequently, higher growth rates in future can indeed be achieved through further deepening of the economic reform process. Government on its part must resist any attempts to delay the process of liberalization and deregulation, no doubt as required under Indian Economic environment and continue to deepen the reforms and remove all obstacles and bottlenecks for unleashing competitive forces in the economic. This would entail removal of the remaining infrastructural constraints, reducing bureaucratic controls in all spheres and removing other barriers to growth.

One important aspect that needs to be mentioned here is that there is a need to develop political consensus around the core reform programme, so that specific reform measures enjoy support cutting across party lines. It needs to stress here that the need for political consensus on economic reforms is no empty slogan. By sheer experience India has demonstrated that there exists broad political support to the reform programmes, as has been proved by the transition of several Governments in last 16 years through the political space. The world at large now does believe that reform process in India is irreversible, but would certainly like to see an acceleration of its momentum, so that goals that seem so easily within reach can be rapidly attained.

While emphasizing the need to build political consensus, it is heartening to note that in recent years several political parties covering the entire spectrum of political thought which have held power in various states and centre have taken up and continued to sustain bold reform programmes embracing a wide ranges of activities. Thus, it may be said, a wide nation-wide and broad-based consensus to reform our economy and to put the individual states and the county as a whole on the path of higher productivity and growth is already in place. What is required now for this is consensus to be built upon and carried over into the realm of policy and implementation.

(RESEARCH PAPER I)

APPENDIX I

Agriculture and Economic Reforms[1]

Agriculture has all along been the most crucial sector of the Indian economy and even today agriculture and allied activities make the single largest contribution to Gross Domestic Product (G.D.P.) accounting for 24.2 per cent of the total. This sector provides employment to 56.7 per cent of country's work force and is the single largest private sector occupation. Agriculture accounts for about 14.7 per cent of the total export earnings and provides raw material to a large number of industries (textiles, silk, sugar, rice, flour mills, milk products, etc.). Besides, the rural areas are the biggest markets for low priced and middle priced consumer goods including consumer durables and rural domestic savings are important sources of resource mobilization. Any change in this sector, positive or negative, has a multiplier effect on the entire economy. In fact, a nation of more than a billion people cannot be dependent on imports for the basic item like food grains. The agriculture sector, therefore, acts as a bulwark in maintaining food security and in the process, national security as well. The allied sectors like horticulture,

---

1. A research paper submitted at National Seminar on "Emerging Challenges In Post-Reform Period," Organized by the Haryana Institute of Rural Development on March 12-13, 2005.

animal husbandry, dairy and fisheries, have importance in improving the overall economic conditions and health and nutrition of the rural masses.[2]

I. FIFTY-FIVE YEARS OF INDIAN AGRICULTURE

India inherited a stagnant agriculture at the time of independence in 1947. The first task of Indian Government in the immediate post-independence period was, therefore, to initiate growth process in agriculture. The agricultural policy was governed by a planning framework. The quantum of plan outlay, its financing and the targets set for the agricultural sector were all decided through the planning process at the state and central levels. The first three Five Year Plans concentrated on growth with some institutional changes including abolition of intermediaries in agriculture, like Zamindars and Jagirdars. In the mid-sixties. a new technology in the form of high yielding varieties (HYVs) was also introduced for cereals. Apart from the new technology, public investment in agriculture particularly in irrigation was stepped up significantly. The public sector played an important role in promoting agricultural research and education. Large investments were made for the development of research system under the aegis of the Indian Council of Agricultural Research (ICAR) and the State Agricultural Universities (SAUs). Simultaneously, a well designed extension network was created for disseminating new technologies to the farmers and the system of administered price provided incentives to the farmers. Successive five year plans aimed at improving the infrastructure through irrigation, stepping up the use of fertilizers, improved varieties of seed implements and machinery and supply of credit. In short, the last 55 years of agriculture

2. Govt. of India, Planning Commission: Tenth Plan 2002-07, p. 195.

development in the country could be divided into following four phases.[3]

- When the expansion of net sown area (NSA), irrigated area, development of rural infrastructure and land reforms played an important role (1947-67).
- When high yielding dwarf varieties, agricultural inputs like fertilizers, pesticides and improved crop production technologies ushered in the Green Revolution; (1967-75).
- When minimum support prices (MSP) and procurement of agricultural commodities were ensured and the foodgrains shortage and distribution system was expanded at the national level; and (1975-90).
- When the thrust was on liberalisation and globalisation with the establishment of the World Trade Organization (WTO). (1990 onwards)

In the present chapter of the study the emphasis is on post-reform scenario in agricultural development.

II. AGRICULTURAL GROWTH IN POST-REFORM PERIOD

A major criticism of the process of economic reforms is the neglect of agriculture. The economic reforms initiated in 1991 largely focussed on fiscal adjustment, foreign trade and investment, industry and financial sector. Some of the measures—notably reduction of subsidies, tariff reduction and trade liberalisation have impact on Agriculture for e.g. the reduction in fertilizer subsidies has raised the input costs for agriculture giving rise to apprehensions that fertilizer use and therefore agricultural product will be adversely affected. Tariff reduction and import

---

3. *Ibid.*, p. 514.

liberalisation is expected to have reduced the cost and improved the availability of imported materials and product, entering agricultural production. The relaxation in restrictions on import and export of farm products surely must also have benefited agriculture. The magnitude of the impact of these measures however remains to be established. It may however, be held that no attempt at a comprehensive revamp in agricultural strategy is made in first generation economic reforms. A major cause of concern in recent years has been deceleration in agriculture in the post-reform period. To highlight this fact the agricultural growth is analysed in terms of following indicators:

(A) GDP and Agricultural Growth Rates.
(B) Annual Growth Rates in Area, Production and Productivity in 1980s and 1990s.
(C) Gross capital formation in Agriculture.
(D) Annual growth rates of various Development Programmes.

(A) GDP and Agricultural Growth rates

The deceleration in agriculture is best reflected in fluctuating growth rates of Agriculture Sector in post-reform period. It is shown in Table I.

Table II shows that growth rate of agriculture and allied sector has shown wide fluctuations in post-reform period. The growth rate of Agriculture and Allied sector was 5.8 per cent in 1992-93. It turned into negative growth of 0.9 per cent in 1995-96. It jumped to 9.6 per cent in 1996-97 on account of good monsoon, but it again registered negative movement of 2.4 per cent in 1997-98. This rate again rose to 6.2 per cent in 1998-99 but was only 0.3 per cent in 1999-2000 and -0.4 per cent in 2000-01. It recovered in the form of 5.7 per cent in 2001-02 but again slipped to -3.1 per cent in the year 2002-03.

From the above analysis it can be fairly concluded that in 12 years of post-reform period the growth of

TABLE I

GDP and Agricultural Growth Rates (At 1993-1994 Prices)

(Percent)

Year	*G.D.P.*	*Agriculture and Allied Sector*
1992-93	5.1	5.8
1993-94	5.9	4.1
1994-95	7.3	5.0
1995-96	7.8	-0.9
1996-97	7.8	9.6
1997-98	4.8	-2.4
1998-99	6.5	6.2
1999-00	6.1	0.3
2000-01	4.4	-0.4
2001-02	5.6	5.7
2002-03*	4.4	-3.1

*Advance estimate.
Source: *Economic Survey*, 2002-03, p. 158.

agriculture and allied sector has not been stable. It is still more or less dependent on monsoon which shows the backwardness of the agriculture sector and failure of new reforms to develop the strongness of agricultural sector.

(B) Annual Growth Rates in Area, Production and Productivity in 1980s and 1990s

The deceleration of agricultural growth can be better analysed by analyzing the annual growth rates of production of foodgrains in Pre and Post-reform period.

It is clear from the table that the rates of growth of production of rice, wheat, coarse cereals, and pulses have all declined in the nineties *vis-à-vis* the eighties. The overall growth rate of production of rice and wheat which was 3.59 per cent per annum during the eighties

TABLE II

Annual Compound Growth of Crop Area, Production and Productivity

(per cent)

Crop	*1980-81 to 1989-90*			*1990-91 to 2000-01*		
	Area	*Production*	*Yield*	*Area*	*Production*	*Yield*
Rice and Wheat	0.43	3.59	3.15	0.84	2.27	1.42
Rice	0.41	3.62	3.19	0.63	1.79	1.16
W heat	0.47	3.57	3.10	1.21	3.04	1.81
Coarse Cereals	-1.34	0.40	1.62	-1.84	0.06	1.62
Pulses	-0.09	1.52	1.61	-1.02	-0.58	0.27
Total Foodgrains	-0.23	2.85	2.74	-0.20	1.66	1.34
Non-Food Crops	1.12	3.77	2.31	0.84	1.86	0.59
Oilseeds	-1.51	5.20	2.43	0.44	0.66	0.61
Sugarcane	1.44	2.70	1.24	1.72	2.62	0.89
Cotton	-1.25	2.80	4.10	2.21	0.92	-1.26
All Crops	0.10	3.19	2.56	0.08	1.73	1.02

Source: *Economic Survey*, 2001-02, p. 189.

fell to only 2.27 per cent per annum during nineties which is just marginally above the rate of growth of population. Pulses and cereals have recorded little or no growth in the 1980s and 1990s. Some area expansion under non-food crops in the 1990's is attributable mainly to the growth in area under cotton and sugarcane, perhaps at the cost of shrinkage in area under coarse cereals. However, the growth in yield of non-food crops in the 1990's has been lower than that in 1980s.

(C) Gross Capital Formation in Agriculture

The pace and pattern of agricultural development are largely conditioned by growth of infrastructural facilities of irrigation, road, market, power, cold storage, etc. Infrastructure plays a critical role on both input and output sides, while on the input front, it helps to

TABLE III

Gross Capital Formation in Agriculture (At 1993-94 Prices)

(Rs. crores)

Year	*Gross Capital Formation*				*Percentage Share of*			*Investment in Agri-culture as Percentage of GDP*
	Agriculture	*Total economy*	*Public sector in agriculture*	*Private sector in agriculture*	*Public sector in Agriculture*	*Private sector in agriculture*	*Agriculture to total*	
1993-94	13,523	181.133	4,457	9,056	33.0	67.0	7.47	1.6
1994-95	14,969	229,879	4,947	10,022	33.0	67.0	6.51	1.6
1995-96	15,690	2,74,557	4,849	10,841	30.9	69.1	5.51	1.6
1996-97	16,176	2,48,631	4,668	11,508	28.9	71.1	6.51	1.5
1997-98	15,942	2,56,551	3,979	11,963	25.0	75.0	4.77	1.4
1998-99	14,895	2,43,697	3,869	11,026	26.0	74.0	6.11	1.3
1999-00	17,304	2,68,374	4,222	13,082	24.4	75.6	6.18	1.3
2000-01	16,687	—	3,919	12,768	23.5	76.5	—	1.3
2001-02*	18,057	—	4,794	13,263	26.5	13.4	—	1.3

* Advance estimates.

Source: *Economic Survey*, 2002-03, p. 172.

integrate local markets with national and international markets, whereas on the output front it is the base for increasing productivity. Therefore, an adequate and efficient infrastructure system is essential for realizing the potential of the sector. However, one of the most disquieting developments in agricultural sector during post-reform period has been the neglect of capital formation, particularly in public sector. It is indicated by Table III.

Table III reveals that investment in agriculture declined from 1.6 per cent of G.D.P. in 1993-94, to 1.3 per cent in 2000-01. The decline was due to fall in public investment from Rs. 4,457 crore in 1993-94 to Rs. 3,869 crore in 1998-99. There has infact, been a continuous decline in public investment in agriculture from 1995-96 till 1998-99. Although the declining trend in public investment was halted in 1999-2000 with the public sector capital formation rising to Rs. 4,222 crore from Rs. 3,869 crore in the preceding year, there has not been any improvement in the share of investment in agriculture as percentage of GDP from the preceding year's level of 1.3 per cent. The advance estimates for year 2001-02 also present a dismal picture with the share of investment in agriculture to GDP remaining at 1.3 per cent. This calls for review of policies which led to diversion of scarce resource away from the creation of productive assets to subsidies for fertilizers, small electricity, irrigation, credit and other agricultural inputs.

Another disturbing fact is that not only the public and private investment in agriculture is declining but the share of agriculture and allied sector in total gross capital formation of the economy has also shown declining trend in post-reform period as indicated by Table IV.

The Table IV shows that share of Agriculture and allied sector in total G.C.F. was 9.9 per cent in 1990-91 which declined to 8.4 per cent in 1994-95 and ultimately to 7.1 per cent in 2000-01. Over the same period the public sector contribution declined from 7.1

TABLE IV

Share of Agriculture and Allied Sector in Total Gross Capital Formation

(per cent)

Year	*Pre-Reform Period*			*Year*	*Post-Reform Period*		
	Public Sector	*Private Sector*	*Total*		*Public Sector*	*Private Sector*	*Total*
1980-81	17.7	13.6	15.4	1990-91	7.1	11.9	9.9
1981-82	14.1	9.2	11.2	1991-92	6.6	9.9	8.7
1982-83	13.1	12.3	12.7	1992-93	6.7	10.5	9.1
1983-84	13.5	14.4	13.9	1994-95	6.7	9.4	8.4
1984-85	11.8	11.5	11.7	1994-95	6.7	7.7	7.3
1985-86	10.2	9.5	9.8	1996-97	7.0	7.5	7.4
1986-87	8.9	10.1	9.6	1997-98	6.2	7.5	7.1
1987-88	10.1	13.2	11.7	1998-99	5.7	7.8	7.2
1988-89	8.8	9.7	9.3	1999-00	5.1	8.2	7.2
1989-90	7.5	9.1	8.4	2000-01	4.9	8.2	7.1

Source: Government of India, Planning Commission, 10th Plan, p. 519.

per cent in 1990-91 to 4.9 per cent in 2000-01, while the share of private sector declined from 11.9 per cent in 1990-91 to 8.2 per cent in 2000-01.

The declining trend in capital formation will need to be reversed by better targeting of subsidies, increasing investment in productive assets such as irrigation, power, credit and developing rural infrastructure. According to Economic Survey, 1999-2000,[4] "the decline in public investment in agriculture is mainly due to the diversion of resources to current expenditure in the form of subsidies for food, fertilizers, electricity, irrigation, credit and other agriculture inputs rather than as creation of assets."

---

4. *Economic Survey,* 1999-2000, p. 134.

(D) Annual Growth Rates of Various Development Programmes

One of the important method of assessing development of agriculture in post-reform period is to assess the growth of various development programmes in agriculture *vis-à-vis* in pre-reform period. In the present analysis the assessment is made with respect of three important variables namely:

(a) High Yield Varieties.
(b) Irrigated Area.
(c) Fertilizer Consumption.

The annual growth rates of these three programmes is shown in Table V.

The table reveals that during the decade 1970-71 to 1980-81, irrigated area indicated an annual average

TABLE V

Annual Growth Rate of Various Development Programmes

	1970-71 to 1980-81	*1980-81 to 1990-91*	*1990-91 to 2000-01*
High Yield Varieties			
Total HYV	**10.5**	**4.2**	**4.4**
Paddy	12.5	4.1	2.3
Wheat	9.5	2.7	1.1
Irrigated Area	**3.6**	**2.7**	**2.1**
Rice	1.4	1.7	1.6
Wheat	4.6	2.3	1.1
Total Cereals	2.4	1.7	2.0
Pulses	0.0	2.7	1.8
Major Irrigation	2.7	1.3	1.2
Minor Irrigation	4.2	3.5	2.3
Fertilizer Consumption	**9.6**	**8.5**	**3.7**

Source: Compiled from the data given in Economic Survey, (2001-02).

growth rate of 3.6 per cent which declined to 2.7 per cent during the decade 1980-81 to 1990-91 and further to merely 2.1 per cent during 1990-91 to 2000-01. Since irrigation is the basic input which helps the fuller utilization of other inputs like seeds and fertilizers, we also observe declining growth rates in irrigated area under rice and wheat from seventies to eighties and nineties. In case of pulses also, irrigated area growth experienced a declining trend (From 2.7 per cent in the decade of eighties to 1.8 per cent in the decade of nineties. A similar trend was observed in case of extension of area under HYV in case of paddy and rice. The growth rate of fertilizer consumption indicated a sharp decline from 8.5 per cent annual average growth rate during the eighties to just 3.7 per cent during the nineties.

In this connection, it is relevant to consider the trend in major and minor irrigation. Major irrigation acts as a supplement to minor irrigation in keeping the water level high, while minor irrigation provides water security to the peasant in case of failure of rains. The slowing down of the growth rate of irrigated area under minor irrigation from 3.5 per cent during eighties to 2.3 per cent during nineties is another contributing factor to slow down of over-all agricultural growth. Economic reforms did not pay adequate attention to expansion of irrigation and this is a major sin responsible for low growth of agricultural production and productivity during nineties.

III. CAUSES FOR DECELERATING GROWTH IN AGRICULTURE SECTOR DURING 1990'S

The Tenth Plan document has stated that there are region-specific causes for the decelerating growth in agriculture sector during the 1990's. Some of these are:[5]

5. Govt. of India, Planning Commission: Tenth Plan, p. 524.

- Low public investment in irrigation and poor maintenance.
- Poor maintenance of rural infrastructure, specially canals and roads.
- Decline in investments in rural electrification and in its availability. This has greatly affected production in eastern India, where huge groundwater potential remains untapped.
- Rising level of subsidies for power, water, fertilizers and food are eating into public sector investments in agriculture, besides encouraging inefficient use of scarce resources such as water. This further aggravates environmental problems leading to loss of soil fertility and decline in groundwater, which reduces return on capital. Farmers then demand further subsidies to maintain the same level of production.
- Inadequate credit support.
- Continuing imbalanced use of NPK fertilizers, (6.69:2.59:1.0) in 2001-02 as against the desirable norm of 4:2:1) and increasing deficiency of micro-nutrients in the soil.
- Stringent controls on movement, marketing, credit, stock and export of agri products that affect their profitability. In the face of pressure from the WTO, there is apprehension that without speedy domestic market reforms, an opportunity to capture world markets would be converted into a threat to the future growth of Indian agriculture. The classic case is that of sugar where imports were opened at zero duty when controls on domestic markets remained widespread.
- Demand constraints (slow growth of the urban economy, restriction on exports, lack of land reforms, failure of poverty alleviation schemes, slow growth in rural wages).
- Controls on the agro-processing industry.
- Poor extension service.

IV. NEGLECT OF AGRICULTURE—THE MAJOR SIN OF ECONOMIC REFORMS

Mahesh V. Joshi stated that in Economic Reforms[6] "Agriculture is being neglected although it is the decisive field in the economy of our country. The Government approved the policy of urban development at the cost of rural and industrial expansion and at the cost of agriculture. This is suicidal policy and yet no concrete or effective steps have been taken to boost agriculture which is facing a great crisis. The India economy is burdened with foreign domination, industrial expansion and the Indian farming and farmers are decapitating the villages dedication and the country is in the grip of economic, social and political whirlpool. The time is ripe for us to ask what will happen to the rural economy and the Indian farmer on whose shoulder rests the future of the country."

The upshot of the entire analysis is that the major sin of economic reforms is gross neglect of agriculture —the mainstay of livelihood of over two-third of the population. Although the Tenth Plan has fixed a target of over 4 per cent for annual growth in agriculture, this target appears to be somewhat difficult to achieve. This is more so in view of the fact that though India had seven good monsoon years in succession, agricultural production indicated year-to-year fluctuations. This casts a shadow on sustainability of agricultural growth, unless there is a re-orientation of priorities with much greater emphasis on agriculture and rural industrialization. The state, instead of withdrawing from investment in agriculture, irrigation and rural infrastructure, has to strengthen public sector investment in these areas. In case, this is not done, bulk of the population dependent on agriculture will suffer and the country would also endanger long-term prospects of food security.

---

6. Mahesh V. Joshi: "Economic Reforms in India—A critical evaluation", A.P.H. Publishing Corporation, New Delhi, 1999.

V. NEW INITIATIVES FOR AGRICULTURAL DEVELOPMENT

In recent years, the government has realized the need for restructuring of agricultural sector. Several new initiatives have been taken for development of agriculture and allied sectors, some of them are discussed below:

(1) National Agricultural Policy (2000)

Agriculture Minister Mr. Nitish Kumar presented the National Agricultural Policy (2000) in the Parliament on July 28, 2000. The policy has been necessitated due to the relatively poor growth of agriculture during the nineties. The Policy document stated[7]: "Capital inadequacy, lack of infrastructural support and demand side constraints such as controls on movement, storage and sale of agricultural products, etc., have continued to affect the economic viability of agriculture sector. Consequently, growth has also tended to slacken during the nineties."

The National Agricultural Policy aims to attain the following objectives:[8]

- Privatisation of agriculture and price protection of farmers in the post-QR regime would be part of the Government's strategy to synergise agricultural growth. The focus of the new policy is on efficient use of resources and technology, adequate availability of credit to farmers and, protecting them from seasonal and price fluctuations. Over the next two decades the policy aims to attain a growth rate in excess of four per cent per annum in the agriculture sector.

---

7 Govt. of India, National Agricultural Policy (2000), Document, p. 1.

8. *Economic Survey*, 2000-01, p. 170.

- Private sector participation would be promoted through contract farming and land leasing arrangements to allow accelerated technology transfer, capital inflow, assured markets for crop production, especially of oilseeds, cotton and horticultural crops.
- Private sector investment in agriculture would be encouraged, particularly in areas like agricultural research, human resource development, post-harvest management and marketing.
- In view of dismantling of quantitative restrictions (QRS) on imports as per WTO agreement on agriculture, the policy has recommended formulation of commodity-wise strategies and arrangements to protect farmers from adverse impact of undue price fluctuations in the world market and promote exports.
- Government would enlarge coverage of futures markets to minimize the wide fluctuations in commodity prices as also for hedging their risks. The policy hoped to achieve sustainable development of agriculture, create gainful employment and raise standards of living.
- The Policy envisages evolving a "National Livestock Breeding Strategy" to meet the requirement of milk, meat, egg and livestock products and to enhance the role of draught animals as a source of energy for farming operations.
- Plant varieties would be protected through a legislation to encourage research and breeding of new varieties. Developmental of animal husbandry, poultry, dairy and aquaculture would receive top priority.
- High priority would be accorded to evolve new location-specific and economically viable improved varieties of farm and horticulture

crops, livestock species and aquaculture. Domestic agriculture market would be liberalized.

- The restrictions on the movement of agricultural commodities throughout the country would be progressively dismantled. The structure of taxes on foodgrains and other commercial crops would be reviewed.
- The excise duty on materials such as farm machinery and implements and fertilizers used as inputs in agricultural production, post-harvest storage and processing would be reviewed.
- Appropriate measures would be adopted to ensure that agriculturists, by and large, remained outside the regulatory and tax collection system.
- Rural electrification would be given high priority as a prime mover for agricultural development.
- The use of new and renewable sources of energy for irrigation and other agricultural purposes would be encouraged.
- Progressive institutionalization of rural and farm credit would be continued for providing timely and adequate credit to farmers.
- Endeavour would be made to provide a package insurance policy for the farmers, right from sowing of crops to post-harvest operations, including market fluctuations in the prices of agriculture produce.

The New Agricultural Policy promises Green Revolution, White Revolution (pertaining to milk and dairy products) and Blue Revolution (pertaining to açqua/fish culture). It has, therefore, been described as a policy of promising Rainbow Revolution.

However, the new policy suffers from following drawbacks:-

1. Firstly, there is no doubt that the 4 per cent growth of agricultural production is very necessary but the basic question is that but for making certain platitudinous statements, the New Agricultural Policy does not specify in quantitative terms the targets so that the objective can be achieved.
2. Secondly, the New Agricultural Policy does talk of growth with equity meaning thereby widespread coverage across regions, but fails to identify the states, which have lagged behind in the utilization of their agricultural potential. It would have been far better had the policy recommended a special package in the form of development in infrastructure in these states so that the process of rapid agricultural growth could be accelerated in them. This appears to be a serious shortcoming of the policy.
3. Thirdly, the policy speaks of encouraging private investment in agriculture. There is no doubt that private investment in the form of tubewells, agricultural implements, human resource development, etc. does help big farmers to improve their levels of productivity. But the small farmers who constitute the bulk of Indian farming community are unable to undertake private investment effectively to boost their productivity. They have to depend more and more on public investment, which has been declining over the years. Moreover, in backward states where the bulk of the peasantry is poor, public investment alone can provide big push to agriculture. The New Agricultural Policy does not make any serious commitment in this regard.
4. Lastly, the Government after making comprehensive recommendations in all areas of agricultural development has not outlined

any machinery of implementation. It has to be realized that agriculture in India is a state subject and the role of State Governments, which are the real implementing agencies of the various schemes, projects and programmes, becomes critical. In the absence of a blue print for action and also in the absence of a package for agriculturally backward states, how shall the New Agricultural Policy enthuse the states to implement it, is another important question. If the Centre intends the states to implement it, it must provide for schemes of Governments. This shall enable the Centre to institute a monitoring mechanism. In case this is not done, the policy will remain a statement of pious intentions.

2. Free Trade in Agri Products—A Major Step towards Agricultural Reforms

In a liberalized trade environment and with an emerging situation of oversupply of many agro-commodities, the incongruity of continuing draconian restrictions such as licensing of dealers, placing limits on stocks and control on movement of commodities—all under the Essential Commodities Act, 1955—had become a noose around the farmers' and traders' neck. Government has, therefore, issued a Central Order under section 3 of the Essential Commodities Act, 1955 to remove the requirement of licensing of dealers and restrictions on storage and movement in respect of foodgrains, sugar, oilseeds and edible oils. Twelve items such as cement, textile machinery, etc. have also been deleted from the purview of the Act bringing down the total number of essential commodities from the existing 29 to 17.

3. Kisan Credit Card Scheme

The Government of India introduced the Kisan Credit Card Scheme in 1998-99 so as to facilitate access to credit from Commercial Banks and Regional Rural Banks to the farmers. The salient features of the scheme are as given below:

(a) Farmers eligible for production credit of Rs. 5,000 or more are eligible for issue of Kisan Credit Card.
(b) Eligible farmers are to be provided with a Kisan Card and pass book or card-*cum*-pass book.
(c) Provision of revolving cash credit facility involving any number of drawals and repayments within the limit is introduced.
(d) Entire production credit needs for full year plus ancillary activities related to crop production is also considered.
(e) Limit is to be fixed on the basis of operational land holding, cropping pattern and scale of finance.
(f) Sub-limits may be fixed at the discretion of banks.
(g) The credit card is valid for three years subject to annual review.
(h) Each drawal is to be repaid within 12 months.
(i) Conversion/reschedulement of loans are also permissible in case of damage to crops due to natural calamities.
(j) As an incentive for good performance, the credit limits could be enhanced to take care of increase in costs, change in cropping pattern, etc.
(k) Security, margin and rate of interest against credit is fixed as per RBI norms.
(l) Operations may be run through issuing branch or at the discretion of bank, through other designated branches.

(m) Withdrawals can be made through slips/ cheques accompanied by card and passbook.

The Kisan Credit Card scheme is an innovative mechanism for facilitating access to short-term credit to farmers. The scheme has gained popularity and its implementation has been taken-up by 27 Commercial Banks, 378 Co-operative Banks and 196 Regional Rural Banks throughout the country. Upto September 2002, 271 lakh cards involving credit sanction of Rs. 64000 crore had been issued. Co-operative Banks accounted for 66 per cent of Kisan Credit Cards followed by Commercial Banks (27 per cent) and RRBs (7 per cent). The scheme announced in 2002-03 Budget for personal insurance cover for accidental death or permanent disability for the KCC holders has been operationalised by a number of banks.[9]

4. National Seed Policy, 2001

The use of quality seeds is vital for high per acre productivity in agriculture. The National Seeds Policy, 2001 provides a framework for ensuring the growth of the seed sector in a liberalized economic environment. It seeks to provide the Indian farmers with a wide range of superior seed varieties, and planting materials in adequate quantity. Some legislative measures are taken in respect of seeds in the form of Draft Seeds Act, 2001. The salient features of this legislation are:[10]

- Establishment of National Seeds Board (NSB).
- Compulsory registration by NSB of any seed for purpose of sowing or planting.
- Registration to be granted for new varieties on the basis of multi-locational trials over a minimum period of three seasons.

---

9. *Ibid.*, 2002-03, p. 166.
10. *Ibid.*, 2000-01, p. 162.

- The NSB will accredit ICAR Centres, State Agriculture Universities and private organizations to conduct Value for Cultivation and use trial for purpose of registration for a fixed period.
- Registration of seed producers and seed processing plants.
- Import and export of seeds will be regulated under this Act.
- Import for sale of seeds will be permitted only for registered varieties. Any person who imports seeds or planting material will declare whether such material is a product of transgenic manipulation or involves Genetic Use Restriction Technology.
- Import of seeds in limited quantity of unregistered variety is to be permitted for research and trial.

5. National Agricultural Insurance Scheme[11]

The National Agricultural Insurance Scheme (NAIS) has been introduced in the country from 1999-2000 Rabi season, replacing the comprehensive crop insurance scheme (CCIS) which was in operation in the country since 1985. The scheme is being implemented by the General Insurance Corporation on behalf of the Ministry of Agriculture. The main objective of the scheme is to protect the farmers against losses suffered by them due to crop failure on account of natural calamities, such as, drought, flood, hailstorm, cyclone, fire, pest, diseases, etc. so as to restore their credit worthiness for the ensuing season. At present the scheme is being implemented by 21 States/UTs.

---

11. *Ibid.*, 2002-03, p. 167.

6. Legislation on Plant Variety Protection and Farmers' Rights

The Protection of Plant Varieties and Farmer's Rights Legislation has been passed by Parliament. The salient features of this legislation are:[12]

- The objective of this legislation is to provide an effective system for the Protection of Plant Varieties and Farmers' Rights which will also stimulate investment for research and development both in public and private sector for development of new plant varieties by ensuring appropriate returns on such investment.
- The legislation recognizes the role of farmers as cultivators and conservers and the contribution of traditional, rural and tribal communities to the country's agro-bio-diversity by rewarding them for their contribution through benefit sharing and protecting the traditional rights of the farmers.
- The Act has some unique features like benefit sharing, community rights and establishment of gene funds, which will support conservation and sustainable use of agro-bio-diversity.
- The Act has provision to set-up a Protection of Plant Varieties and Farmers' Right Authority to perform all functions related to the protection of plant varieties.

7. Watershed Development Fund[13]

In order to channelize greater resources for rainfed areas, the Watershed Development Fund (WDF)

---

12. Govt. of India, Planning Commission: Tenth Plan 2002-07, p. 195.
13. *Ibid.*, p. 584.

was set-up in 2000-01 at the National Bank for Agriculture and Rural Development (NABARD) with a corpus of Rs. 200 crore. The fund is to be used for integrated watershed development in 100 priority districts across in states in a phased manner through a participatory approach. Six states—Andhra Pradesh, Maharashtra, Gujarat, Madhya Pradesh, Orissa and Uttar Pradesh—would be covered in the first phase. In the second phase, the programme would be extended to Bihar, Kerala, Rajasthan, Tamilnadu, Jammu and Kashmir, West Bengal, Himachal Pradesh and Haryana.

8. Agri-Export Zones[14]

In the EXIM Policy 2001-02, the Government announced the proposal to set-up Agri-Export Zones for the purpose of developing and sourcing raw materials and their processing/packaging leading to final exports. The concept essentially embodies a cluster approach of identifying the potential products and the geographical region in which such products are grown and adoption of an end to end approach of integration of the entire process, right from the stage of production of consumption.

Under the Scheme, the State Governments would identify products with export potential which have comparative advantage in local production. Agricultural and Processed Food Products Development Authority (APEDA) is the nodal agency of the Central Government to promote setting up of Agri-Export Zones.

Till December 2002, the Central Government has sanctioned and notified 41 Agri Export Zones (AEZs) which are being set-up in 17 States—West Bengal, Uttaranchal, Karnataka, Punjab, Uttar Pradesh, Tamilnadu, Maharashtra, Andhra Pradesh, Tripura, J&K, Madhya Pradesh, Bihar, Gujarat, Sikkim, HP, Orissa and Jharkhand—Covering products like Lychee, Pineapple, Potatoes, Onion, Garlic, Mangoes (Kesar, Chausa,

---

14. *Economic Survey* 2002-03, p. 174.

Dusshari, Alphonso, etc.), Grapes, Flowers, Apples, Vegetables, Walnuts, Gherkins, Wheat, Ginger and Turmeric, Basmati Rice and Seed Spices.

9. Towards Agricultural Diversification[15]

In the new phase of economic reforms, an attempt is being made to diversify agriculture. The Ministry of Food Processing is setting up food parks in different parts of the country. The idea behind setting up of food parks is to enable small and medium entrepreneurs find access to capital intensive facilities, such as cold storage, warehouse, quality control labs, effluent treatment plants, etc. Development of such facilities is expected to make the food processing units in the food parks cost competitive besides improving their market accessibility. So far 30 food parks have been sanctioned in different parts of the country. The Ministry is also in the process of introducing a new Plan Scheme for development of infrastructure like cold chain, storage, etc. for the benefit of food processing units in addition to the scheme of food parks already in existence.

The ministry is also operating Plan Schemes on the Promotion of Total Quality Management including ISO 9000, ISO 14000, Hazard Analysis and Critical Control Points (HACCP), Good manufacturing practices, Good Hygienic Practices, etc. with the following objectives:

- To motivate the food processing industries for adoption of food safety and quality assurance mechanism.
- To prepare them to face the global competition in the international trade in the post-WTO era.
- To enable adherence to a stringent quality in hygiene norms.

---

15. *Ibid.*, p. 161

- To enhance product acceptance by overseas buyers.
- To keep Indian Food industry technologically abreast of international best practices.

In addition, Ministry of Food processing is also working towards the promotion of bar coding on food packages, as the bar coding is on its way to become almost a compulsory requirement in the global market.

VI. WTO AGREEMENT AND AGRICULTURE SECTOR

No other issue in recent times has generated so much heat than the likely repercussions of the new international economic order under WTO on World economy in general and developing countries in particular. According to supporters the setting up of WTO is expected to bring about substantial gains in world trade and increased income from liberalization improved market access and greater export opportunities, besides greater predictability of the trading environment. The Government of India has also been harping on this tune. However, the critics have pointed out that the entire negotiation process in various meetings of WTO was ruthlessly dominated by the developed countries (Particularly the USA) and the results that have emerged are highly tilted in their favour. The poor countries operated on the periphery, seldom consulted until the rich ones had completed negotiations among themselves. As noted by Kevin Watkins, "Whatever the skills of negotiators from the South, for the most part they are like extras on the GATT Stage: the show cannot go on without them, but nobody is remotely interested in what they have to say."[16]

---

16. Quoted by Biplab Dasgupta, "Structural Adjustment, Global Trade and the New Political Economy of Development", New Delhi, 1998, p. 147.

Herein, an attempt has been made to highlight the likely favourable and unfavourable effects of the new economic order on agriculture sector of Indian economy. The foremost benefit that India expects relates to the improved prospects for agricultural exports as a result of likely increase in the world prices of agricultural products due to reduction in domestic subsidies and barriers to trade. While on the one hand earnings from agricultural exports are likely to increase, on the other hand, India has ensured that all major programmes for the development of agriculture will be exempted from the disciplines in the agricultural agreement. Thus, the operation of the public distribution system will not be affected by the provisions of the Agreement, agricultural subsidies granted by developing countries need not be withdrawn till such time they remain within the prescribed limits specified in the Agreement; and protection necessary for development of the agricultural sector in the underdeveloped countries might be continued.

Secondly, as per agreement, it is not expected to raise India's imports of foodgrains. It is stated in the treaty that the poor countries facing balance of payments problem may continue to impose Tariff on the imports of foodgrains. India can avail of this provision and avoid imports of food stuffs thereby stay off easy imports of foodgrains.

However, the critics point out to various adverse implications of WTO for India, which are stated as under:

1. Firstly, the extension of intellectual property rights to agriculture (via the patenting of plant varieties) has serious consequences for India. In India, plant breeding and seed production are largely in the public domain. Plant breeding is undertaken by agricultural universities and units of ICAR (Indian Council of Agricultural Research), whereas seed multiplication is in the hands of the National

and State Seed Corporations. This is due to the reason that India being a poor country where agriculture is the livelihood of the majority of the population, the government must bear the responsibility of ensuring the supply of adequate quantities of seeds at reasonable prices to the farmers. The aim is not to maximize profit as would be the case in the private sector, but to sustain the livelihood of the majority of the population on the one hand, and to achieve self-sufficiency in foodgrains on the other hand. Patenting of plant varieties will transfer all the gains to the multinational companies. Almost all new varieties will belong to MNCs simply by virtue of their massive financial resources. As noted by Suman Sahai, "Research is unfortunately as much a matter of talent as of money. More money means more resources to invest in breeding and it means greater speed in putting varieties on the market."[17] In terms of financial resources, there is absolutely no comparison between MNCs and Indian companies. In fact, the research budgets alone of some of these MNCs are more than the budget of Indian Union. If Indian research institutions are unable to compete financially and are denied access to patented genetic material (as TRIPs Agreement is designed to ensure), the Indian scientists will find it extremely difficult to breed new varieties. This will gradually become the sole privilege of the large foreign companies. As a result, the control over our genetic resources will pass onto the hands of MNCs who will not find it difficult to control

17. Suman Sahai, "American Pressure to Open Up Indian Agriculture", *Economic and Political Weekly*, February 24, 1996, p. 443.

the seed production in this country. Since control of seed production implies control over food supply, the entire Indian food security system will be jeopardized and thrown out of gear.

2. Secondly, another area of controversy has been the limits on the extent to which farmers can be provided subsidies. Dunkel Final Act stipulates that developing countries can subsidise upto 10 per cent of their value of output, while developed countries have a lower ceiling of 5 per cent. In case, in a country subsidies are higher than the limits set by the Final Act, then they should be reduced by 20 per cent within a period of six years. In that sense, there is an effort to introduce "subsidies discipline." In this connection, it needs to be pointed out that a uniform treatment to subsidies for both developed and under-developed countries is not rational. The reason being the difference in the nature of subsidies in different countries. Developed countries subsidise their agriculture so that they can dump cheap grains in the markets of other countries, while in contrast, developing countries use subsidies to help the farmers to buy inputs at lower prices so that they can increase their production and thus reduce their dependence in food and agricultural raw materials on foreign countries. Another crucial function of the subsidies is to make foodgrains available to the people at affordable prices and thus food subsidies play a crucial role in controlling food grain prices so that the masses get food at cheap rates.
3. Thirdly, under TRIPs (Trade Related Intellectual Property Rights), patenting has been extended not only to plant varieties but to the large area of micro-organism as well.

> Micro organisms refer to very small forms of life. In this category are included such living creatures as bacteria, virus, fungus, algae, small plants and animals, and even genes. Patents in the field (agriculture, pharmaceuticals and industrial bio-technology) linked to micro-organisms are either already with the multinational companies or are likely to be acquired at a much faster rate *vis-à-vis* the developing countries. Thus, the multinational companies belonging to developed countries are likely to dominate the global economy that will emerge in the coming years.

Negotiations on agriculture, which have been taken taking place in special sessions of the WTO Committee on Agriculture, have focused on achieving progressive and substantial reforms in agriculture trade. While the discussion leading to Cancun had centered around bridging the divergence between the common positions taken by the European community (EC) and the US and those of the G-20 alliance, the post-Cancun deliberations strengthened the G-20 alliance and emphasized their outreach to others, in particular the G-33 alliance of developing countries on special products, the Africa group, and the Cairns group of agriculture exporting countries. The G-20 was successful in exposing the EC and the US as demanders of substantial market access in developing countries, in Particular, the large and relatively more advanced among them, and without regard to their legitimate food and livelihood security and rural development concerns, with only minimal market access commitments being called forth from themselves. The G-20 also emphasized the requirement to eliminate all forms subsidies within a credible time-frame and to achieve substantial reductions in trade-distorting domestic support. In the lead-up to the WTO General Council Decision of August 1, 2004 (Framework Agreement), the negotiations among the five interested

Parties (FIPs), comprising the EC, the US, Australia, Brazil and India, resolved the divergent positions on key aspects of each of the three pillars in the agriculture negotiations.

The framework agreement explicitly agrees to eliminate export subsidies by a credible date. It imposes a down payment of 20 per cent on overall trade-distorting domestic support in the first year of implementation, besides containing a combination of cuts, disciplines and monitoring requirements in the various elements of the domestic support pillar, and a tired formula for tariff reductions based on proportionately lower commitments by the developing countries *vis-a-vis* those by the developed countries. The Framework also recognizes the critical importance of agricultural policies that are supportive of their developmental goals, poverty reduction strategies, food security and livelihood concerns, through instruments such as Special Safeguard mechanism against likely import surges. The Framework, thus, provides a useful basis for further negotiations on detailed modalities that could help market access opportunities for products of export interest and safeguard small and vulnerable producers of farm products.

However, it must be realized that WTO is a new emerging reality of 21st century. It should be seen as a gate-way to free trade, foreign investment, foreign technology and foreign ideas which can be and shall be made available to the Indian economy. Our Indian Economy needs it most for growth, self-reliance and for making people acquainted with new objects and the easier acquisition of things which they have not previously thought to be attainable. Indian farmer on its part must look not only to the domestic market but also seize opportunities in global market for improved value added realization and diversification opportunists offered by WTO. Dr. Manmohan Singh has rightly observed.[18] "GATT Treaty is expected to diversify Indian

---

18. Manmohan Singh, "India's Export Trend', Oxford University Press, London.

agriculture, encourage India's multilateral transactions of scientific knowledge and raise productivity standard and output manifold."

To sum up, it may be said that agriculture still employs two-thirds of India's labour force. There is enormous scope for increasing employment and production in agriculture through higher private and public investment, more and better infrastructure, faster dissemination of best-practice cropping techniques and improvements in water management. The bias against agriculture in the overall incentive framework has been greatly reduced in recent years and should be eliminated. Remaining restrictions on internal and external trade in agricultural commodities should be removed. The sector of agro-industry, still subject to licensing control should be delicensed so that competition between manufacturers can work to the benefit of farmers and rural workers. Irrigation is the life-blood of rural economy, but the funds allocated in the state budgets are usually insufficient for maintenance of irrigation canals and channels and the bureaucratic functioning of irrigation departments often impedes best use of water resources. Institutional innovations should be sought to make the provision and maintenance of irrigation services much more responsive to farmer interests. Conversely, farmers must be prepared to shoulder a growing proportion of the costs of irrigation services.

(Research Paper II)

Appendix II

Globalisation in Retailing: Causes, Impact and Trends in India[1]

1. INTRODUCTION

Retailing provides a crucial link between producers and consumers in a modern market economy. The performance of this sector has a strong influence on consumer welfare. Retailers not only provide consumers with a wide variety of products, but also a wide range of complementary services (such as assurance of product delivery), which can lead to more informed choice and greater convenience in shopping. They also provide producers with the much needed information on consumer demand pattern. Productivity and efficiency in retail operations and lower price levels and reduce distortions in the price structure. Through backward and forward linkages, performance of retailing services affects the performance of interlinked sectors such as tourism, recreational and cultural services, manufacturing of consumer goods, agro-food processing industries, etc.[2]

---

1. A Research Paper presented at National Seminar on "Foreign Direct Investment in Retail Business", at G.N. Khalsa College, Karnal on Feb. 18, 2006.
2. FDI in Retail Sector in India, Department of Consumer Affairs, Ministry of Consumer Affairs, Public and Food Department, Government of India, p. 21.

The objective of this paper is to analyse the global developments in retailing and to identify the reasons for globalisation of retailing, besides, the paper will analyse the impact of retailing on developing countries and finally the analyses of FDI in retailing in India is undertaken.

II. DEFINITION OF RETAILING

In India, the definition of retail trade is still evolving with changes in technology, integration of the various modes of operation. For the purpose of this paper, the following definition of retailing has been used. This definition takes into account the evolving formats and is derived in consultation with various retailers, industry representatives and retail experts:

> "Retailing is defined as all activities involved in selling goods or services directly to final consumers for their personal, non-business use via shops, markets, door-to-door selling, mail order or over the internet, where the buyer intends to consume the product through personal, family or household dues."

Retailing can be divided into two parts:

(a) Organized Retailing

Any retail outlet chain (and not a one shop outlet) which is professional managed (even if it is family run), has accounting transparency (with proper usage of MIS and accounting standards) and organized supply chain management with centralized quality control and sourcing (certain part of the sourcing can be locally made) can be termed as an organized retailing in India.[3]

---

3. U.S. Department of Labour, Bureau of labour statistics. http// stats.bls.gov/iag/whole retailtrade.htm

(b) Unorganized Retailing

Any retail outlet which is run locally by the owner or the caretaker of the shop, such outlets lack technical and accounting standardization. The supply chain and the sourcing are also done locally to meet the local needs.

III. GLOBAL DEVELOPMENTS IN RETAILING

The structure of the retail sector of a country reflects its socio-demographic characteristic. The size and density of retail outlets are determined by demand-related phenomenon such as population density, level of urbanisation, participation rate of women in the labour force, access to cars, taste, personal consumption expenditure, etc. The structure also varies with the level of development of the country and speed of adaptation of new technology such as use of credit cards. In the early stages of development, bulk of the retail enterprises consists of the single shop or sole proprietorships. As the economy diversifies and the per capita income increases, these traditional small shops are gradually replaced by larger enterprises. This, in turn, results in consolidation and currently more than 50 fortune 500 companies and around 25 Asian Top 200 companies are retailers. Retailing with total sales exceeding US$ 8 trillion in 2003, is one of the biggest private industries in the world. It is extremely difficult to analyse nationally, globally and on a cross-country basis the growth in output and employment in retailing since only a few countries have reliable data on retail trade. Moreover, statistical information collected by various sources are often contradictory and mutually conflicting. Nevertheless, it is estimated that this sector accounts for more than 10 percent of GDP in the western economies. Among developing countries, the sector accounts for around 10 percent of GDP of India and 8 percent of GDP of China. The sector is labour-intensive and contributes significantly to employment.

Contribution of retailing to employment of the selected countries is presented in Table I. In the US, retail trade represents around 11.7 percent of all employment and about12.9 percent of all establishments. Retailing is the UK's top service industry, employing around 2.8 million people (around 11 percent of the UK's workforce) as on March 2004. In 2002, the sector had £ 230 billion in sales (35 percent of total consumer spending). Over the five years period (1999-2004), employment in UK's retail sector grew by over 230,500.

TABLE I

Share of Retailing in Total Employment in Selected Countries

Country	*Share of retails in Total Employment (%)*
India	6-7
China	6
Poland	12
Brazil	15
USA	11.7
Korea	18
UK	11
Malaysia	7

Source: Extracted from Mckinsey, 2000.

In developed countries, more than three-fourths of the total retail trade is being handled by the organised sector 5. The share of organised sector is also increasing in many developing countries (Table II) but it is very low in the case of India (Only 2 percent).[4]

Food and grocery constitute the large segment of retailing and major proportion of sale of top global

4. *Ibid.*

TABLE II

Organised Retailing as a Percentage of Total Retailing

Country	*Current Share of Organised Retailing (in percentage)*
USA	80
Western European countries	70
Argentina	40
Brazil	40
Thailand	40
Korea	35
Taiwan	35
China	20
Malaysia	20
Poland	20
India	20

Source: Extracted from Mckinsey, 2000.

retailers. The top 30 global retailers together with their percentage of sale from grocery and the percentage of sales in domestic and foreign markets for the year 2003 are given in Table III. The number of stores and countries of operation of some large retailers in 2002 is given in Table IV.

IV. REASONS FOR GLOBALISATION OF RETAILING: SUPPLY AND DEMAND SIDE FACTORS

Unlike manufacturers, most retailers prefer to operate in the domestic market. This is because retailing is taste driven and it is difficult to understand the consumer behaviour in a foreign country. This localised nature of the industry has gradually changed in the 20th century with increased globalisation, convergence of tastes and removal of trade barriers to

TABLE III

Top 30 Global Retailers with their Sales in Grocery and Percentage Share of Domestic and Foreign Sales in Total Retail Sales, 2003

Rank	*Company*	*Country of Origin*	*Net Sales 2003 (USD mn)*	*Grocery Sales (%)*	*Domestic SalesS (%)*	*Foreign ales (%)*
1.	Wal-Mart	USA	256,329	43.7	79.1	20.9
2.	Carrefour	France	79,609	77.4	50.7	49.3
3.	Ahold	Neth.	63,325	84.0	15.8	84.2
4.	Metro Group	Germany	60,532	50.5	52.9	47.1
5.	Kroger	USA	53,791	70.2	100.0	0.0
6.	Tesco	UK	50,326	74.6	80.1	19.9
7.	Target	USA	48,163	17.8	100.00	0.0
8.	Rewe	Germany	44,251	7.6	71.4	28.6
9.	Aldi	Germany	41,011	83.6	63.0	37.0
11.	ITM (Intermarche)	France	37,723	77.3	72.2	27.8
12.	Safeway (USA)	USA	35,552	75.5	85.3	14.7
13.	Schwarz Group	Germany	33,357	83.0	66.2	33.8
14.	Schwarz Group	Germany	33,357	83.0	66.2	33.8
15.	Walagreens	USA	32,505	380	100.00	0.0
16.	Auchan	France	32,422	57.2	57.5	42.5
17.	AEON	Japan	30,574	47.2	91.7	8.3
18.	Ito-Yokado	Japan	30,541	62.5	73.8	26.2
19.	Edeka	Germany	29,670	83.8	91.2	8.8
20.	Sainsbury	UK	27,995	73.3	85.1	14.9
21.	Tengelmann	Germany	27,721	69.7	49.1	50.9
22.	Leclerc	France	27,332	59.9	95.7	4.3
23.	CVS	USA	26,588	31.2	100.0	0.0
24.	Casino	France	25,958	73.3	58.9	41.1
25.	Kmart	USA	23,253	14.0	100.0	0.0
26.	Delhaize Group	Belgium	21,256	77.1	20.1	79.9
27.	Loblaw	Canada	18,002	77.5	100.0	0.0
28.	JC Penney	USA	17,786	16.9	99.4	0.6
29.	Coles Myer	Australia	17,523	58.5	99.4	0.6
30.	Daiei	Japan	17,158	43.3	98.9	1.1
	Total Top 30		1,287,382			
	Others		2,612,618			
	Total Worldwide		3,900,000			

Source: Extracted from M+M Planet Retail.

TABLE IV

Number of Stores and Countries of Operation of the Few Global Retailers in 2002

Company/ Country of Origin	*No. of Stores*	*Countries of Operation*
Wal-Mart Store/ United States	5.164 (1)	Argentina, Brazil, Canada, China, Germany, Japan, Maxico, Singapore, Republic of Korea, United Kingdom, United States, Vietnam.
Carrefour/ France	10,704	Argentina, Balgium, Brazil, Chile, China, Colombia, Czech Republic, Dominican Republic, Egypt France, Greece, Indonesia, Italy, Japan, Malaysia, Mexico, Oman, Poland, Portugal, Qatar, Romania, Singapore, Slovakia, Republic of Korea, Spain, Switzerland, Taiwan Province of China, Thailand, Tunisia, Turkey, United States.
Ahold/ Netherlands	9,407	Argentina, Brazil, Chile, Costa Rica, Czech Republic, Denmark, Ecuador, El Salvador, Estonia, Guatemala, Honduras, Indonesia, Latvia, Lithurania, Malaysia, Netherlands, Nicargua, Orway, Paraguay, Peru, Poland, Portugal, Slovakia, Spain, Sweden, Thailand, United States (2).
Metro/ Germany	2,411	Austria, Belgium, Bulgaria, China, Croatia, Czech Republic, Denmark, France, Germany, Greece, Hungary, India, Italy, Japan, Luxembourg, Moracco, Netherlands, Poland, Portugal, Romania, Russian Federation, Slovakia, Spain, Switzerland, Turkey, United Kingdom, Ukraine, Vietname
Tesco/ United Kingdom	2,294	Czech Republic, Hungary, Ireland, Malaysia, Poland, Slovakia, Republic of Korea, Taiwan Province of China, Thailand, United Kingdom, United States

Costco/ United States	400	Canada, Japan, Mexico, Republic of Korea, Taiwan Province of China, United Kingdom, United States.
Rewe Zentrale/ Germany	12,077	Austria, Bulgaria, Croatia, Czech Republic, France, Germany, Hungary, Italy, Poland, Romania, Slovakia, Ukraine.
Aidi/ Germany	6,609	Australia, Austria, Belgium, Denmark, France, Germany, Ireland, Luxembourg, Netherlands, Spain, United Kingdom, United States.

Source: Extracted from M+M Planet Retail.

retail expansions. Also, the markets in developed countries are becoming more and more saturated, competition is driving down profits and forcing the retailers to expand their operation in never markets. The main reason for globalisation of retailing are:

- Saturated domestic market.
- Convergence of taste.
- High competition in domestic market leading to lower profit.
- Need to set-up global sourcing networks and supply chain.
- Liberalisation and removal of other trade barriers in developing countries.
- Rapid liberalisation, improvement in infrastructure, increase in per capita income and purchasing power, entry of women into workforce, etc. in developing countries have encouraged globalisaton of retailing.[5]

V. FDI IN RETAILING AND ITS IMPACT

In recent years the destination sectors of FDI have become more varied. FDI inflows have shifted from

5. http://www.brc.org.uk/latesdata.asp

infrastructure, natural resources and export driven manufacturing to other areas such as retailing, tourism, construction and offshare services. A World Bank study[6] showed that cumulative FDI inflows to the retail sector in the 20 largest developing countries amounted to US $45 billion in 1998-2002 (about 7 percent of the total of these countries). The study showed that after liberalisation, countries such as Brazil, Poland and Thailand have received significant FDI in retailing. In another study Bajpai and Dasgupta[7] presented a comparative analysis of FDI flows from multinational companies into China and India over 1992-2001 and concluded that one of the reason why China has received more FDI than India is that the country has allowed FDI in retailing while in India there is FDI cap.

Due to paucity of data, there are hardly any empirical studies on the impact of FDI in retailing on the developing countries. In general, FDI in retailing have following impact:

- Improved productivity and efficiency in retail sector. The foreign firms transferred advanced management know how in merchandising and inventory managements and introduced new technologies which improved productivity. The simplest example of increase in efficiency is that technology such as bar coding has now trickled down to small retailers. Moreover, small retailers that like large retailers are adopting such techniques as printing promotional leaflets, price tags and shopping bags for participating members.

---

6. Bajpai and Das Gupta (2004) 'Multinational companies and FDI in China and India', CGSO Working Paper No. 2, January. The Earth Institute of Columbia University.
7. Palmade, V. and Andrea Anayiotas (2004), "Foreign Direct Investments Trends: Looking Beyond the current gloom in Developing Countries." *Public Policy Journal*, September 2004.

- The impact of the entry of foreign retailers on employment is controversial while some studies show that they have led to unemployment by forcing the local players out of business, others have countered the claim by asserting that they have created more jobs, not just in their stores but also in supporting industry. In Thailand, when foreign retailers entered the country during Asian Crisis, there presence increased the pace of unemployment. However, when the economy recovered, employment in retailing increased. Low salary and long working hours characterized the Malaysian retail sector, but with the advent of foreign players salary level became at per with other industries and working conditions improved.[8] In India, direct selling format companies such as Amway, Tupperware and oriflame have created significant employement.
- Entry of large low-cost retailers is likely to lower prices. Prof. Basker[9] estimated the impact of entry of Wal-Mart on retail prices and found that prices declined by 2-10 percent in short-run and approximately twice the size in the long-run.
- The modernisation of retail sector and entry of foreign retailers benefited consumers at all levels. Consumer are assured of product quality, they have better shopping experience and have access to better customer services.

---

8. Bajpai and Das Gupta (2004), 'Multinational companies and FDI in China and India' CGSO Working Paper No. 2, January. The Earth Institute of Columbia University.
9. Domestic Trade Forum, "Towards a study growth of Domestic Trade Economy, presentation by Malaysia Retailer Association, 19 May, 2003 quoted in "FDI in retail sector"; Department of consumer affairs, Govt. of India, p.34.

- FDI in retailing linked local suppliers, farmers, manufacturer to global market. For farmers and producers who can meet the quality and safety standards of super markets, entering the supply chain of supermarket ensures a reliable and profitable market for goods and even access to the global market through chain of international retailer. The global retailers are directly sourcing their products from the producers. This has benefited the producers with the better price of their produce.
- FDI in retailing has encouraged investment in the supply chain. As multinational retailers are spreading their operation, regional players are also developing their supply chain, differentiating their strategies and improving their operations to counter the size of international players. Regional players key advantage lie in their understanding of the retail market and knowledge of supply market, while international retailers have advantage of technology, management and marketing skills, purchasing power and new formats. In order to compete with global rivals, the regional players attempt to consolidate their position through mergers and acquisition and are rapidly increasing the number of hypermarkets, supermarket, and other store formats.[10]

VI. FDI IN RETAILING IN INDIA—POLICY AND ENTRY ROUTES

In India, till recently, FDI is not allowed in retailing, but the Union Cabinet on January 24, 2006 rationalised and simplified the FDI policy and allowed

10. Basker, E., "Job creation or destruction; labour market effects of Wal-Mart Expansion", Department of Economics, University of Missouri, Working Paper No. 0215.

the contentious issue of foreign investment in retail sector by allowing FDI upto 51 percent with prior government approval for retail trade in single brand products. This would imply that foreign companies would be allowed to sell goods sold internationally under a single brand, viz. Reebok, Nokia, Adidas. Retailing of goods of multiple brands, even if such products are produced by same manufacturer would not be allowed. But, due to strong opposition of left parties, it remains to be seem whether the policy will be implemented or not.

Although FDI is not allowed in retailing, many international players are operating in the country. Some of these entry routes re discussed in details below:[11]

(a) Manufacturing and Local Sourcing

Companies that set-up manufacturing facilities are allowed to sell the products in the domestic market. Consumer durable companies such as Sony and Samsung have entered the retail sector through this route. Due to high labour cost in their domestic market, many international brands are setting up manufacturing bases in developing countries such as India and China and/or are sourcing products from local manufacturers. For example, Levi's and Tommy Hilfiger are sourcing products from Indian manufacturers like Arvind Mills. Benetton has a manufacturing unit in India. Other international brands like GIVO from Italy have set-up export-oriented manufacturing facilities. These companies are allowed to sell products to Indian consumers through franchising, local distributors, existing Indian retailers, own outlets, etc.

(b) Franchising

Franchising is the most preferred mode through which foreign players have entered the Indian market. It

---

11. *The Tribune*, Chandigarh, Jan. 25, 2006.

is the easiest route to enter the Indian market. Franchising is often used as a mode to expand the market of a particular retail enterprise outside domestic economy since it allows firms to expand without investing their own capital, is based on local expertise and enables firms to crub local oppositions and regulations. This is the most common mode for entry of fast food chains across the world. Apart from fast food chains like Pizza Hut, players such as Lacoste, Mango, Nike and Marks and Spencer, have entered the Indian market through this route.

For setting up franchising operation, the foreign players are required to take permission from the Reserve Bank of India (RBI). RBI often imposes the condition that franchisers have to bring in foreign investment and set-up a base for carrying on operational activities. A foreign franchiser not wishing to make a direct investment would have to render technical assistance to the franchisee. Some franchisee, such as Pizza Hut have made significant investment in the supply chain.

The arrangements between franchisee and franchiser are found to be extremely flexible and are based on negotiation between the two. Some Indian franchisees have complained about high franchising fees together with high real estate costs, high import duties and other costs escalate the prices. For instance, the cost of a Marks and Spencer product is higher than not only the brands produced domestically but also in comparison to the price of the product in the UK. The high prices restrict the ability of the foreign players to penetrate the market but they have entered the country to make their brands visible to the huge Indian market.

If FDI is allowed in retailing, franchisees are not very sure whether they would hold the retailing rights for the brands. According to industry representatives, since franchisees largely constitute of domestic traders (even some unorganised retailers have take up franchising rights) who have made significant investment in infrastructure, government through legislation must ensure that they do not loose out their franchising rights if FDI is allowed in retailing and the franchisers decide to change the mode of operation. The existing franchisees have also expressed an interest in entering into joint venture with the franchisers if FDI is allowed in retailing.

(c) Test Marketing

Test marketing is another route through which many foreign players have entered the Indian market. Foreign Investment Promotion Board (FIPB) allows foreign companies to test market products for a two-year period by the end of which they are required to set-up manufacturing facilities in India. Direct selling companies like Amway and Oriflame entered the Indian market through this route. Initially, Amway got an approval for test marketing for a period of two years but they managed to secure an extension of one more year. At the end of the third year, they set-up contract manufacturing facilities and brought in foreign investment and technical know-how. Oriflame too extended its test marketing license for a third year and at the end of which had set-up a manufacturing facility in Noida (UP) for producing certain specific products. Other products are imported and would continue to be imported from abroad.

Nokia came to India through the test marketing route in mid-1990s. Initially they got a license for two years to test their products in the Mumbai circle. After three months of their entry they tied up with the service providers to provide integrated services to their customers. Due to pressure from the FIPB, Nokia had tied up with the HCL Infotech as a strategic partner for all India distribution of Nokia products. After the success of its products in the country, Nokia had opened up an office but had not set-up a manufacturing facility and continued to import all products (even models made specifically for India). After another two years they divided the country into four zones and entered into a strategic alliance for distribution with Supreme for East and West India while HCL continued with North and Southern zone. Nokia had also applied for the cash and carry license from the FIPB and has recently got the license. Nokia is aggressively targeting the Indian consumers and plan to capture 75 percent of the mobile market in the next seven years. The company, which currently operates as a wholesale cash-and-carry, recently announced that it would set-up manufacturing facilities by 2006.

The test marketing route allows foreign players to test the demand for their products in Indian market before undertaking investment. Even if FDI is allowed in retailing, many foreign players would like to enter the Indian market through this route.

(d) Wholesale Cash-and-Carry Operation

This is the route through which large international retailers such as Germany's Metro Cash and Carry GmbH and Shoprite Checkers of South Africa have entered the Indian market. The wholesale cash-and-carry operation is defined as any trading outlets where goods are sold at the wholesale rate for retailers and businesses to buy. The transactions are only for business purposes and not for personal consumption as in the case of retailing.

(e) Distributor

Companies such as Swarovski and Hugo Boss have set-up distribution offices in India and these offices supply the products to local India retailers. All products of Hugo Boss are imported and distributed through the company's distributor.

(f) Special Cases

The Sri Lankan retailers have entered the India market through the initiatives of Export Development

Board of Sri Lanka (EDB) which obtained special permission from the RBI to set-up retail operations in India. The EDB has leased 17 retail outlets in Spencer Plaza in Chennai in which Sri Lankan retailers are showcasing and selling their products. The Sri Lankan products showcased in these stores are mostly at the higher end of the quality spectrum and can be brought into the country free of duty. This gives an advantage to large Sri Lankan retailers like Hameedia not only to establish a global presence but also to access the large customer base of India at competitive prices. The EDB is also exploring the possibilities of setting up similar trade centres in other cities like Delhi and Mumbai. Although this mode has allowed retailers from Sri Lanka to enter the Indian market without domestic manufacturing and sourcing conditions and some products sold by these traders are similar to those sold by Indian retailers, EDB did not face any opposition from Chambers, retailers and the trading houses.

Although the official policy is that as yet FDI is not allowed in retailing, but it has not acted as an entry barrier. Foreign players have a substantial presence in the country and have used different routes to enter Indian Trading Sector. Some of the existing foreign players and prospecting entrants are listed below in Table V.[12]

VII. CONCLUSION

In the end, FDI Retailing is likely to lead to more investment in organised retailing and allied sectors. It would lead to establishment of sophisticated supply chains, inflow of technical know-how, investment in up-gradation of human skills and increasing souring from India. Yet following precautions are required for permitting FDI in Retailing:

---

12. FDI in Retail Sector in India, Department of Consumer Affairs, Ministry of Consumer Affairs, Public and Food Department, Government of India, pp. 107-111.

TABLE V

Some Existing Foreign Players and Prospective Entrants

Retailers	*Type*	*Status*
7-Eleven	Supermarket	Evaluating
Amway	Direct selling	Already in
Auchan	Hypermarket	Evaluating
Carrefour	Multi-format retailer	Postponed entry
Dairy Farm	Multi-format retailers	Tied up with RPG
JC Penny	Product sourcing	Already in
Landmark	Department Store	Already in
Lee Cooper	Product sourcing	Already in
Levi's	Product sourcing	Already in
Mango	Apparel retailer	Already in
Marks and Spencer	Department Store	Already in
Metro	Cash and carry	Already in
Oriflame	Direct selling	Already in
Reebok	Oint venture	Already in
Shoprite	Wholesale cash-and-carry and franchising	Already in
Sony	Manufacturer Retailer	Already in
Wal-Mart	Hypermarket	Wait and watch (has a distribution centre)

Source: FDI in Retail Sector, Department of consumer affairs, Government of India, p. 115.

(a) Foreign players should not be allowed to trade in certain sensitive products like arms and ammunition, military equipment, etc. and the list of excluded products should be clearly stated in the FDI policy.

(b) FDI should not be restricted to certain products types (i.e., branded products) or store formats (large department stores).

(c) Certain zoning restrictions may be imposed by the state government/local bodies for town planning. However, such restrictions should not distinguish between domestic and foreign retailers with similar store formats.

The strategy of opening up should be backed by appropriate reform measures. India can learn from the experiences of other developed and developing countries and develop its own strategies, laws and regulations that would be in the best interest of the country. As of now, there is no proper definition of retailing or retail formats in India. International players are exploiting the situation and are often entering the market and expanding their businesses through multiple routes and are operating in the country with more than one format of retailing. The regulatory regime should address these issues. The entry norms should clearly state the approval requirements, conditions/restrictions if any imposed, etc. The government should also strictly enforce the quality standards for local production and imports.

(Research Paper III)

Appendix III

Perceptions, Concerns and Likely Impact of FDI in Retail on Indian Market[1]

Retailing is the largest private industry in India and second largest employer after agriculture. The sector contributes to around 10 per cent of GDP and 6-7 percent of employment. With over 15 million retail outlets, India has the highest retail outlet density in the world. This sector witnessed significant development in the past 10 years—from small unorganised family-owned retail formats to organised retailing. Liberalisation of the economy, rise in per capita income and growing consumerism have encouraged large business houses and manufacturers to set-up retail formats; real estate companies and venture capitalists are investing in retail infrastructure. Many foreign retailers have also entered the market through different routes such as wholesale cash-and-carry, local manufacturing, franchising, test marketing, etc. With the growth in organised retailing, unorganised retailers are fast changing their business

---

* Based on survey by Arpita Mukherjee and Nitisha Patel, 'FDI in Retail Sector in India', Ministry of Consumers Affairs, Govt. of India.

1. A Research Paper presented at National Seminar on "Foreign Direct Investment in Retail Business," at G.N. Khalsa College, Karnal on Feb. 18, 2006.

models and implementing new technologies and modern accounting practices to face competition.

In spite of the recent developments in retailing and its immense contribution to the economy, retailing continues to be one of the least evolved industries and the growth of organised retailing in India has been much slower as compared to the rest of the world. Over a period of 10 years, the share of organised retailing in total retailing has grown from 10 percent to 40 percent in Brazil and 20 percent in China, while in India it is only 2 percent. One important reason for this is that retailing is one of the few sectors where foreign direct, investment is not allowed within the country, there has been protests by trading associations and other stakeholders against allowing FDI in retailing. On the other hand, the growing market has attracted foreign investors and India has been portrayed as an important investment destination for the global retail chains. This is evident from the fact that India has received requests from many important trading partners (such as US, Japan, China, EU, Singapore, Brazil and Korea) in the Doha round of WTO negotiations to allow FDI in retailing.

It is now widely debated whether allowing FDI in retailing would bring in more foreign investment in India. Existing research has shown that the actual inflow of foreign investment would depend on several factors such as size of the market, per capita income growth, macro-economic stability, conductive legislation, access to real estate and availability of retail infrastructure. In the present paper an attempt has been made to analyse the perceptions of foreign retailers about Indian market; arguments for and against FDI in retailing in India. Besides, the paper also analyses the impact of FDI in retailing on various economic activities in India.

II. INDIAN MARKET

Perceptions of Foreign Retailers: Although Indian market is portrayed as an attractive Investment destination, foreign retailers point at that there are several barriers. Some of the barriers are listed as under:

- Foreign retailers point out that although per capita income in India has increased, the purchasing power and brand awareness is still very low in India. In fact, Carrefour a multi format retailers decided against enlarging Indian market because of this reason.
- Heterogeneity in terms of differences in culture and living habits makes it difficult to have a uniform marketing strategy across the country. In India each state is a mini-country and demography of a region varies quite distinctly from the others. To be successful, retailers have to identify with different lifestyles. Hence, there are more regional players in retailing rather than national players.
- The complexity of creating a supply chain, differences in taxes across states and poor infrastructure also makes it difficult to have a nation-wide chain store.
- Food and grocery and apparel and accessories are the two main areas where foreign players have shown an interest in entering the Indian market because these two segments constitute bulk of the consumer spending. Most foreign retailers have done a feasibility study before entering the market. Majority of the studies showed that margins in food and grocery retailing are very low and consumers are satisfied with their neighbourhood kirana stores. These kirana stores offer various facilities like home delivery and purchase on credit which are difficult for international players to offer. Moreover, shopping habits in India are different from that of the developed countries where consumers are willing to

stock food items and travel long distances for shopping. Some international players have pointed out that even if FDI is allowed in retailing, small sized supermarkets in selected neighbourhood of particular regions or discount chains would be more successful than large formats like hypermarket. Others stated that India still does not have so much product variety to have a hypermarket as in countries such as the US. In apparel, players such as Mark and Spencer and Mango are aware that their products have a premium price and they would find it difficult to penetrate the market. They have entered the Indian market only for brand presence.

- Foreign retailers and prospective entrants have pointed out that lack of clarity of government regulation, uncertainties created by political pressure from trading associations, high and multiple taxes, requirement for multiple clearances, bureaucratic red-tapism and high real estate prices is making it difficult for them to enter the Indian market and expand operations.
- The rigidity in labour laws, scarcity of allied infrastructure facilities such as power, high electricity tariff, logistic problems, high bank lending rates, bureaucratic red tapism, etc. is preventing foreign retailers from setting up manufacturing facilities.

III. ARGUMENT BY THOSE OPPOSED TO FDI IN RETAILING

Many trading association, some political parties and other industry associations have argued against FDI in retailing due to following reasons:

(i) Indian retailers are yet to consolidate their position. The existing retails scenario is characterised by the presence of a large number of fragmented family-owned businesses, who would not be able to survive the competition from foreign players.

(ii) The entry of foreign players drives unorganised retailers out of business, it would lead to wide-spread unemployment. The example of south-east Asian countries show that they allowed FDI, the domestic retailers were marginalized and this led to unemployment.

(iii) FDI in retailing can upset the import balance, large international retailers would prefer to source majority of their products globally rather than investing in local products.

(iv) Global retailers might resort to predatory pricing. Due to their financial clout, they often sell below cost in the new markets. Once the domestic Players are wiped out of the market foreign players enjoy a monopoly position which allows them to increase prices and earn profits.

(v) Indian retailers have argued that since lending rates are much higher in India, Indian retailers, especially small retailers, are at a disadvantageous position compared to foreign retailers who have access to International funds at lower interest rates. High cost of borrowing forces the domestic players to charge higher prices for the products.

(vi) FDI in retail trade would not attract large inflows of foreign investment since very little investment is required to conduct retail business. Goods are bought on credit and sales are made on cash basis. Hence, the working capital requirement is negligible. On the contrary; after making initial investment on basic infrastructure, the multinational retailers may remit the profits earned in India to their own country.

IV. ARGUMENTS BY THOSE FAVOURING FDI IN RETAILING

- Experience of other countries shows that retailing has attracted significant FDI.
- FDI would bring in technical know-how and skill.
- It would speed up the growth of organised retailing, set-up supply chains and lead to implementation of information technology.
- Joint ventures would ease capital constraints of existing organised retailers.
- Domestic retailers would get access to global best management practices.
- Sourcing from India would increase.
- There will be more investment in upstream activities and allied sectors.
- Competition would drive down prices.
- Protection leads to inefficiency.
- FDI would lead to development of different retail formats and modernisation of the sector.

V. IMPACT OF FDI IN RETAILING ON INDIAN SCENE

What impact FDI in retailing will have on Indian scene can be best analysed by looking into its impact on following activities.

(a) Impact of Foreign Retailers on Indian Manufactures

- Existing foreign players such as metro and Mc Donald's have made significant investment in India. By 2004, Mc Donald's had invested arranged Rs. 8 billion in creating the supply chain, cold storage facilities, real estate for restaurant. Six years prior to setting up its operation in India, Mc Donald's started setting up the supply chain and in the process has transferred state-of-the art processing technology Mc Donald's international suppliers worked with India companies to implement and develop products that meet Mc Donald's quality standards. For example, Cremica Industries worked with one of the Mc Donald's suppliers from Europe to develop technology and expertise, which allowed it to expand business from baking to also providing breads to Mc Donald's India and other companies. Mc Donald's and its suppliers worked closely with farmers in places like Qoty and Pune to cultivate high quality lettuce. This includes sharing advanced agricultural technology and expertise like utilisation of drip irrigation systems that reduces overall water consumption and agricultural management practices, which result in greater yields.

- Entry of foreign retailers in forcing the domestic suppliers to upgrade scale of production and quality standards to match international competition.
- Indian manufacturers/suppliers are entering international markets through foreign retailers.
- Presence of foreign brands is leading to development of Indian brands for instance, in the case of textiles, shoes, etc. foreign brands are passing a technical know-how to the Indian manufacturers, and in the process many Indian brands have up-graded themselves and are now ready to export their products.

(b) Impact on Sourcing

One of the arguments against FDI in retailing is that foreign players would not source their products from India. Contrary to this argument, India has significant competitive advantage in terms of low cost of labour, availability of raw materials, etc. and many foreign retailers such as Arrow, Levi's, JC Penny, Wal-Mart, Gap are already sourcing their products from India. With rising labour cost in the developed countries, many companies are shifting their labour cost in the developed countries, many companies are shifting their operations to developing countries such as India and China. The Indian government has also shown keen interest in developing the country as an international sourcing hub for certain products like shoes, textiles, etc.

(c) Impact on Prices

There is difference of opinion about the likely impact on Prices. On one hand, it is held that prices will rise became products sold by foreign retailers are high priced. However, high priced products will have limited market shown in India since purchasing power is low in India. On the other, load according to another opinion prices will be lower as foreign retailers would invest in supply chain, reduce intermediaries and wastage. Competition from foreign retailers would force domestic retailers to upgrade and improve productivity. This will lead to lower prices presently, there is no price competition the consumers would gain from such competition.

(d) Impact of Consumers

Consumers are the major beneficiaries of the retail boom. They now have a choice of wide range of products, quality and prices. Shopping has become a pleasurable experience. Organised retailers are initiating various measures such as tracing of consumer behaviour, consumer loyalty programmes, etc. to retain their market share. It is predicted that entry of foreign retailers would further increase the range of products available to Indian consumers and improve the quality of services offered [these include consistency, standardisation, branding (including private labels), pricing, pre-sale activities, after sale support, etc.].

(e) Impact on Employment and Training

It is argued that organised retailing will reduce the number of intermediaries, distributors and middlemen since organised retailers tend to source products directly from manufacturers, farmers, etc. The entry of foreign players would further reduce the number of intermediaries, distributors and middlemen since international retailers would first set-up their supply chains by sourcing directly from manufacturers and middle men, but since foreign retailers are likely to source most of their products domestically, it would create more employment.

(f) Impact of Farmers, Manufacturers, Suppliers

- With setting up of supply chain and removal of intermediaries farmers/manufacturers, etc. would get better prices for their products—income would increase.
- Global retailers would link Indian farmers/ manufacturers to their international chain.
- Farmers and manufacturers would have access to state-of-the-art technology.
- There would be upgradation in production technology and improvement in quality.

(g) Impact of Other Sectors

The growth of inter-linked sectors such as tourism is dependent on the growth of organised retailing and if FDI is allowed in retailing, it is expected to boost the Indian tourism industry. Highly developed retail formats in countries such as Singapore, Hong Kong, Malaysia and UAE (Dubai) have made them important shopping destinations and, in turn, led to the growth of their tourism industry.

If FDI is allowed in retailing, it would provide an impetus to the growth of recreational and entertainment services. The shopping malls offer a wide range of entertainment such as multiplexes, food courts and children play areas, apart from shopping experiences.

Respondents are of the view that international retailers would invest heavily in promotions and advertisement. This would promote the advertising industry.

Entry of foreign players would provide impetus to the growth of Indian IT sector. (Information Technology) majors such as TCS and Infosys have already come up with a variety of packages for supply chain management and retail practices which are implemented by global retailers.

CONCLUSION

Although Indian consumers are benefiting from the development of organised retailing in terms of wide range of products, better shopping ambiance, etc. and majority of them support FDI in retailing, the country does not have a strong consumer association which can place their views before the government. The protectionist attitude of some trading associations does not take into consideration the gains to consumers from entry of foreign players in retailing. The study found that organised retailers in India are not yet exposed to price competition. Even though many of them have reorganised their supply chains, the benefits have not percolated down to the consumers in terms of lower prices. It is likely that foreign players would practice price competition. If they do so, it will not only force the existing domestic players to improve their performance, but consumers would gain in terms of lower prices. However, government should have an appropriate regulatory regime to safeguard against the anti-competitive practices such as predatory pricing.

(RESEARCH PAPER IV)

APPENDIX IV

Trends of FII Inflows to India*

The strong trends towards globalization in many countries during 1990s have brought about significant developments in the world economy. One of them is the tremendous increase in the mobility of capital across national borders. Globalization had led to widespread liberalization and implementation of financial market reforms in many countries, mainly focusing on integrating the financial markets of these countries with the global markets. These reforms included deregulation of markets like eliminating foreign exchange controls, reducing taxes imposed on foreign investors, relaxing the restrictions on the purchase of domestic securities by foreign Investors, the issuance of bonds by foreign borrowers in the domestic markets and so on. These measures have allowed the free flow of capital from developed markets to emerging markets, from capital surplus countries to capital scarce countries, seeking the highest rate of return and thereby, enhancing the productivity and efficiency of capital at the global level.

I. TRENDS IN GLOBAL CAPITAL FLOWS

Between 1942 and 1970, the capital flows were

---

* A Research paper presented at Seminar on "FII Inflows to India: Determinants, Causes and Volatility of Indian Stock Market" at G.N. Khalsa College, Yamunanagar on 30th March 2007.

only among industrialized countries and the flows towards the developing countries were only marginal. But after the first oil price shock in 1973, capital started flowing to developing countries. These flows were generally in the form of syndicated bank loans. This trend continued unabated resulting in increased interest burden on the developing countries till the Latin American debt crisis in 1982. The size of the capital flows to developing countries was averaging around US $ 163 billion per annum between 1973 and 1982. There was a considerable slow down in the international capital flows to developing countries after 1982. It was around US $ 103 billion per annum in the period 1983 to 1989. After 1982 the debt flows started registering a decline and the Foreign Direct Investment (FDI) flows started picking up slowly. However, the FDI flows remained lower than the debt flows in quantum till 1987. With worldwide trends towards globalization and improved economic performance by developing countries, there was a surge in capital flows during 1990 to 1997. The net capital flows to developing countries were at the peak at US $ 325 billion representing 5.5 percent of GDP of developing countries in 1997. There has been a steady slide in capital flows from 1997 due to various reasons like Asian crisis in 1997-98, turmoil in the global fixed income markets, collapse of the Argentine currency board peg in 2001 and the spate of corporate failures and accounting irregularities in US in 2002. However, the global capital flows to developing countries have bounced back and have registered a sharp increase in 2003 reaching US $ 228 billion representing about 3.6% of the gross domestic product of developing countries.[1]

The composition of capital flows to emerging market economies have gone through significant changes over time. As mentioned earlier, bank loans

---

1. Batra, Amita, 2003, 'The Dynamics of Foreign Portfolio Inflows and Equity Retuns in India', ICRIECR Working Paper 109.

TABLE I

Net Capital Flows to Developing Countries

Year	*Net capital flows to developing countries US$ billion*
1970	11.3
1980	82.8
1990	100.8
1995	237.2
1996	281.6
1997	324.3
1998	266.5
1999	236.7
2000	193.7
2001	206.1
2002	190.6
2003	228.2

Source: Global Development Finance, Various issues.

TABLE II

Composition of Capital Flows to Developing Countries

Year	*FDI Flows*	*Portfolio Flows*	*Debt Flows*
1970	2.2	0.0	6.9
1980	4.4	0.0	65.2
1990	24.5	3.7	43.4
1995	95.5	32.1	77.0
1996	119.0	45.88	87.6
1997	171.1	22.6	105.3
1998	175.6	6.6	57.6
1999	181.7	12.6	13.8
2000	162.2	12.6	-9.8
2001	175.1	4.4	-1.2
2002	147.1	4.9	7.3
2003	135.2	14.3	44.3

Source: Global Development Finance, Various issues.

were the major component of capital flows in 1970s. The FDI flows which started picking up in early 1980s gained real momentum between 1987 and 1997. In 1994, these flows were in excess of net debt flows for the first time. The portfolio flows, which were non-existent till 1980s, have become a major component of international capital flows from the early 1990s.

II. CAPITAL FLOWS TO INDIA

Till the beginning of 1991, India had a highly regulated financial system with a restrictive foreign exchange regime. It had a closed capital account and capital mobility was restricted through administrative controls. According to Y.V. Reddy (2002)[2], the environment in financial sector was characterized by segmented and under-developed financial markets, coupled with paucity of instruments before 1991. The trade and investment policies did not encourage foreign capital. FDI was tightly regulated and small compared to other Asian economies and foreign portfolio flows was totally prohibited. Initially till early 1980s India was totally dependent on multilateral and bilateral concessional forms of finance for external flows. Since the current account deficit widened subsequently the country started supplementing the traditional forms of borrowing with commercial borrowing including short-term borrowings and deposits from non-resident Indians (NRIs). As a consequence, in 1991, India was faced with a balance of payments crisis and had to devalue money. Since official assistance was not available because of its global decline, India had to embark on economic reforms programme to transform the controlled economy into a market-oriented one. The financial

---

2. Reddy, Y.V., 2002, 'Monetary and Financial Sector Reforms in India: A Practitioner's Perspective' presented at the Indian Economy Conference Program on Comparative Economic Development (PCED) at Cornell University, USA, on April 19-20, 2002.

liberalization strategy, which was a part of the general economic reforms, included dismantling of capital controls, reforms in trade and investment policies and so on. India's foreign investment regime was liberalized. FDI was confined to a narrow group of industries with majority control and to a large number with a 40% equity control with foreign investors till 1991.

In 1991, Industrial policy statement permitted majority control in a large number of industries and 100% control in several industries. These lists have been subsequently puffed up and from 1995 most of the industries are open to FDI. In 1992, the foreign portfolio investments by Foreign Institutional Investors (FIIs) are allowed. Indian companies with high credit rating were allowed to float Global Depository Receipts (GDRs) and the American Depository Receipts (ADRs). These measures, which were conscious efforts to integrate the Indian financial markets with the global markets, brought about a radical transformation in the quantum and nature of capital flows to India.

Ever since the introduction of economic reforms, India has become one of the chosen destinations of the international capital flows. The net capital flows were averaging around US $ 4 billion during the 1980s. After the reforms they shot up to an average around US $ 9 billion during 1993-2000, registering an increase of more than double. During the ten years between 1990-91 and 1999-00, India has mobilized around US $ 40 billion in foreign investment. The cross border capital flows have recorded a tremendous increase from 1999-2000 crossing US $ 10 billion mark every year. As it can be noticed from Table III, the composition of capital flows has also gone through a transformation over time in line with the global trends. The non-debt capital flows have slowly become a major component of total net capital flows replacing debt-creating capital flows. The ratio of non-debt creating capital flows to debt creating capital flows has changed from 1.5 to 83.3 in 1990-91 to 44.6 to -6.6 in 2002-03, thereby reducing the incidental interest burden on the economy.

TABLE III

Composition of Capital Inflows to India

Year	*Total net capital inflows (US$ billion)*	*Non-debt creating inflows as a percent of total flows*	*FDI flows as a percent of total flows*	*Portfolio flows as a percent of total flows*	*Debt creating flows as a percent of total*
1990-91	7.1	1.5	1.4	0.1	83.3
1995-96	4.1	117.5	52.4	65.1	57.5
1996-97	12.0	51.3	23.7	27.6	61.7
1997-98	9.8	54.8	36.2	18.6	52.4
1998-99	8.4	28.6	29.4	-0.8	54.4
1999-00	10.4	49.7	20.7	29.0	23.1
2000-01	10.0	67.8	40.2	27.6	59.4
2001-02	10.6	77.1	58.0	19.1	9.2
2002-03	12.1	46.6	38.5	8.1	-10.6

Source: Reserve Bank of India, Report on Currency and Finance, 2002-03.

The portfolio flows that were negligible in 1990-91 have gained momentum over time and have come to play a significant role on the economy.

III. FOREIGN PORTFOLIO INVESTMENT FLOWS TO INDIA

As mentioned above, a major force that has changed the quantum and nature of international capital flows to India is the portfolio investment flows. India has witnessed a decade of portfolio flows and they are gaining more significance with every passing year. It has come to play a dominant role in the Indian economy.

Portfolio investments include investments in American Depository Receipts (ADRs)/Global Depository Receipts (GDRs) and offshore funds in addition to investments by FIIs. Foreign portfolio investments in India have received importance and are allowed in the

Indian stock markets as a follow up of the recommendation of the Narasimham Committee report on financial system. The committee recommended their entry and stated:[3]

"The committee would also suggest that the capital market should be gradually opened up to foreign portfolio investments and simultaneously efforts should be initiated to improve the depth of the market by facilitating the issue of new types of equities and innovative debt instruments." The Government of India issued the guidelines for FII investments on September 14, 1992. Prior to 1992, only Non-resident Indians (NRIs) and Overseas Corporate Bodies (OCBs) were allowed to undertake portfolio investment in India. Three years later in November 1995, Securities and Exchange Board of India (SEBI) notified the Foreign Institutional Investors' Regulations, which are largely, based on the earlier guidelines issued in 1992. The country's stock markets are opened up for direct participation by FIIs such as pension funds, mutual funds, investment trusts, asset management companies, nominee companies and incorporated institutional portfolio managers or their power of attorney holders (providing discretionary and non-discretionary portfolio management services). These investors are welcome to invest in all the securities traded on the primary and secondary markets including the equity and other securities/instruments of companies listed/to be listed on the stock exchanges in India including the OTC exchanges in India. These would include shares, debentures, warrants and schemes offered by domestic mutual funds. SEBI requires the FIIs to register with them and to obtain approval from RBI under the Foreign Exchange Regulation Act, 1973 to enable them to buy and sell securities, open foreign currency accounts and permits and repatriates funds. For all practical purposes, full convertibility of rupee is

---

3. Narasimham Committee Report, p. 121.

available to FII investments. Gradually the scope of FII operations in India has been expanded and presently the ceiling for overall investment for FIIs is 24% of the paid up capital of the Indian company which can be raised up to the sectoral cap/statutory ceiling subject to the approval of the board and the general body of the company passing a special resolution to that effect[4] .

IV. TRENDS IN PORTFOLIO FLOWS TO INDIA

The table below gives the source specific foreign portfolio investment in India during the period 1992-93 to 2002-03.

TABLE IV

Composition of Foreign Portfolio Investment in India

Year	*GDRs/ ADRs**	*FII investment*	*Off shore funds*	*Total*
1992-93	240	1	3	244
1993-94	1520	1665	382	3567
1994-95	2082	1503	239	3824
1995-96	683	2009	56	2748
1996-97	1366	1926	20	3312
1997-98	645	979	204	1828
1998-99	270	-390	59	-61
1999-00	768	2135	123	3026
2000-01	831	1847	82	2760
2001-02	477	1505	39	2021
2002-03#	600	377	2	979

Provisional.

* Represents the amount raised by Indian corporates through Global Depository Receipts (GDRs) and American Depository Receipts (ADRs) represents fresh inflows of funds by FIIs.

Source: Reserve Bank of India.

4. National Stock Exchange of India Ltd., 2003, Securities Markets in India: An Overview, www.nseindia.com

Portfolio flows in India have become synonymous with FIIs investment. The FII flows, which were only US $ 1 million in 1992-93, have risen over time and are at US $ 1505 million in 2001-02 and at US $ 377 million in 2002-03. The net investment flows by FIIs have always been positive every year from the year of their entry except in the year 1998-99. The net investment flows by FIIs were negative during 1998-99 primarily because of the uncertainty that prevailed after India tested a series of nuclear bombs in May 1998 and the imposition of economic sanctions by the US, Japan and other industrialized countries.

This increase in FII flows to India reflects the strong economic fundamentals of the country, as well as the confidence of the foreign investors in the growth with stability of the Indian market. The year 2003 marked a watershed in FII investment in India. FIIs started the year 2003 in a big way by investing Rs. 985 crore in January itself. Meanwhile, corporate India continued to report good operational results. This, along with good macro-economic fundamentals, growing industrial and service sectors led FIIs to perceive great potential for investment in the Indian economy. In April 2003, prices of commodities like steel and aluminium went up, propelling FII investment in May 2003 to Rs. 3,060 crore. Around the same time, Morgan Stanley Capital International (MSCI) in its MSCI Emerging Markets Index gave a weight of 4.3 per cent to India among the emerging markets of the world.[5] Calendar year 2004 ended with net FII inflows of US $ 9.2 billion, an all-time high since the liberalisation.

---

5. MSCI Emerging Markets Index SM is a free float-adjusted market capitalisation index that is designed to measure equity market performance in the global emerging markets. As of December 2003 the MSCI Emerging Markets Index consisted of the following 26 emerging market country indices: Argentina, Brazil, Chile, China, Colombia, Czech Republic, Egypt, Hungary, India, Indonesia, Israel, Jordan, Korea, Malaysia, Mexico, Morocco, Pakistan, Peru, Philippines, Poland, Russia, South Africa, Taiwan, Thailand, Turkey and Venezuela.

The buoyant inflows continued in 2004-05. This weight was further increased to 5.9 per cent in April 2004. In 2004-05, after reversing direction briefly during the period May-June, FII inflows became robust again, leading to net inflows of US $ 10.25 billion during the year The buoyancy continued in 2005-06, with net inflows aggregating to US $ 3.26 billion in the first seven months up to end-October 2005.[6]

TABLE V

Trends in FII Investment

Year	*Gross Purchase (Rs. Crore)*	*Gross Sales (Rs. Crore)*	*Net Investment** (Rs. Crore)*	*Net Investment* (US $ mn.)*	*Cumulative Net Investment** (US $ mn.)*
1993-94	5593	466	5125	1634	1638
1994-95	7631	2835	4796	1528	3167
1995-96	9964	2752	6942	2036	5202
1996-97	15554	6979	8575	2432	7634
1997-98	18695	12737	5958	1649	9284
1998-99	16115	17699	-1584	-386	8898
1999-00	56856	46734	10122	2339	11237
2000-01	74051	64116	9934	2160	13396
2001-02	49920	41165	8755	1846	15242
2002-03	47060	44371	2689	562	15804
2003-04	144858	99094	45765	9949	25754
2004-05	216953	171072	45881	10172	35926

** Net Investment in US $ mn. at monthly exchange rate.
Source: Handbook of SEBI, p. 35.

6. Report of the Expert Group on Encouraging FII Flows and Checking the Vulnerability of Capital Markets to Speculative flows, Govt. of India, Ministry of Finance, p. 5.

Trends in FII Investment (A)

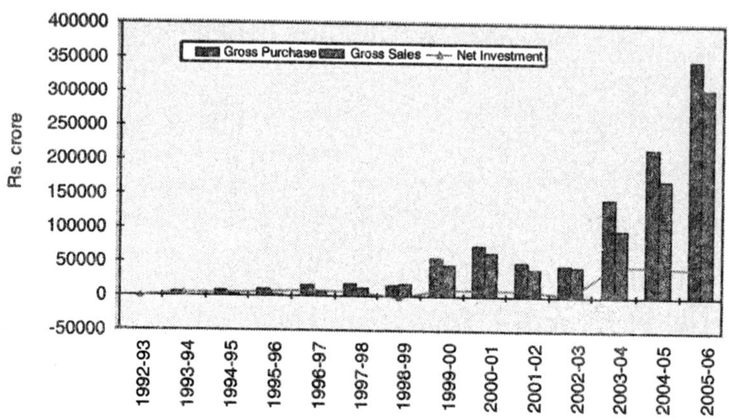

Trends in FII Investment (B)

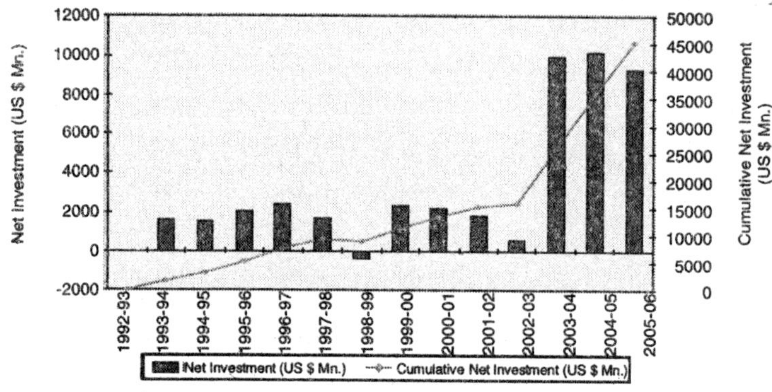

The FII flows, which were only US $ 1638 million in 1992-93, have risen over time and are at US $ 35926 million in 2004-05. The net investment flows by FIIs have always been positive every year from the year of their entry except in the year 1998-99. The net investment flows by FIIs were negative during 1998-99 primarily because of the uncertainty that prevailed after India tested a series of nuclear bombs in May 1998 and the imposition of economic sanctions by the US, Japan and other industrialized countries. FII investment soon recovered and touched US $ 35926 million in 2004-05. This reflects the strong economic fundamentals of the country, as well as the confidence of the foreign investors in the growth with stability of the Indian market.

V. TRENDS IN FII'S REGISTRATION

The rise in FIIs inflows into the country coincides with the rise in the number of FIIs registered with SEBI. The FIIs registered with SEBI come from as many as 28 countries including money management companies operating in India on behalf of foreign investors. US-based institutions account for slightly over 41%, those from UK constitute about 20% and the institutions from the western European countries account for another 17%. These national affiliations may not essentially mean that the funds are from these particular countries. They may be on behalf of the residents in other countries. Nevertheless, the regional break down of the FII affiliations does give an indication of the relative importance of these regions of the world to FII inflows to India.

These developments have given rise to a keen interest in understanding the impact and the implications of the FII investment on Indian companies. Since these portfolio investments are made in the securities offered by the Indian companies and since the magnitude of these flows have recorded a sharp increase over the last decade it would certainly have implications for the Indian companies.

The diversity of FIIs has been increasing with the number of registered FIIs in India steadily rising over the years (Table VI). In 2004-05, with 145 new FIIs registering with Securities and Exchange Board of India (SEBI), as on March 31, 2005, there were 685 FIIs registered in India. The names of some prominent FIIs registered during 2004-05 are: California Public Employees' Retirement System (CalPERS), United Nations

TABLE VI

Trends in FII's Registration

Financial year	*During the year*	*Total registered at the end of the year*
1992-93	0	0
1993-94	3	3
1994-95	153	156
1995-96	197	353
1996-97	99	439
1997-98	59	496
1998-99	59	450
1999-00	56	506
2000-01	84	528
2001-02	48	490
2002-03	51	502
2003-04	83	540
2004-05	145	685
2005-06*	131	803

* As on October 31, 2005.

Source: Report of the Expert Group on Encouraging FII Flows and Checking the Vulnerability of Capital Markets to Speculative flows, Govt. of India, Ministry of Finance, p. 5.

for and on behalf of the United Nations Joint Staff Pension Fund, Public School Retirement System of Missouri, Commonwealth of Massachusetts Pension Reserves Investment Trust, Treasurer of the State North Carolina Equity Investment Fund Pooled Trust, the Growth Fund of America, and AIMFunds Management Inc.[7]

In terms of country of origin), the USA topped the list with a share of 40 per cent of the number of FIIs

---

7. Report of the Expert Group on Encouraging FII Flows and Checking the Vulnerability of Capital Markets to Speculative flows, Govt. of India, Ministry of Finance, p. 5.

Country-wise Breakdown of FIIs Registered in India (November 2003)

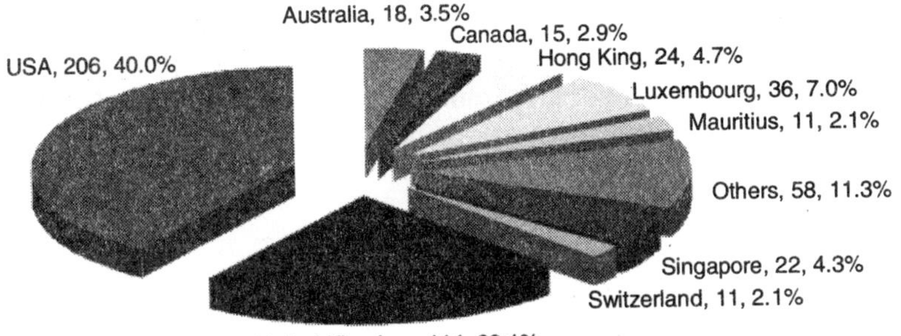

Source: Securities Exchange Board of India.

registered in India, followed by UK's 17 per cent. Other countries of significance in terms of origin of FIIs investing in India are Luxemburg, Hong Kong, and Singapore. In terms of net cumulative investments by FIIs, US-based FIIs dominate with 29 per cent of the net cumulative FII investments in India, followed by UK at 17 per cent. In recent months, European and Japanese FIIs have started to evince an increasing interest in India, and of the FIIs that registered with SEBI in October 2004, a significant number belonged to Europe and Japan. These developments have helped improve the diversity of the set of FIIs operating in India.[8]

To conclude with increased global financial integration and liberalization, emerging economies are increasingly attracting capital from developed economies. India being one of the fastest growing economies in Asia, with an expected growth rate of more than 8 percent per annum, has been witnessing consistent inflows from foreign institutional investors. Given that India is one of the fastest growing economies in South Asia, promising a growth of over 8

8. *Ibid.*

percent, second only to China, it would not be a surprise to see increased FII flows to India in the future. Factors like a strong currency, key reforms in the banking, power and telecommunications sector, increased consumer spending and stable policies are expected to play a major role in attracting foreign institutional investors to India.

(RESEARCH PAPER V)

APPENDIX V

Services Led Growth in India—Some Issues

I. INTRODUCTION

The evolution of sectoral shares in output, consumption and employment as economies grow has been studied by economists for well over fifty years. During the 1950s and 1960s, research by Kuznets and Chenery[1] suggested that development would be associated with a sharp decline in the proportion of GDP generated by the primary sector, counter balanced by a significant increase in industry, and by a more modest increase in the service sector. Sectoral shares in employment were predicted to follow a similar pattern.

With the benefit of more data on development than was available to Kuznets and Chenery, recent literature has tended to emphasize the growing importance of service sector activity (Inman 1985, Kongsamut, Rebelo and Xie, 2001)[2]. For example,

---

1. Chenery, Holis, B. 1960, Patterns of Industrial Growth, *American Economic Review*, Vol. 57, pp. 415-26.
2. Inman, Robert P., 1985, Interaction and overview in managing, The service economy: Prospects and problems, Cambridge University Press, Cambridge. Kousgsamut, Piyaba, SergioRebolo and Danyang Xie, 2001, Beyond Balanced Growth, IMF Working Paper, WP/01/85.

Kongsamut, *et al*, (2001) analyze a sample of 123 countries for 1970-1989 and show that rising per-capita GDP is associated with an increase in services and a decline in agriculture both in terms of share in GDP and employment. In other words, the sectoral share given up by agriculture as the economy matures goes more to the services sector and less to industry than the Kuznets-Chenery work had suggested. The modern view is that as an economy matures, the share of services (in output, consumption, and employment) grows along with a decline in agriculture. By contrast, the share of industry first increases modestly, and then stabilizes or declines.

II. SHARE OF SERVICES IN GDP

Such a pattern of growth is visible in the cross-country data on shares in GDP presented in Table I. These data suggest two stages of development. In the first, both industry and services shares increase as countries move from low income to lower middle income status, while in the second, the share of industry declines and that of services increases as the economy moves to upper middle and higher income levels.

TABLE I

Sectoral Shares in GDP in 2001, Global Averages

	Agriculture	*Industry*	*Services*
Low income	24	32	45 Stage-I
Lower Middle Income	12	40	48 Stage-I
Upper Middle Income	7	33	60 Stage-II
High Income	2	29	70 Stage-II

Source: World Bank's WDI, 2003 Table 4.2. Defination: Low income: Per capita GDP<$745: Lower Middle: $746-2975 and Upper Middle: $2976-9205; and High ->$9206.

FIGURE 1

Sectoral Shares in GDP by Various Income Categories

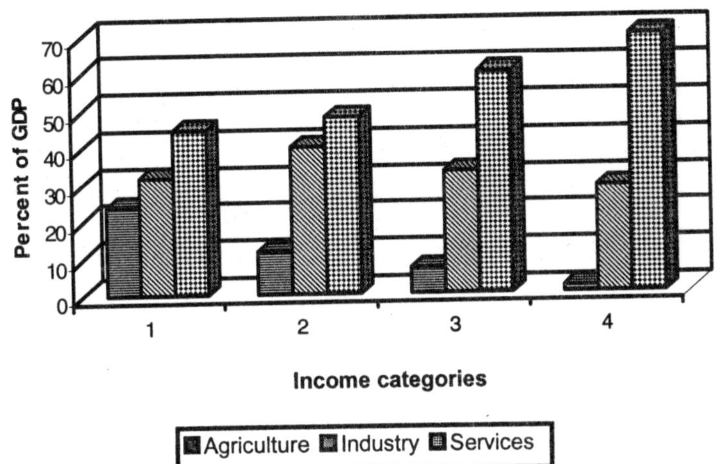

TABLE II

India, Sectoral Shares in GDP, 1950-2003

(Percent of GDP)

	Agriculture	*Industry*	*Services*
1950	58	15	28 Stage-I
1980	38	24	38 Stage-I
1990	33	27	41 Stage-I
2000	24	27	49 Stage-II
2003	22	27	51 Stage-II

Source: CSO Data for India.

How does the Indian experience fit in with this pattern? Through the 1980s atleast, the fit is quite close. Table II shows that in the four decade period, 1950-90, agriculture's share in GDP declined by about 25 percentage points, while industry and services gained equally. The share of industry has stabilized since 1990,

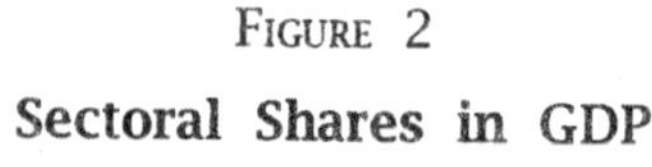

FIGURE 2

Sectoral Shares in GDP

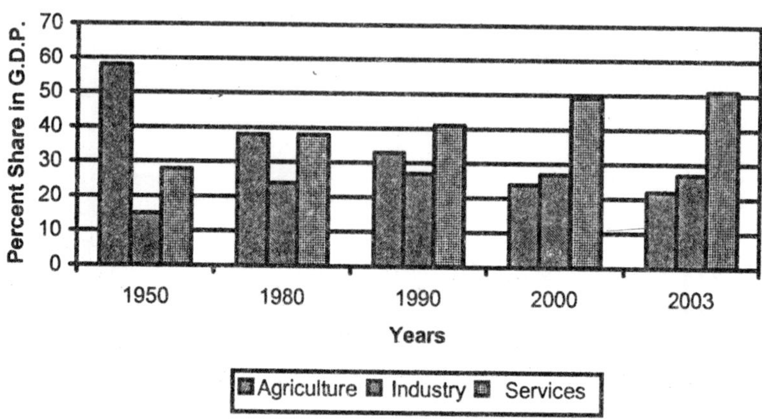

and the entire subsequent decline in the share of agriculture has been picked up by the services sector. Thus, while over the four decades, 1950-90, the services sector gained a 13 percent share, the gain in the 1990s alone was 8 percentage points.

The conventional wisdom about the stages of development process suggests that an economy evolves from being agriculture-dominated to industry-dominated, and then to services-dominated. History suggests that the dominance of services sector is unlikely to be sustained without strong growth of industry and agriculture.[3] The Indian growth experience, however, appears to negate the stylised Rostowian stages of growth hypothesis, since transition in India has been marked by the rapid movement from agriculture-dominated growth to services-dominated growth bypassing the stage of industry-dominated growth.

Although the share of services activity in overall activity has increased in India in line with the

3. Acharya, Shankar (2002), "Macro-economic Management in the Nineties", *Economic and Political Weekly*, April 20.

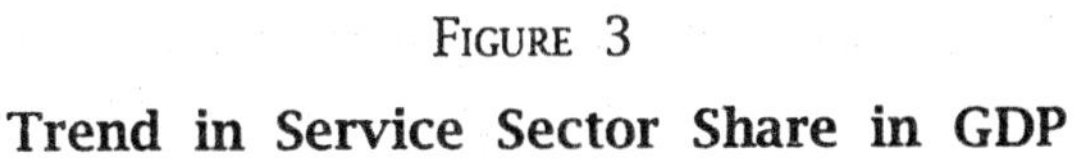

FIGURE 3

Trend in Service Sector Share in GDP

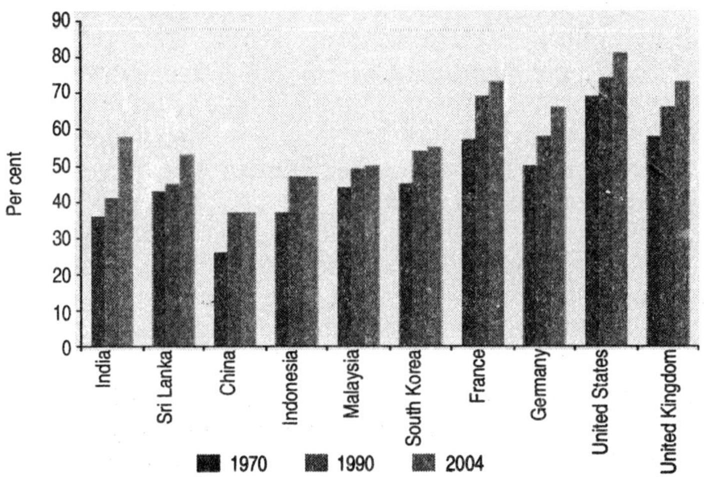

international experience, the Indian experience is somewhat a typical, since the share of manufacturing in GDP has remained broadly unchanged. For example, in China, the decline in the share of agriculture from 27 per cent in 1990 to 15 per cent in 2004 was completely cornered by rise in the share of mining, manufacturing and utilities sector from 37 per cent to 46 per cent; the share of the services sector remained stagnant at 37 per cent during the period. Similarly, in the case of Malaysia, decline in agriculture's share from 15 per cent to 10 per cent over the period 1990 to 2004 was absorbed by rise in manufacturing sector's share from 24 per cent to 31 per cent.[4] This is in line with the general pattern of development wherein transformation from agriculture to modern economy is intercepted first by rise of industrial sector and subsequently dominance of services sector prevails with economic maturity. On the other hand, in India, the entire decline in the share

4. RBI, Annual Report, 2005-06, pp. 26-27.

of agricultural sector from 41 per cent in 1970-71 to 20 per cent in 2005-06 has been more than absorbed by the services sector, as its share rose from 36 per cent to 61 per cent. Manufacturing sector's share has recorded only a modest rise from around 13 per cent in 1970 to 15 per cent in 2005-06. India has, however, a unique opportunity to be a major global player in both knowledge-based services as well as knowledge-based manufacturing. With a massive human resource-base, a large proportion of young people and a strong foundation in technical education, India is well positioned to capitalise on the worldwide potential in the knowledge economy and the services sector is expected to continue to remain the driver of economic growth in India. However, some economists caution that if the service sector bypasses the industrial sector, economic growth can be distorted. They say that service sector growth must be supported by proportionate growth of the industrial sector, otherwise the service sector grown will not be sustainable. It is true that, in India, the service sector's contribution in GDP has sharply risen and that of industry has fallen (as shown above). But, it is equally true that the industrial sector too has grown, and grown quite impressively through the 1990s (except in 1998-99). Three times between 1993-94 and 1998-99, industry surpassed the growth rate of GDP. Thus, the service sector has grown at a higher rate than industry which too has grown more or less in tandem. The rise of the service sector therefore does not distort the economy.

III. GROWTH IN SERVICES IN INDIA

The emergence of India as one of the fastest growing economies in the world in the 1990s can be attributed, to a large extent, on the rapid growth of its service sector. The growth of output in the service sector in the 1990s has been much higher than the growth of output in agriculture or industry. Consequently, contribution of services to GDP in the period 2001-04, has been more than 60 per cent per annum. (Figure 5) However, this growth in the service sector has not been uniform. In order to arrive at some policy direction it is imperative to examine the performance of different services and assess the economy's potentials and constraints in these services. We examine the performance of aggregate as well as disaggregated services in terms of their growth rates; share in GDP, employment, trade and FDI. We find that the service sector in India witnessed a phenomenal growth in the decade of 1990s.

During 1980s, its output grew at the rate of 6.6 per cent per annum, while during 1990s the growth rate increased to 7.5 per cent per annum. In the last ten years (1994-04), the service sector has grown on an average by 7.9 per cent per annum, ahead of agriculture with growth of 3 per cent per annum and manufacturing sector with growth of 5.2 per cent per annum [as seen in Figure 4]. In contrast to this, we find that in the same period in countries like Thailand, Indonesia and China, agriculture sector has grown at an average rate of 1.5%, 1.9% and 3.8% while manufacturing sector has grown at the rate of 7.2%, 6.6% and 12.2% respectively. Corresponding growth rates in service sector has been 3.9%, 4.5% and 8.9%. Most of the developing countries witness a lower growth rate in the

FIGURE 4

Average Sectoral Growth Rates (1994-2004)

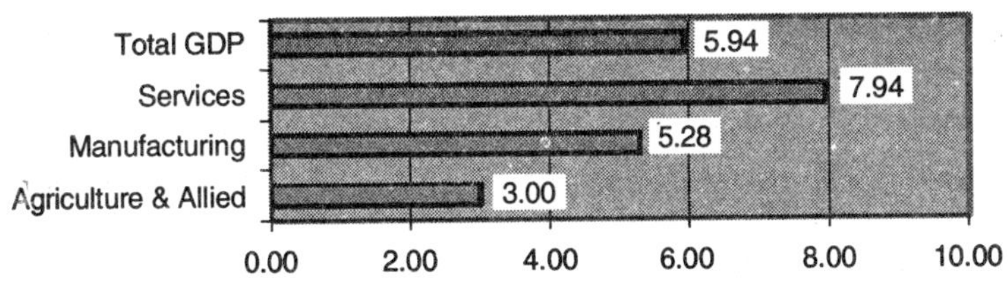

Source: Author's estimates using CSO.

FIGURE 5

Changing Composition Of GDP since 2000-01

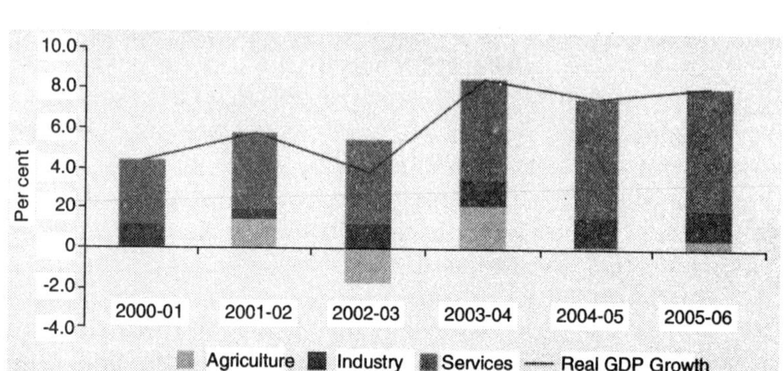

service sector as compared to the manufacturing sector. Higher growth rate in the service sector is therefore a unique feature witnessed by India.[5]

IV. WHICH SERVICES HAS GROWN FASTER[6]

A closer scrutiny of India's service sector reveals that amongst services, business services has been one of the fastest growing services in the 1980s closely followed by banking and insurance (as seen in Table III). In the 1990s, we find that a similar trend continues for business services, which grows by almost 20 percent, but while the growth in banking has increased growth in insurance sector has slowed down in the 1990s. The prime drivers of growth in services, apart from business services in the 1990s, are found to be communication services (with average growth of around 13.6%) and hotels and restaurants (with average growth of around 9%). However, there is a fall in the growth rates of

---

5. Gordon, Jim and Gupta, Poonam, "Understanding India's Service Revolution", IMF-NCAER Conference, New Delhi, Nov. 14, 2005.
6. Banga Rashmi, "Critical Issues in India's Service-led Growth". A Report prepared by consultants for Asian Development Bank.

TABLE III

Average Annual Growth Rate in Services

Sl. No.	*Service*	*1980s*	*1990s*
1.	Trade (Wholesale and Retail trade)	5.9	7.3
2.	Hotels and Restaurants	6.5	9.3
3.	Railways	4.5	3.6
4.	Transport	6.3	6.9
5.	Storage	2.7	2
6.	Communications	6.1	13.6
7.	Banking	11.9	12.7
8.	Insurance	10.9	6.7
9.	Dwellings, real estate	7.7	5
10.	Business services	13.5	19.8
11.	Legal services	8.6	5.8
12.	Public administration and defense	7	6
13.	Personal services	2.4	5
14.	Community services	6.5	8.4
15.	Other services	5.3	7.1

Source: Central Statistical Organisation.

railways, dwellings and real estate, legal services and public administration and defense in the 1990s.

Further we find that increase in the share of services in GDP has not been the same across the board for different services in India [as seen in Figure 6]. Figure VI compares share of different sectors in GDP in the last ten years, i.e., 1993-94 and 2002-03. The most important services in terms of their share in GDP in early 1990s were trade (12%), insurance (11%), community services (6.5%), but in 2002-03 we find that the sectoral contributions have changed. Share of trade has increased to 14% and community services to 8.4%. But share of insurance has declined to 7%. Other services that have witnessed a fall in their shares in 2002-03 are railways, real estate and dwellings.

What emerges from the above trends is that, services sector has grown in importance as compared to

FIGURE 6

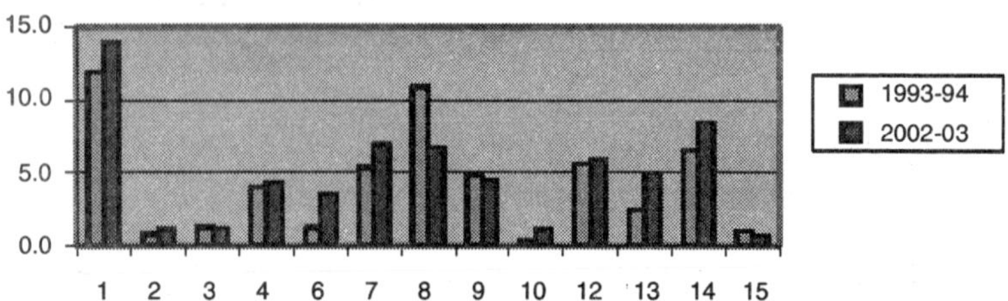

1. *Trade* (Wholesale trade and retail trade in commodities both produced at home (including exports) and imported, purchase and selling agents, brokers and auctioneers)
2. *Hotels and Restaurants* (services rendered by hotels and other lodging places, restaurants, cafes and other eating and drinking places)
3. Railways
4. *Transport by other means* (roads, water, air transport, services incidental to transport)
5. *Storage*
6. *Communications*
7. *Banking* (banks, banking departments of RBI, post-office saving bank, non-bank financial institution, cooperative credit societies, employees provident fund)
8. *Insurance* (life, postal life, non-life)
9. *Dwellings, real estate*
10. *Business services*
11. *Legal services*
12. *Public administration, defense*
13. *Personal services* (domestic, laundry, barber, beauty shops, tailoring, others)
14. *Community services* (education, research, scientific, medical, health, religious and other community)
15. *Other services* (recreation, entertainment, radio, TV broadcast, sanitary services.

Note: Services with share less than one percent has not been shown.
Source: Author's estimates based on Economic Survey and CSO.

other sectors in terms of its contribution to GDP and also its growth rates since 1990s. But this growth in share of GDP differs for different services. The most important service in terms of its share in GDP in the last decade has been wholesale and retail trade. But in terms of growth, we find that business services and communications have experienced the maximum growth in the 1990s, but their share in GDP is still quite low. Community services (which include education and health) on the other hand, have improved their share in GDP and also their growth rates in the 1990s.

V. SHARE IN FDI

Along with trade, there has been a large inflow of FDI into India since 1990s onwards. India has been ranked in top ten FDI destinations in the World Investment Report (2004). However, this increase in FDI inflows has been accompanied by a change in the structure of FDI. Following the international trend, FDI inflows into India are also shifting increasingly away from manufacturing sector, towards services sector. The average share of services in total FDI in the period 1990-94 increased from 10.5 per cent to 28.3 per cent in the period 1995-1999 (World Investment Report, 2004).

But, the inflow of FDI into services sector has been biased towards few of the services sectors (see Figure 7). Sectors that have received largest approvals are telecommunications and financial services. Within telecommunication, the largest recipient is cellular mobiles.

One of the striking features of India's FDI flows is the growing proportion of outward FDI from the services sector. The share of services in total FDI outflow increased to around 45 percent in the period 1999-2003, in which non-financial services constitute around 36%, trade is around 5% and the rest was from financial and other services. It is interesting to note that the sectors that received higher FDI in services, i.e., telecommunications, financial and consultancy services are also the fastest growing services sectors in the economy.

FIGURE 7

Share of Services in Inward FDI (1991 to 2002)

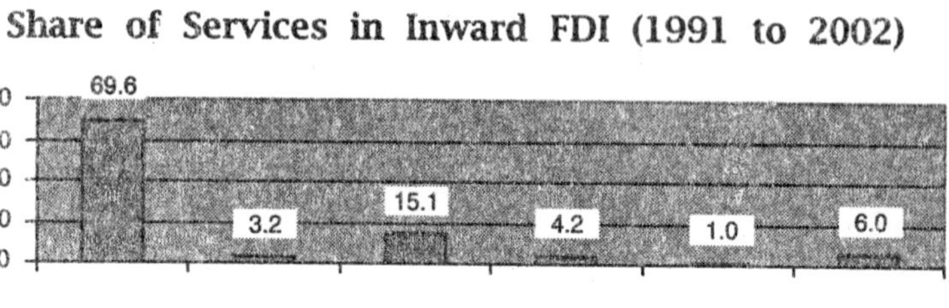

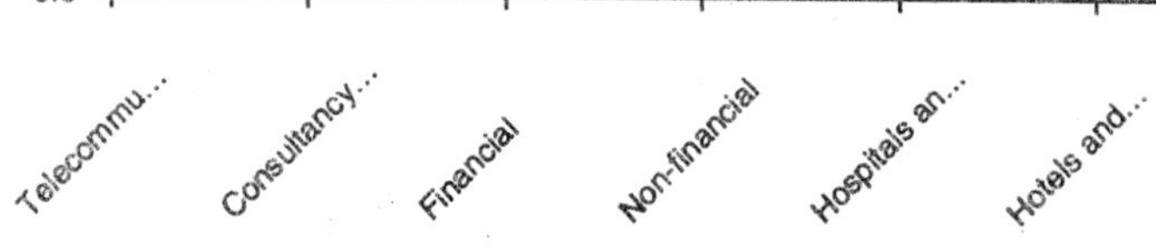

VI. WHAT EXPLAINS GROWTH IN INDIA'S SERVICE SECTOR?

The literature on growth in service sector primarily argues that when an economy grows, both demand side and supply side factors operate that lead to higher growth in the service sector as compared to the other sectors and also lead to a larger share of service sector in total employment. These factors are:

(a) High-Income Elasticity of Demand for Final Product Services

Arising share of services in GDP is regarded as an outcome of higher income elasticity of demand for services. The empirical studies have shown that the income elasticity of demand for services could be greater than or equal to unity. Income elasticity of demand for services increases with rising income which favours the fulfilment of more sophisticated desires.

The empirical estimates of price and income elasticity for various categories of services sector in real GDP depends on the relative strength of coefficients of income and price elasticity

The income elasticity of demand is greater than unity and price elasticity is negative and significant for total services. In other words, demand for overall services rises with increase in per capita GDP and decreases with increase in prices of services. The higher income elasticity of demand in case of producer services underscores its forward linkages. This is corroborated by the emergence of producer services comprising advertising, publicity, marketing and other IT-related activities in the recent period as important services industries in India. Therefore, producer services can be regarded as amajor source of economic growth.

TABLE 4

Income and Price Elasticities for Services Sector

Sector	*Income elasticity*	*Price elasticity*
Services	1.20	(-) 0.68
Producer services	1.22	(-) 0.78
Consumer services	1.00	(-) 0.10
Government services	1.41	(-) 1.05

Note: Statistically significant at 1 percent.

Source: Raj Kapila and Uma Kapila, "India's Economy in 21st Century", pp. 165-66.

(b) Trade Liberalization and Reforms

The set of trade liberlisation and reforms initiated since 1991 also impacted the performance of the services sector in following way:

(i) Firstly, reforms in the domestic industrial environment which resulted in rising manufacturing growth provided synergies to the services sector in form of increased demand for producer services

(ii) The liberalization of the financial sector provided an environment for faster growth of financial services.

(iii) Reforms in certain segments of infrastructure services also contributed to the growth of services. Consequently, the services sector posted a much higher growth during reform period as compared with the pre-reform period with its share touching nearly 55 percent mark.

(iv) The rapid growth in services sector appears to have benefited from external demand; the typical example of which is the software industry and call centers. Interestingly, the decelerating trend in manufacturing and overall GDP seems to have been much less pronounced in case of services. Nevertheless, there are apprehensions about its sustainability in view of the contribution of "public administration and defence" to growth in services.

VII. SYNERGY BETWEEN SERVICES AND INDUSTRY

In the end it will be prudent to explore the synergy between services and industry which is found to be quite significant in India. Services can be classified as producer, consumer and Government services. While the producer and consumer services have recorded higher growth rates and shares in the post-reform period, the share of Government services witnessed a decline mainly due to curtailment of revenue expenditure (Table V).

The increasing share of producer services reflects the growing complementarity between services and manufacturing (Banga and Goldar, 2004; Hansda, 2001).[7]

Concomitantly, there also exists a positive relationship between use of services input and industrial productivity in the manufacturing sector (Banga and Goldar, 2004). In this context, as the cross-country

---

7. Banga, R. and B. Goldar (2004), "Contribution of Services to Output Growth and Productivity in Indian Manufacturing: Pre- and Post-Reforms", ICRIER Working Paper.

TABLE V

Gross Value Added in Services

Services	*1981-82 to 1990-91*	*1992-93 to 2004-05*
Producer services	7.7 (67.5)	8.4 (70.0)
Consumer services	6.2 (18.1	8.6 (17.6)
Government services	6.5(14.4)	5.9 (12.4)

Note: Figures in brackets are shares of sub-sectors in gross value-added of services.

Source: RBI, *Annual Report*, 2005-06, p. 27.

experience suggests, investments in the ICT sectors contribute to productivity gains across other sectors of the economy such as manufacturing. Productivity gains in manufacturing, of course, also reflected benefits of increased competition following the reforms in the 1990s which, *inter alia*, led to declines in import tariffs and domestic barriers to entry. In brief, evidence suggests that the services activity could be leading to higher growth in manufacturing sector by providing sustained demand for manufactured goods as well as by raising the productivity. Further research is, however, required to have a clearer understanding of the sources and significance of the role of service sectors in propelling India's recent growth and the marked differences in this respect from other countries. In this context, it also needs to be noted that the nature of services sector activity is evolving quite rapidly with the emergence of new services as well as innovations in the delivery of these services. Accordingly, issues of appropriate measurement of services activity in national accounts along with their productivity assume importance. Services-led growth should, however, not assume a lopsided nature. Policies to accelerate the current pace of growth in manufacturing activity and raise agricultural growth would need to be pursued for a further step-up in the economy's overall growth rate. An economy of India's size and scope cannot ignore the manufacturing sector. A substantial manufacturing base is essential to absorb the workforce moving out of agriculture. Finally, the advanced skill-intensive part of the Indian economy may be bidding up scarce skills in such a way as to slow the growth of labour-intensive manufacturing. Greater attention may need to be paid to improve the quality of education so as to enhance the supply of skilled labour.

Bibliography

A. BOOKS

Arun Banerji: "Finance in Early Raj: Investment and External Sector", Sage, New Delhi, 1995.

A. Vaidyanathan: "The Indian Economy since Independence", in Dharma Kumar (ed.) 'The Cambridge Economic History of India', Vol. 2, Cambridge University Press, 1983.

A.K. Bagchi: "Private Investment in India," 1900-1939.

Ajit Kumar Sinha: "New Economic Policy of India", Deep & Deep Publication, New Delhi, 1995.

Bipin Chandra: "The Rise and Growth of Economic Nationalism in India", PPH, New Delhi, 1966.

B.R. Tomlin: "Historical Roots of Economic Policy", in Subroto Roy and William E. James (ed.) "Foundations of India's Political Economy, towards an Agenda for 1990's", Sage, New Delhi, 1992.

Bhagwati and Desai: "India: Planning for Industrialisation", 1970 Oxford University Press, London.

Bimal Jalan: "India's Economic Policy: Preparing for Twenty-first Century", New Delhi, Penguin, 1996.

Bishwa Nath Singh, Mohan Pd. Shrivastava and Narendra Prasad: "Economic Reforms in India", New Delhi, APH, 2003.

Dutt and Sundharam: "Indian Economy", S. Chand and Sons, 2002".

Deepak Nayyar: "Economic Liberalisation in India", 1996.

Debentra Kumar Das: "Economic Development Opportunities through Liberalisation", 1998.

D.H. Robertson: "Essays in Monetary Theory", King and Stables Ltd., London, 1940.

Gurcharan Das: "India Unbound", New Delhi, 2000.

I.C. Dhingra: "Indian Economy", S. Chand and Sons.

Jagdish Bhagwati and Padma Desai, "India: Planning for Industrialisation", London.

Jawahar Lal Nehru: "Discovery of India".

John P. Lewis, "Quiet Crisis in India", Bombay, Reprint 1970.

K.L. Gupta: "भारत में लोक उद्योग", Navyug Sahitya Sadan, Agra, 1998.

Karanti Lingaich and T. Satyanarayana: "Indian Economy", Sterling, New Delhi, 1990.

Kiriti Parikh: "Learning from Tigers and Cubs: Economic Restructuring in East Asia: Lessons for India", Indira Gandhi Institute of Development Research, Bombay, 1992.

Kewal Khanna: "Current Economic Issues and Trends", Printwell, Jaipur, 1997.

Michael Kidron: "Foreign Investment in India", Oxford University Press, London, 1965.

M.Y. Khan: "Indian Financial System", Tata McGraw - Hill Publishing Co. Ltd., New Delhi.

Menjor Singh: "Economic Reforms in India: Problems and Prospects", New Delhi, 2001.

Mahesh V Joshi: "Economic Reforms in India: A Critical Evaluation", A.P.H. Publishing Corporation, New Delhi, 1997.

Manmohan Singh: "India's Export Trend", Oxford University Press, London.

N.K. Sengupta: "Government and Business", Vikas Publishing House Pvt. Ltd., Delhi, 2002.

Om Parkash: "Economics of Liberalisation: The Indian Drama", 1996.

P.N. Dhar, "Indian Economy", Kalyani Publishers, 2002.

D.K. Ghosh and G.K. Kapoor: "Business Policy and Environment", 1996.

P.V. Sharma: "Emerging Issues of Indian Economic Development", New Delhi, Kanishka, 2001.

Rashmin Sanghvi, Naresh Ajwani and K.G. Choudhury, "Guide to Foreign Exchange Management Act, 1999", New Delhi.

Rajesh Chadha, Alan V. Deardorff, Sanjib Pohit and Robert M. Stern: "The Impact of Trade and Domestic Policy Reforms in India—A CGE Modeling Approach", University of Michigan, 1998.

Ratnakar Gedam: "Economic Reforms in India—Experience and lessons" Deep and Deep, New Delhi, 1999.

R. Arunachalam: "Agricultural Growth and Economic Reforms", Deep and Deep, New Delhi, 2002.

Reeta Mathur: "Economic Reforms and Poverty Alleviation", Jaipur, Sublime Pub., 2002.

Rudder Dutt: "Economic Reforms in India—A Critique", S. Chand and Co. Ltd., New Delhi, 1997.

Raj Kapila and Uma Kapila: "Economic Development in India", Vol. 25, Academic Foundation, Delhi.

R.N. Tripathy: "Public Finance in Underdeveloped Countries."

Rudder Dutt: "Second Generation Reforms: Need for Changing Growth Strategy", Second Generation Economic Reforms in India, Deep & Deep Pub., 2002.

Saxena and Gupta: "भारत में उद्योगों का संगठन वित व्यवस्था तथा प्रबन्ध", Navyug Sahitya Sadan, Agra.

Shankar Acharya: "India's Fiscal Policy", Robert, E.B. Lucas and Gustav F. Papanek (ed.) "The Indian Economy—Recent Development and Future Prospects."

Subramaniam Swamy: "India's Economic Performance and Reforms: A Perspective for the New Millennium", Konark Publishers, 2000.

Shuji Uchikawa: "Economic Reforms and Industrial Structure in India", New Delhi, Manohar, 2002.

Shubhashis Gangopadhyaya and Willima Wadhwa: "Economic Reforms for the Poor", Delhi, Konark, 2000.

Saxena and Gupta: "Indian Economy", 1997.

Vijay Joshi and I.M.D. Little: "India's Economic Reforms 1991-2000", Oxford University Press, Delhi, 1999.

V.B. Bhise: "Economic Reforms and Ninth Five Year Plan", New Delhi, 1998.

V.S. Mahajan: Economic Reforms and Liberalisation", Deep & Deep Publications Pvt. Ltd., New Delhi, 2002.

B. ARTICLES

A.S. Kanta Wala: "Trends and Structure in Foreign Investment", *The Indian Journal of Commerce*, Vol. L, No. 192, 1997, pp. 89-98.

A.T. Pannir Selram: "The Future of Indian Financial Sector—Foundation Paper for National Debate", *Journal of Indian Institute of Bankers*, Platinum Jublee Special.

Ajit Kumar Shukla: "Globalisation of Indian Economy", *The Indian Journal of Commerce*", Vol. XLVI, No. 177, 1993, pp. 17-19.

Alak Ghosh: "Industrial Policy: A Critical Appraisal", quoted in "New Economic Policy of India" edited by Ajit Kumar Sinha, Deep & Deep Publications, 1999.

Ambhuti Shukla: "Impact of Import Liberalisation on Export Performance of Indian Economy", *Economy Affairs*, Dec. 2001.

Amresh Bagchi: "India Tax Reforms—A Progress Report", *EPW*, Oct. 17, 1998.

Arjun Sen Gupta: "India's Economic Reforms and the Art of the Feasible", *Economic and Political Weekly*, Dec. 16, 2000, pp. 4485-97.

Ashok V Desai: "A Decade of Reforms", *Economic and Political Weekly*, December 15, 2001, pp. 4627-30.

B. Bhattacharyya and Satinder Palaha: "Foreign Direct Investment in India: Facts and Issues", Occasional Paper 2, 1996, Indian Institute of Foreign Trade, New Delhi.

Barbara Lee and John Nellis (1990): "Enterprise Reform and Privatisation in Socialist Economies", World Bank Discussion, Paper 104.

Biswajit Dhar and Mritunjay Mohanty, "FEMA": A Closer Look", *Economic and Political Weekly*, Oct. 3, 1998.

D.K. Rangnekar, "Industrial Policy", *The Economic Times*, Annual Number, 1975.

D.M. Nanjundappa: "PSU Banks Reform: A New Package", *Yojana*, July 2000, pp. 4-9.

D.P. Agrawal and K.S. Jaiswal: "Globalisation of Indian Economy", *The Indian Journal of Commerce*, Vol. 177, 1993, pp. 35-48.

Deepak Nayyar, "Indian Economy at the Crossroads - Illusions and Realities", *Economic and Political Weekly*, April 10, 1993.

G. Thimmaiah: "Relevance of the Kelkar Report", Dec. 2, 2002.

George Cherian: "Export Policy, In Need of A Re-look", *Economic Times*, 25 Sept. 2002.

H.A.C. Prasad: "Impact of Economic Reforms on India's Major Exports"—Policy Guidelines", Occasional Paper, IIFT, New Delhi, 1997.

H.K. Paranjape: "New Industrial Policy: A Capitalist Manifesto", *Economic and Political Weekly*, Oct. 26, 1991.

Hans Binswanger and S.R. Khandker: "The Impact of Formal Finance on the Rural Economy of India", World Bank Policy Research Working Paper No. 949 (Washington DC, 1992).

I.G. Patel: "New Economic Policy: Historical Perspective", quoted in "*New Economic Policy of India*", edited by Ajit Kumar Sinha, Deep & Deep Publications, 1999.

Indira Rajaraman: "Restructuring Direct Taxes", *Economic Times*, December 11, 2002.

J.C. Sandesara, "New Industrial Policy: Question of Efficient Growth and Social Objectives", *Economic and Political Weekly*, August 3-10, 1991.

K. Chandrasekhar: "Efforts and Achievements under Economic Reforms", Facts for You, December 1995, pp. 13-16.

K.N. Raj: "New Economic Policy—Engine of Growth", *Economic Times*, Dec. 21, 1985.

Keya Sengupta: "Challenges of Second Generation Reforms", quoted in "*Second Generation Economic Reform in India*", edited by Dutt, Deep & Deep Publication, Delhi 2002.

M.C. Bhatt: "Joint Ventures and Technology Trade", *Foreign Trade Review*, Vol. XXVII, Jan.-March 1993.

Mahesh C Purohit: "National and Sub-National VATs", *Economic and Political Weekly*, March 3, 2001, pp. 757-59.

Manmohan Singh: "New Economic Policy", quoted in "*New Economic Policy of India*" edited by Ajit Kumar Sinha, Deep & Deep Publications, 1999.

Meena Krishna: "Indian Agriculture and Globalisation Perspective" quoted in "*Second Generation Economic Reforms in India*" edited by Rudder Dutt, Deep & Deep Publications, Delhi, 2002.

Mihir Rakshit, "Some Macro-economic of India's Reforms", Experience, Paper on line at: http// www.sas.upenn.edu/casi/paper on line.html.

Montek S. Ahluwalia: "Economic Performance of States in Post-Reforms Period", Economic and Political Weekly, May 6, 2000, pp. 1637-46.

Nagesh Kumar: "WTO's Emerging Investment Region", *Economic and Political Weekly*, August 18, 2001.

Narendra Prasad: "Banking and Financial Sector Reforms in India", quoted in "*Banking and Financial Sector Reforms in India*", edited by Amalesh Banerjee and S.K. Singh, Deep & Deep Publications, New Delhi.

Odeyar D. Heggade and M.R. Bharathi: "Second Generation Reforms: Issues and Directions", quoted in "*Second Generation Economic Reforms in India*", Deep & Deep Publications, Delhi, 2002.

P.M. Passah: "Banking and Financial Sector Reforms in India—Rationale, Progress Efficacy and Future Agenda", quoted in "*Banking and Financial Sector Reforms in India*" edited by Amalesh Banerjee and S.K. Singh, Deep & Deep Publications, New Delhi, 2001.

P.N. Singh: "Globalising Indian Economy", *The Indian Journal of Commerce*, Vol. XLVI, No. 177, 1993, pp. 1-12.

Padmabhushan G.L. Tandon: "Anatomy for PSEs", Facts for you, September 2002, pp. 22-25.

Ravindra H. Dholakia and Deepak Kapur: "Economic Reforms and Trade Performance", *Economic and Political Weekly*, December 8, 2001.

Rita Sharma: "Reforms in Agricultural Extension New Policy Framework", *Economic and Political Weekly*, July 27, 2002, pp 3124-34.

Rudder Dutt: "Second Generation Reforms: Need for Changing Growth Strategy", quoted in "*Second Generation Economic Reforms in India*", edited by Rudder Dutt, Deep & Deep Publications, Delhi, 2002.

S.D. Sawant, Vaidehi Daptardar, Sandhya Mhatre: "Capital Formation and Growth in Agriculture", *Economic and Political Weekly*. March 16, 2002, pp. 1068-72.

Sanjaya Lal: "Less Developed Countries and Private Foreign Investment", *Economic and Political Weekly*, Aug. 3, 1974.

Shankar Acharya: "Straight Talk on Direct Taxes", *Economic Times*, 21 Nov., 2002.

Shuji Uchikawa: "Economic Reforms and Foreign Trade Policies", *Economic and Political Weekly*, Nov. 27, 1999, pp. M 138-M 147.

Subir Gokarn: "Guilty Until Proven Innocent", *Business Standard*, Aug. 23, 1999.

Suman Sahai: "American Pressure to Open up Indian Agriculture", *Economic and Political Weekly*, Feb. 24, 1996.

T.K. Velayudham: "Development in Indian Banking: Past, Present and Future", *The Journal of Indian Institute of Bankers*, Platinum Jubilee Special.

Umesh C. Patnaik: "Reforms in the Banking Sector and Task Ahead", *The Indian Journal of Commerce*, Vol. XLVIII, 1994, pp 105-11.

V.V. Ramanandham: "What is this privatization", *The Indian Journal of Commerce*, Vol. L, No. 190, 1997, pp. 26-33.

Vijay L. Kelkar: "India's Reform Agenda: Micro, Meso and Macro-economic Reforms," Paper on Line at: http//www.sas'.upenn.edu/casi/papersonline.htal

Vyuptakesh Sharan: "Reforming India's Foreign Trade", *The Indian Journal of Commerce*, Vol. 51, pp. 17-26.

Y.V. Reddy: "Public Enterprises and Economic Reforms", *The Indian Journal of Commerce*, No. 190, 1997, pp. 34-43.

C. GOVERNMENT PUBLICATIONS

Economic Survey of India—An annual publication of Ministry of Finance and Company Affairs, Government of India.

Public Enterprise Survey—An annual publication of Department of Public Enterprises, Ministry of Heavy Industries & Public Enterprises.

Annual Report of Ministry of Industry—An annual publication of Ministry of Industry.

World Development Report—An annual publication of World Bank and Oxford University Press.

Statistical Abstract of India—An annual publication of Ministry of Statistics and Programmes Implementation, Government of India.

SIA Newsletter—Monthly Publication of Secretariat of Industrial Assistance, Ministry of Industry, Government of India.

Report on Currency and Finance—An annual publication of Reserve Bank of India.

D. WEBSITES

Department of Commerce, Govt. of India. http://commin.nic.in

Directorate General of Foreign Trade, Govt. of India: http://dgft.delhi.nic.in

Secretariat for Industrial Assistance (SIA), Govt. of India: http://indmin.nic.in

Office of the Economic Adviser, Govt. of India: http://eaindustry.nic.in

National Informatics Centre, Govt. of India:
http://www.nic.in
Ministry of Disinvestment, Govt. of India:
http://www.divest.nic.in
Ministry of External Affairs, Govt. of India:
http://www.meadev.gov.in
Department of Public Enterprises, Govt. of India:
http://www.dpe.nic.in
Department of Agriculture Research and Education, Govt. of India
http://dare.nic.in

Index